The Book of Crystal Acupuncture^{sm} & Teragram™ Therapy Diagrams

by
Dr. Margaret Rogers Van Coops
Ph.D., DCH(IM)

authorHOUSE™

1663 LIBERTY DRIVE, SUITE 200
BLOOMINGTON, INDIANA 47403
(800) 839-8640
WWW.AUTHORHOUSE.COM

AuthorHouse™
1663 Liberty Drive, Suite 200
Bloomington, IN 47403
www.authorhouse.com
Phone: 1-800-839-8640

AuthorHouse™ UK Ltd.
500 Avebury Boulevard
Central Milton Keynes, MK9 2BE
www.authorhouse.co.uk
Phone: 08001974150

First published by AuthorHouse 2/13/2006

ISBN: 1-4208-6293-6 (sc)

Printed in the United States of America
Bloomington, Indiana

This book is printed on acid-free paper.

Companion book to:
"Breakthrough Therapies – Crystal Acupuncture[sm] & Teragram[sm] Therapy"

Cover By Teri Kahan
Edited By Stephen Van Coops, Ph.D. DCH(IM)
Graphic Design and Layout By Margaret Rogers Van Coops, Ph.D. DCH(IM)

Table of Contents

Crystal Acupuncture^{sm} Points Diagrams For Healing The Entire Body

New Crystal Stones For The Treatment Of Specific Diseases 107

ACKNOWLEDGEMENT

THANK YOU...

The Book of Crystal Acupuncture^{sm} and Teragram^{sm} Therapy Diagrams is a derivative of *Breakthrough Therapies* and my original booklets, *Crystal Acupuncture^{sm} and Teragram^{sm} Therapy*, which both accompanied the healing stone kits.

I wish to dedicate this book to all the thousands of people who have walked into my life and allowed me to test my theories, experiment with my skills and to watch them as they integrated their energies with mine.

Over the years I have dealt with many illnesses that were considered incurable or beyond medical understanding. With the aid of my Spirit Guide, Chang, and many other Spiritual Master Teachers, I was able to learn how we are matter made from condensed energy that forms a pattern in each individual. This pattern is so rare and unique. It is like each snowflake. No two are the same. Yet, despite this difference many snowflakes have some patterning in common. So too, do humans, animals and plant life. Yes, I have even healed trees and plants after they have been in shock.

I have had the pleasure of exploring many patterns in the human and animal forms. In every case I have found the key to release their fear, pain, anger and guilt. My greatest problem has always been getting the conscious minds of adults to accept transformation and change. Children and animals seemed to always trust me unconditionally, and so many wonderful healings occurred.

I hope that when you read this book and apply the therapies to yourself, that you will always remember how unique your patterning is and how important it is to let your true pattern emerge. Let go of mental patterning that holds you back. Start afresh by creating a new page on which to write your own findings about yourself. Remember, everything you have learned in this life can be challenged and refocused.

I would like to specially thank U.S. graphic artists: Teri Kahan of "Teri Kahan Design", for the cover designs of this book and *Breakthrough Therapies* and Rose Richkind of "Déjà Vu Design" for her formatting advice. I would also like to thank my Japanese friends, Kinko Okamura and Kinko Kajiyama for their support in educating me to become a graphic artist, which made it possible for me to create this book, and lastly, but by no means less important, enormous thanks to my husband, Stephen Van Coops, for his patience and great editing work.

Margaret Rogers Van Coops Ph.D. DCH(IM) O.M.

CRYSTAL ACUPUNCTURE^{sm}

WHY CRYSTAL ACUPUNCTURE^{SM}?

Long ago, early Man found himself to have a great affinity with Mother Earth and, in his quest for guidance and purpose to his existence, he turned to nature. Among the many things this earth offers Man are the magnificent rock formations and the precious minerals that lie encrusted within them. Early Man collected these minerals and used them in ceremonies to heal himself. He found that these minerals seemed to contain a way of soothing his troubles and easing his pain. Small pebbles, rocks and stones were carried in a sacred pouch around his neck and if his pouch was ever lost, it was feared that his life would deteriorate without them. This belief was validated by a mere awareness of lack of energy and movement within his body. New stones would be immediately acquired and blessed to harmonize with him.

Today these mineral rocks and stones are called gems and crystals. Various cultures have learned to integrate their use into everyday life. For example, the Greeks like to hang them as beads and fiddle with them to achieve a calm state while contemplating their problems. The Japanese make meditation rock gardens and fill them with rock ornaments where individuals can achieve serenity. Native Americans like to include them in their ceremonies to rid their bodies of negativity. Westerners like to wear them as pendants and bracelets to make her/himself feel attractive and at ease with themselves. Whatever the reason for their use, rocks can make a person feel better.

When I was a young child, I collected as many varieties of rocks as I could and through inspiration and clairvoyance (the ability to see the stones energy in auric form), would use them to help ease away pains that my friends and family were suffering. I merely placed the rock on the offending part and held it there. After a little while the pain was gone. When I asked if anyone knew the reason why stones worked, nobody seemed to know, nor did they understand that every stone had a color vibration and resonation field, even though I could feel and see it. My curiosity to find the answers set me on my pathway to discover the secret.

I discovered that each rock had its own nature. By that, I simply mean that the way energy flows through it is unique to itself. Some rocks are likened to a battery and can hold a charge, while others disperse energy. Still others amplify energy while their counter-balancers diminish unwanted energy. Further investigation revealed that some rocks were neutral which provided a stabilizing affect. Whether these rocks are used separately or together on a person, an astounding effect in the change of the way the body's energy flows can be felt.

With the growing interest in Metaphysics in the early 1970's, cut rocks and polished stones began to appear in stores. People were drawn to buy them for meditation. It was generally noted that the users felt a change not only in their bodies, but also in their emotional and mental states. At this time, my research into the use of these crystals took me into the world of Acupuncture in order to understand how they could affect the body's energy flow. In 1975 I discovered I had inherited Parkinson's Disease, which made my research all the more intense and personal.

I discovered many answers with the help of Acupuncture. Acupuncture, an ancient art of healing, has isolated four cycles of energy that flow in a healthy body. These are: Digestive system, Circulatory System, Nervous System, Glandular System. These cycles interact with one another to form what is called the Yin and Yang energy of the body. Yang represents the positive force of Fullness and is generally considered to be the active force that creates compressive, cohesive, constrictive, implosive, solidifying, crystallizing and attractive chemical reactions in the body, while Yin represents the negative force which creates and disperses energy by dilating, repelling, expanding, exploding and liquefying chemical changes in a counterbalance force. The Yang-Yin interplay creates harmony within the body that allows normal functioning to occur as well as creating a sense of well being in the mind, body and spirit.

The Yang-Yin force should be perceived as an ever-evolving force of energy that is continually changing within its own rhythmic pattern. Though certain parts of the body are considered primarily Yang or Yin, it should be understood that each has within its make-up a modicum of the opposing force in order to keep a true balance, which results in a healthy body.

The above-mentioned cycles of energy flow around the body in much the same way as blood flows – though much more rapidly and with various pressures. Acupuncturists have been able to locate 16 pathways through which energy flows. These pathways are called meridians and are divided into two categories: 12 organs and 4 vessels. Along each meridian are acupuncture points. These points, when stimulated/sedated, balanced or toned have a direct effect on the organs of the body and the mental/emotional attitude.

In normal Acupuncture treatments, a gold or stainless steel needle is inserted into an Acupuncture point. This needle is then stimulated with an electrical charge, which forces the Yang-Yin energy to move and redirect itself. Afterwards, these same needles are rotated or heated to tone/sedate excess energy.

In my research with crystals, I found that when they were placed on an Acupuncture point, they did in fact effect a greater change than regular Acupuncture could provide. What was even better was the fact that no electrical discharge was needed. It was noted that each crystal allowed the normal Yang-Yin energy to pass through it and to amplify or sedate and tone that energy. In other words, the crystals assisted individuals to redirect and enhance their own energy without outside assistance.

Any disease or discomfort is a direct manifestation of an imbalance in the Yang-Yin force. At the first signs of discomfort, crystal acupuncture should be used to maintain a good balance with harmony in the energy flow. However, if a person is in the advance state of disease, Crystal Acupuncture[sm] can assist them to release negative energy and to rejuvenate and rebuild the body over a period of time. Other therapies, medical treatments and medications can be safely given in conjunction with Crystal Acupuncture[sm]. Crystal Acupuncture[sm] is wonderful therapy to do to self or others and is easily learned.

As I continued my research, I learned that everyone has Five Bodies, which are held together by seven vortices of energy called Chakras. The Chakras rotate in a clockwise direction from the front of the body to the back. Then the return path from the back of the body to the front also returns in a clockwise direction, forming a double helix. These simple rotations stimulate energy to flow throughout the Physical Body, rejuvenating all parts. In the hands and feet, there are Minor Chakras that allow a release of energy into the Earth, or by channeling divine healing, into family and friends. The working combination of all these Chakras governs the condition of the Five Bodies, rather like an old fashion clock, the cogs vary in size and turn precisely to give us the correct time. So, each Chakra rotates at a speed relative to events that have stimulated our emotional responses, which have occurred throughout our life. Being spiritually aware of self and others helps to keep these Chakras in balance. The combined energy of the Chakras and Five Bodies creates what is known as the Aura.

THE FIVE BODIES

THE FIVE BODIES

The Physical (Energy created by function)
The Etheric (Every day thoughts & emotions)
The Spirit (Energy created by emotional consciousness)
The Higher Mind (Wise God-self – Energy created by thought)
The Soul Body (Unconditional loving God-self)

Each body has its own energy flow and is concentrated along the meridians as shown below.

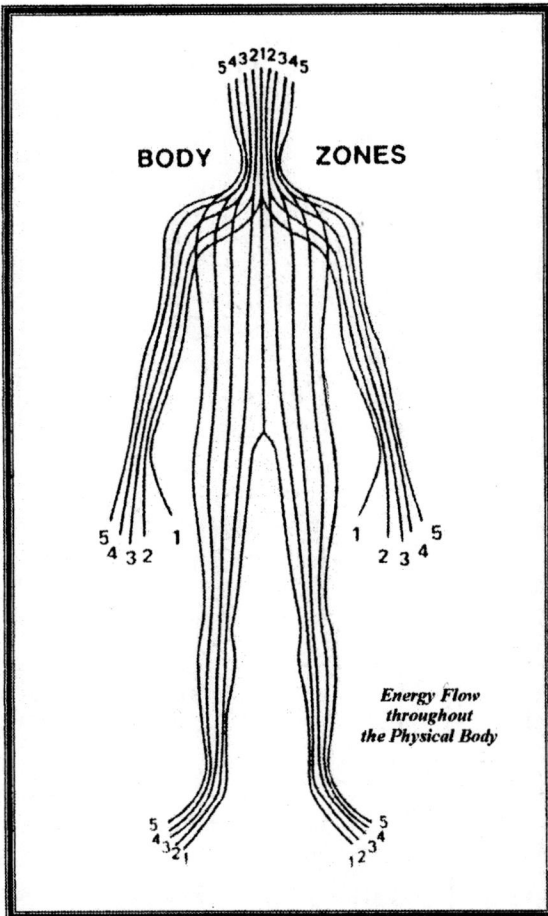

BODY ZONES

Energy Flow
throughout
the Physical Body

Energy from the five bodies shown below, meet at the chakras and radiate outward to form the Aura. See diagram section.

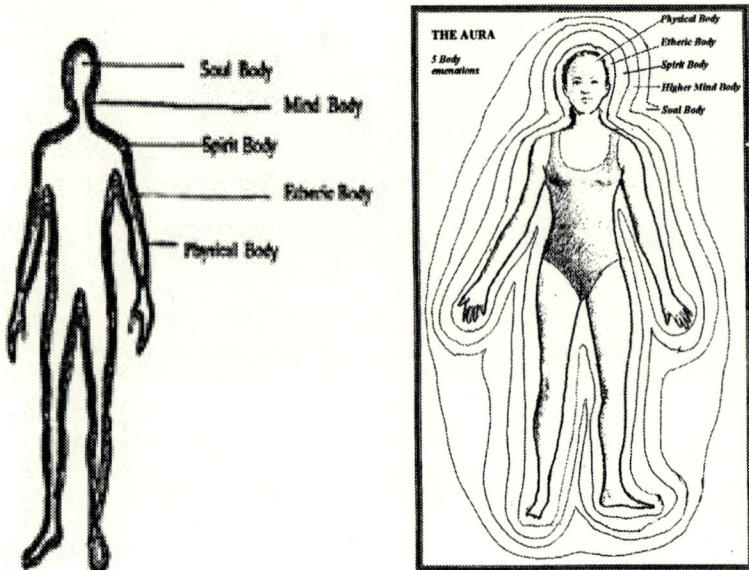

As these energies continually cross one another throughout the body, it can be shown how important is the pressure and intensity of the flow to be in balance. Imbalance creates an arcing and misdirecting of the energy, ultimately resulting in a malfunction of the physical body. Cross-reflex reactions in the physical body can result in pain manifesting away from the actual point of arcing, i.e. Arcing in the heart results in pain in the lower back.

The beauty of working with crystals is that you do not have to know much. Your intuitive self will sense which color crystal to use and how often to use it. With practice, you will also intuitively know where to place it on your body. There are no bad side effects to Crystal Acupuncture[sm]. Any emotional or mental negativity that may temporarily arise after the treatment are old memories of pain, anger, fear or guilt that are released as that blocked energy now flows. Frequent meditation to release old mindsets should accompany Crystal Acupuncture[sm] whenever possible and it will be found that new awareness will automatically fall into place. Sufferers of chronic disorders and diseases should seek counseling to assist rapid release and should continue with medical assistance under the guidance of their doctor.

The convenience of Crystal Acupuncture[sm] is that you do not need anyone else to help you do it. You can be your own therapist and healer. However, you may wish to help someone else with your crystals. If this is the case, be aware that it is your energy that will pass through the crystals and on into your loved one. Always empty your mind and heart of all negativity before using your crystals either on yourself or your loved one and say the declaration/prayer for healing given later in this book.

Once you have learned to sense your own Yang-Yin force, you will be able to attune to it and use the crystal pendulums to assist yourself with making emotional, mental and practical decisions. You will learn to empty your mind and focus on your inner-self as you search for true answers. Following your own guidance will result in a more confident and happy life with far fewer worries as your body makes its journey back to full recovery.

It should be noted that Crystal Acupuncture[sm] is an aide to accomplish good health. The crystals are not a cure-all or miracle wonder. If the user does not relax and attune to their inner-self and the good things in life, then the crystals can be perceived as useless. It should be understood that negative energy when amplified could result in negative side effects.

I have chosen from many different stones, a small collection of crystals that are easily available on the open market. However, if you find it impossible to find your crystals, then I can supply you with your own set. The crystals chosen are available in every part of the world. Each crystal may vary in its ability to act as a conduit for your healing energy. For example: Quartz found in Russia can have a different effect from quartz found in America. This is partly due to the natural formation of rocks and the resonation of the country and the people who have lived in it.

The crystals I have chosen are:

CRYSTAL	COLOR	CAPABILITY	USES
Quartz	clear	energizer/amplifier	general
Rose quartz	pink	toner/harmonizer	circulation
Amethyst	purple	spiritual harmonizer	nervous
Carnelian	reddish orange	etheric harmonizer	glandular
Hematite	black	mind harmonizer	general
Aventurine	green	etheric harmonizer/toner	digestive
Sodalite	blue	stimulant Higher Mind	general
Amazonite	aqua stripe	energizer/harmonizer	general

Properties of the crystals

Amazonite: "Synthesis"
- Harmonizes the Heart and Throat Chakras and balances the Yin and Yang energies.
- Aligns Chakras and regenerates "Power spot" in the center of the physical form.
- Stimulates stamina, strength of character, faith and compassion.
- Improves bone calcium and new tissue growth.
- Stimulates speech with balanced expression.
- Inspires states of perfection, serenity.
- Improves grounding of emotions that result in an acute sense of reality.

Amethyst: "Metamorphosis."
- Cleanses, purifies, restructures and renews all levels of body, mind and spirit.
- It transforms lower energies into a higher refined vibration.
- Protects the user against psychic manipulation, verbal and spiritual attack.
- Improves bone maladies, i.e. arthritis, and stimulates the senses of hearing, smell and taste.
- Frees the Etheric Body of learned conditioning.
- Clears the Aura of negativity and helps in deepening meditation states.
- Releases emotions of anger and pain.
- Opens awareness of the Spirit Body's vibration of pure love.
- Can cause a revolution in the way you live your life.

Aventurine: "Healer Of The Heart & Soul."
- Balances masculine and feminine energies in the Lower Self.
- Stimulates energy to move from front to back connecting with Higher Mind Body
- Balances through the stimulation of cross-reflexes causing a harmonizing of the Spiritual Masculine and Feminine Self.

- Develops levels of creativity and leadership with a passion for the pleasures of life.
- Enables one to make the right decisions.
- Creates a blanket of spiritual love to physically heal the heart, lungs, adrenal and muscular systems so that the liver and pancreas function effectively.
- In meditation, stimulates connection with the Soul Body and spiritually releases heartache from the Etheric Body.
- Arouses passion that motivates one towards success.
- Harmonizes the reproductive system.
- Aligns all Five Bodies, creating a true state of tranquility.

Carnelian: "Ambition And Drive."
- Inspires positive courageous confidence.
- Motivates, activates and energizes personal power.
- Awakens hidden talents.
- It protects from becoming lost in negative emotions, by stimulating insights and awareness that arise from the Spirit Body.
- When worn, it protect from other people's negative emotional outbursts, such as envy, fear and rage.
- Aids in mentally re-assessing self through clear and precise thinking
- Stimulates to be in the moment and to go with the flow.
- Stimulates the inner child to manifest in positive ways.
- Strengthens a belief in the magic of life and the power of the Spirit
- Provides connection to Spirit Guides and their world.
- Balances the glands of the body, as well as the Liver, Pancreas and Spleen.
- Harmonizes with the Spleen Chakra, and therefore, harmonizes all the other Chakras by stimulating the second Chakra (Spleen) to balance and harmonize the five bodies.

Hematite: "Stone Of Mental Mastery."
- Stimulates photographic memory.
- Helps you remember all you have said or heard.
- Brings clarity, with balance and calm reason.

- Dissolves negative ideas and opens channels for receptivity from the Spirit Body to receive unconditional love for self.
- Aids in making truly peaceful, loving relationships.
- Aids the elimination of negative conditioning from the Etheric Body   Learning is made easy.
- Calms the nerves; erases panic symptoms, cools the body and normalizes circulation.
- Controls fear, pain, anger and guilt, while erasing loneliness.
- It transforms negativity into spiritual joy and bonds the Spirit Body with The Etheric and Physical Bodies.
- Prevents states of escapism, suicide or being a recluse in a mental depressive state.

Quartz: "Universal Conduit."
- Amplifies, focuses, stores and transforms energy.
- Aids in focusing on affirmations and prayers.
- Stimulates psychic perception.
- Effectively releases surfacing negative ideas and emotions.
- Opens up awareness for a need to change for the better.
- Empowers and stimulates action in procrastinators.
- Opens up all the meridians, allowing the energy of all Five Bodies to flow, directly affecting every part of the body
- In meditation, personal history can be erased, along with negative mindsets.
- Releases Lower Self mental and emotional trauma from the Etheric Body.
- Aids in harmonizing the Lower Self-perceptions with the Higher Mind Body.
- Stimulates inspiration and psychic development.
- Lifts the spirit towards love and peaceful union with God.

Rose Quartz: "Stone Of Warmth And Love."
- Balancer of the Yin and Yang energy.
- Aids in the release of emotional pain like a gentle calming salve.
- Opens the heart to beauty within and without.

- **Cherubic energies are attracted to the user, protecting, and dissolving negativity.**
- **Stimulates the Spirit Body to harmonize with the Etheric Body through inspirational ideas, full of positive passion and enthusiasm.**
- **Creates a desire to manifest self-love and enjoy romance.**
- **Clears the body of excess fluids and promotes healing by releasing tension and stress.**
- **Aids in the circulation of blood, and strengthens the lymphatic system.**
- **Lifts depression.**

Sodalite: "Stills The Mind."
- **Creates a lightness of being by stimulating the mind to face truths.**
- **It assists in the growth of self-esteem, worth and value, by releasing negativity directly connected to learned opinions and judgment.**
- **Connects the energies of the Higher Mind and Soul Bodies and to integrate them all the way into the Physical Body.**
- **Aids one to sleep peacefully.**
- **Cleans the Digestive System and balances the metabolic rate by stimulating the glands in the body.**
- **Effectively harmonizes the Etheric Body.**
- **Aids in controlling the rate of flow of energy and can be used to calm and relax the mind and the emotions, which results in a sense of wellness.**

The above descriptions for the stones and their properties reflect the wonderful knowledge and research presented in the book, *Love is in the Earth* by Melody, Copyright 1995 and published by Earth-Love Publishing House. Please refer to this wonderful work for more complete descriptions of these stones and hundreds of others that have Metaphysical properties.

Often I find my students wondering which crystals to use on various parts of their bodies, or they simply wish to ask him/herself a question. Since all things are known and our Spirit Self has all the answers, dowsing, a form of Radionics, is a very good way to find the truth. I always advise my students to find a pendulum stone that harmonizes with their energy. Since most individuals have emotional, mental and physical questions, I suggest that Aventurine be used for physical/practical questions, Rose Quartz for emotional questions and Sodalite for mental ones. If you are unable to find these crystals in drop form for dowsing, then once again I am able to supply you with these as well as a silver chain.

Care of your Crystals

A most frequent question asked is "How can I clean my crystals?" Like all stones on this planet, they are usually quite hardy, however, some of the more fragile stones should be handled and stored with care. The crystals that I suggest be used through this book are hardy and can be cleaned with warm soapy water, and briefly soaked in an antiseptic solution between clients/patients. It is important to remember that "Cleanliness is next to Godliness" But, in more Earthly terms, germs abound, and so it is important to keep your crystals clean. After each session, wash each crystal and hand dry. They should be stored in a padded container that allows them to lie separate from one another preventing breakage.

Crystal Techniques

Crystals may vary in size. However, size is not important. Even the tiniest piece can be helpful. Since some crystals are very expensive or extremely rare does not make it better than the less expensive one. Whatever your choice of stone, the crystal will always be cut to a point and used in Crystal Acupuncture[sm] with the three techniques shown below.

Impound:

Apply firm pressure of the tip of the crystal point into the Acu Point on the skin. Hold for 1 second and then make a quick release. This should be done in a rhythmic pattern several times with pauses between indentations to allow energy to flow. (The crystal should not lose contact with the skin and a slight small impression should be seen on the surface of the skin). This impulse technique moves and disperses blocked energy. (Never press too hard – be gentle).

Toning/Balancing:

With very slight pressure, the crystal tip should rest comfortably on the Acu Point, allowing your energy to make a complete circuit. When this is done, a tingling electrical sensation will be felt.

Releasing and Harmonizing:

The point of the crystal should be rotated in a clockwise direction on the Acu Point. This creates a spiral flow of the energy that causes your energy levels to harmonize throughout the Five Bodies. Then cease rotation and impound again. Repeat this pattern until you feel energy flowing evenly.

Take deep breaths and relax as you feel your Five Bodies lifting in vibration and your Chakras synchronizing.

There is no set time allotted for each placement of the crystals used. You must use your own intuition and physical senses to know when to cease using the crystal. On completion of working with each Acu Point, gently massage the point to close it and seal the energy in.

You can work on yourself with the crystals as often as is required. However, it is suggested that time be allowed between each treatment. An ideal time to treat self would be early morning and late evening before retiring. If you have a simple complaint, such as a headache, then a one-time treatment should prove ample. However, for more serious ailments, once every other day should be sufficient. On the rest day, meditation with a focus on awareness of energy being released from the cellular-neuro-muscular memory should be carried out. It is not unusual to find old memories emerging with old history feelings. Simply release them and reprogram, using the idea that tomorrow is a new beginning. You have a new diary and a clean page to start afresh. Writing down your ideas for the future will be helpful in setting the meridians into a new dynamic.

In cases of extreme urgency, such as life or death, treatments may be given to the feet once or twice a day. This will stimulate the life force energy, which will return vitality to the body and improve chances of survival.

To use the crystals

Before beginning any treatment it is always essential to instill a focus on inner peace. You may find it easy to focus on a prayer of your own choosing relative to your religion and faith. But should you have difficulty I have prepared a simple prayer that embraces all religions. Sit quietly in a comfortable position. Take several deep breaths and read the declaration/ prayer that follows.

I call upon my highest good to flow through me.
I call upon God's eternal love to caress me.
I call upon all that is good to embrace me.
I surrender my conditioned mind to the wisdom of God and the Universe.
I surrender my will to that of the Holy Spirit.
I surrender my life and its negativity.
In its place I accept healing, enlightenment
and the rejuvenation of my life.
So be it.

Beginning Treatment

Take several more deep breaths and then attune to your illness or discomfort. Then select the necessary crystal following instructions from the diagrams or simply use your intuition and begin the procedure. Though the diagrams are extremely effective, it may be your desire to use other crystals that you own. It is quite in order to experiment. There are no harmful affects. Below is a simple way to begin healing yourself.

Get your energies circulating

(1) Take the clear quartz crystal and place it on your thumb or big toe point (center top 1-3 mm behind nail). Impound your crystal 3- 5 times. (6 - 10 times is the maximum for serious ailments). Allow the crystal to sit on the point and let your energy flow through the crystal. Breathe deeply and release negativity. When you feel intuitively ready, rotate the crystal on the Acu Point 6 - 10 times to create balance and harmony. Breathe deeply again. (This technique may be repeated several times if necessary). Repeat this procedure with the remaining fingers or toes.

Correct your energy flow and treat your ailment.

(2) (Find the Diagram relative to your complaint and the crystals indicated in the key. Then locate the Acu Point(s) on your skin that are shown in the diagram and place indicated crystal(s) on point(s), (one at a time).-

Hold each crystal in turn in position and allow your energy to flow through the crystal until you feel your energy flowing in the physical form. (Always focus on one point at a time). Rotate the crystal 3 - 6 six times and then remove it from point. There is no special order for each point to be treated. Use your intuition. When you have used the same crystal on all the points shown, then begin to use the second crystal. Continue until you have used all the crystals indicated.

N.B. If energy does not flow, impound this point 5-6 times again and then hold the crystal in position while allowing your energy to flow and release. It may be necessary to do this several times until every movement of the crystal can be felt as energy movements elsewhere in the body.

What to expect

Your body may give you a various number of signals that something is happening inside:

(1) Static electrical sensations in the hands and feet.
(2) Prickling sensations in various parts of the body.
(3) Cold shivers or heat sensations.
(4) Sharp pin prick-like pains along the meridian.
(5) Awareness of emotions: anger, guilt, fear, loneliness etc.
(6) Muscle twitches, tension in muscles before relaxing.
(7) Pins and needle sensations anywhere in the body.
(8) Strong senses of energy change for the better.
(9) Light headiness. (Breathe and relax).
(10) Shuddering and spasmodic reflex jumps.
(11) A quieting of brain activity/need for sleep.
(12) A stimulating of brain activity/need for exercise.
(13) Change in breathing pattern.
(14) Facial sensations.
(15) With closed eyelids, rapid eye movement can occur.
(16) Sneezing, coughing and choking throat reactions
(17) Short term panic and anxiety releases

All the above are forms of stress stored in the body through cellular neuro-muscular memory. As a child you made lots of mindsets based on your emotional experiences. These mindsets are often negative and need to be eliminated together with their accompanying emotions. Go with the flow of what occurs. Always be positive about everything you feel. Tell yourself often that you are releasing old memories. Be ready to replace them with new thoughts and attitudes about yourself along with visual images. Build up your self-esteem, self-worth, and self-value in the days that follow. If necessary, take metaphysical workshops to help yourself improve.

There will be times, usually within three days of treatment, when your energy flow will be excessively slow or fast. Don't panic. You're ready to let go of something. Warn your friends and don't hold back. Cry, laugh, yell, scream etc., but be careful not to hurt yourself or anyone else. These basic outbreaks of repressed energy will release all of your blocked energy and leave you feeling free to start over. Love yourself and love your friends for being there for you and start building a new life.

Crystal Acupuncture[sm] is a therapy and should be taken seriously as such. Your crystals can also be used during meditation. Simply hold one or more in each of your hands and breathe deeply. Always remember to maintain a positive attitude when you meditate and to say the declaration/prayer.

Dowsing with your stones and your questions

First relax in a comfortable chair. Sit upright and allow your energies to flow. Select your question pendulum, Blue for mental problems, pink for emotional problems and green for practical problems. With your elbow wedged firmly into your waist, allow your upper arm to extend outward so that the pendulum can hang downward.

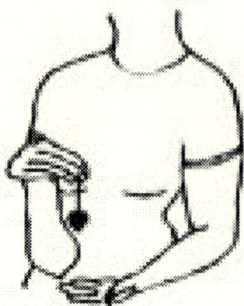

Accept that the pendulum is an extension of your energy. The pendulum will begin to swing back and forth and then to rotate. In order to establish which direction is negative, ask yourself a simple question to which you know the answer i.e. "Is my name Sheila?" The direction the pendulum flows is your positive. To double check, ask a second question that you know to be false i.e. "Is my name John?" The pendulum will swing in the opposite direction.

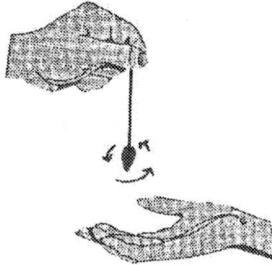

Now that you have established your polarities, trust that your deep-subconscious knows the truth and that your true energy flow will reveal the truth. Empty your mind of everything but your problem. Ask the question very simply. E.g. "Is Tom the man I will marry?" Do not ask confusing questions that may warrant several answers. E.g. "Does Tom feel the same about me tonight?" This type of question is loaded with sub-questions dependent on a variety of factors. Tom's feelings may be deep but very different in perspective from yours. He may not love you as much this night as yesterday, which doesn't mean he won't love you even more tomorrow. What is your opinion about the meaning of the word "same?" His opinion could be very different.

Your insight into yourself from within the deep-subconscious is complete. You have all the answers you need. However, you cannot know the deep-subconscious of your friends/colleagues unless their lives are karmically entwined with yours. If this is the case then you will receive positive affirmations to your questions. If not, the pendulum may vacillate between negative and positive, which reveals uncertainty. If this is the case, sit and wait for more physical occurrences to either confirm or negate your question.

If you have had experience in Radionics (dowsing) you may like to dowse a friend's energy to become aware of their Aura. It is possible to find the edges of each of the Five Bodies and to establish weak points in each of them that need to be healed. If you decide to do this kind of work, it is essential that you protect yourself from negativity and remain in a higher state of consciousness and in harmony with your Spirit Guides.

THE FIVE BODIES
& THEIR ENERGY FLOWS

PHYSICAL BODY

The natural flow of energy in this body is always flowing perpendicularly from the feet or hands up to the head and down again. Similar to the natural blood flow in the body, energy circulates in less than 3 seconds. Earthly physical experiences are always processed through the five senses, which will then allow the brain to program each miniscule sensation within the cellular-neuro-muscular systems. If this body does not flow correctly, deformity occurs.

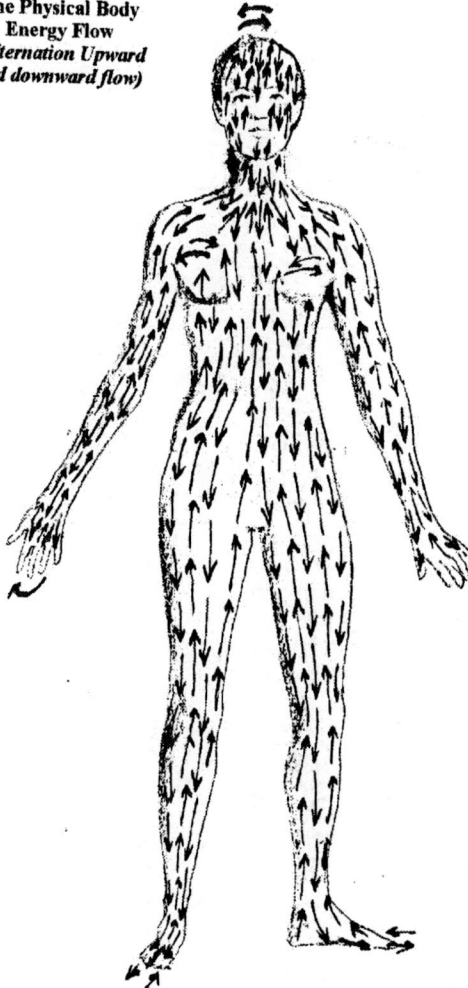

Fig. I
The Physical Body
Energy Flow
(Alternation Upward
and downward flow)

ETHERIC BODY

Energy flows in this body in a clockwise horizontal spiral, ascending and then descending, rotating throughout all cells in the Physical Body. This body is programmed with every positive and negative emotional and mental experience. If this body does not flow correctly, energy will block causing a backflow that can manifest in deformity, physical illnesses and biochemical abnormalities, which usually is caused by hatred, pain, fear, anger and guilt.

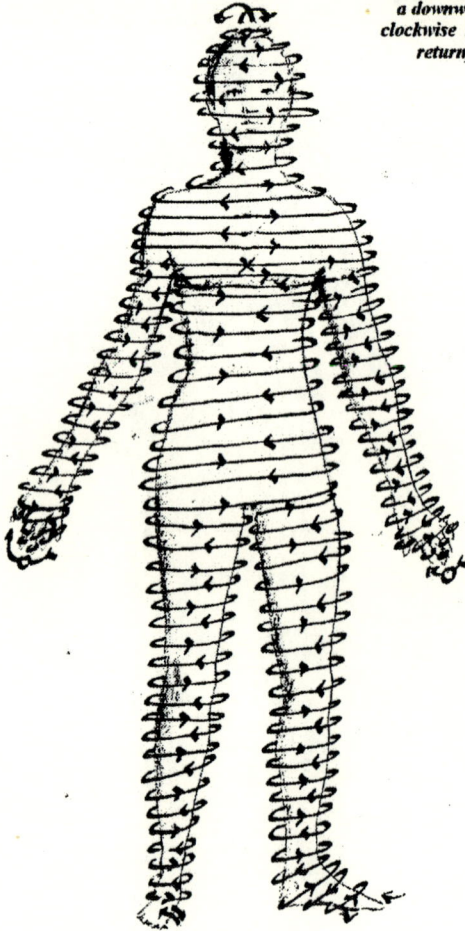

**Fig. II
The Etheric Body
Energy Flow
*(Ascending anti-
clockwise spiral with
a downward
clockwise spiral
return)***

SPIRIT BODY

The natural flow of energy in the Spirit Body descends from the Crown Chakra in a large clockwise horizontal spiral rotation than the Etheric Body. It flows to the feet and hands, where it affects the Etheric and Physical Bodies, bringing on changes at the cellular level. As these changes occur, the energy flowing back to the Crown Chakra brings a sense of resolve to the surface, allowing healing to occur. If this body becomes blocked, obsession with suppression, repression and depression will occur.

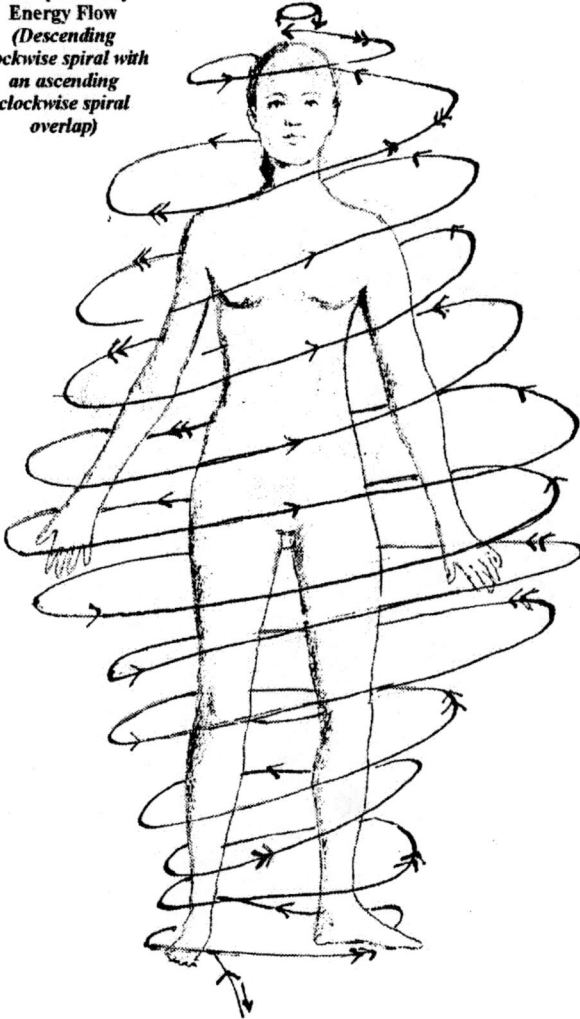

Fig. III
The Spirit Body
Energy Flow
*(Descending
clockwise spiral with
an ascending
clockwise spiral
overlap)*

HIGHER MIND BODY

Flow of energy in this body always begins in a clockwise descending diagonal spiral to the feet and hands where it shifts to return in an opposing clockwise diagonal to the head. Energy from this body passes through al cells of the Physical Body causing reflex reactions that in turn stimulate the Etheric and Physical Bodies to shift their energy flows. This shift allows The Spirit Body to generate healing energy. The Higher Mind Body brings wisdom form the Universal Consciousness into the physical awareness, resulting in a change of mind and heart. If the Physical, Etheric & Spirit Bodies are simultaneously blocked, then the will to live will be lost.

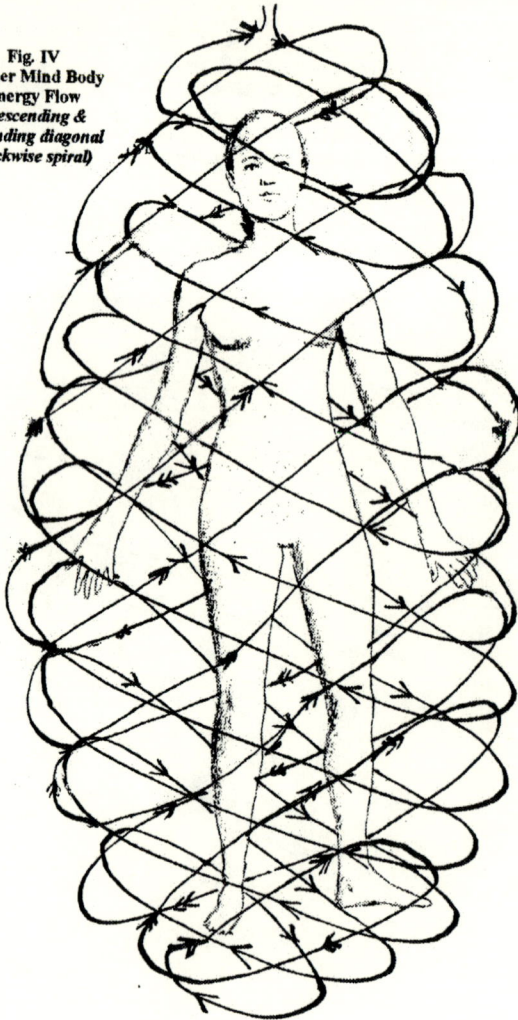

Fig. IV
Higher Mind Body
Energy Flow
(Descending &
ascending diagonal
clockwise spiral)

SOUL BODY

The natural flow of energy in this body is always in a downward and outward directional flow throughout the other Four Bodies. Energy from this body fills every cell in the Physical Body. This loving healing energy from God revitalizes and rejuvenates the lower bodies constantly. The Soul Body allows the Spirit to stay in the Physical Body. This energy is a refined vibration of light that resonates, tones and harmonizes all five bodies.

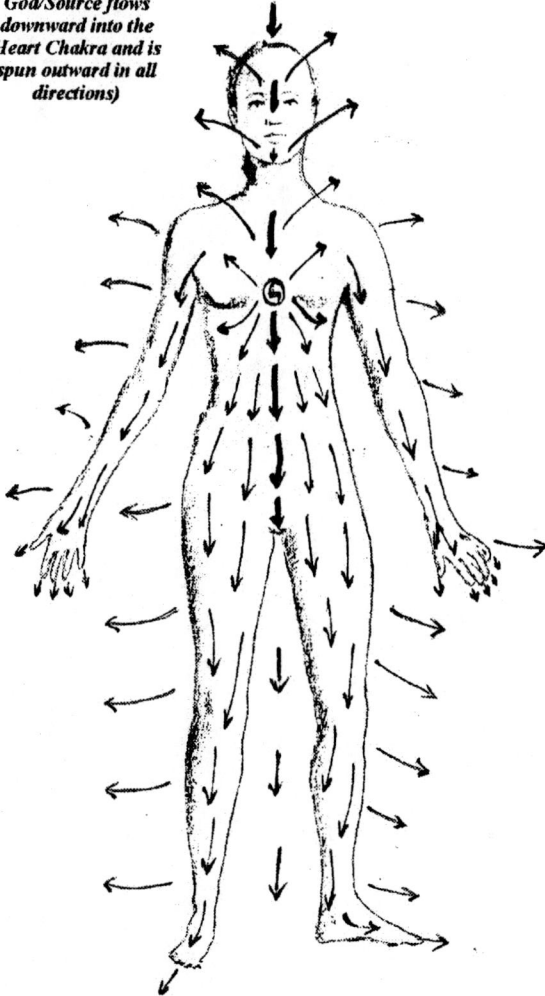

Fig. V
The Soul Body
Energy Flow
(Energy from God/Source flows downward into the Heart Chakra and is spun outward in all directions)

MAJOR & MINOR CHAKRAS

THE MAJOR & MINOR CHAKRAS

Each chakra rotates in a clockwise direction from the front to the back, and then has a return pathway in another clockwise direction over the originl pathway, creating a double helix. The Minor Chakras cause all excess energy to leave the body or to receive energy from the Earth, while the Crown Chakra receives energy from The Universe. The Spleen Chakra balances all energy flows of the Five Bodies and aligns the rotations of the other Chakras. If everything is rotating at the right resonation, then a healthy body with mental and emotional balance in keeping with the harmony of the spirit is the result.

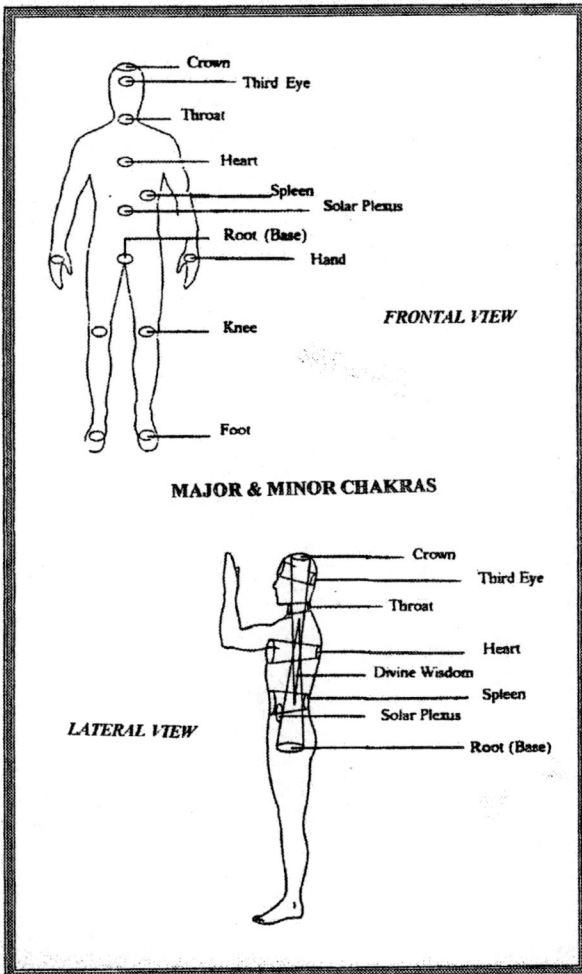

FRONTAL VIEW

MAJOR & MINOR CHAKRAS

LATERAL VIEW

Each Chakra carries energy from each of the Five Bodies in a clockwise rotation, spinning it on to the next chakra that is above and below. Rather like a spinner in a washing machine, energy is forced to move. The front of the Chakra is stimulated to relate to Earthly ways, while the back of the Chakra is stimulated by Higher Awareness. The Chakras have several cones within each one, the center core being the force of concentrated power. If each Chakra is well balanced, then like a fine watch, the cogs keep accurate time, so these Chakras will maintain a healthy body. The Crown and Root Chakras exchange energy within the other five chakras that harmonize the Higher & Lower Selves.

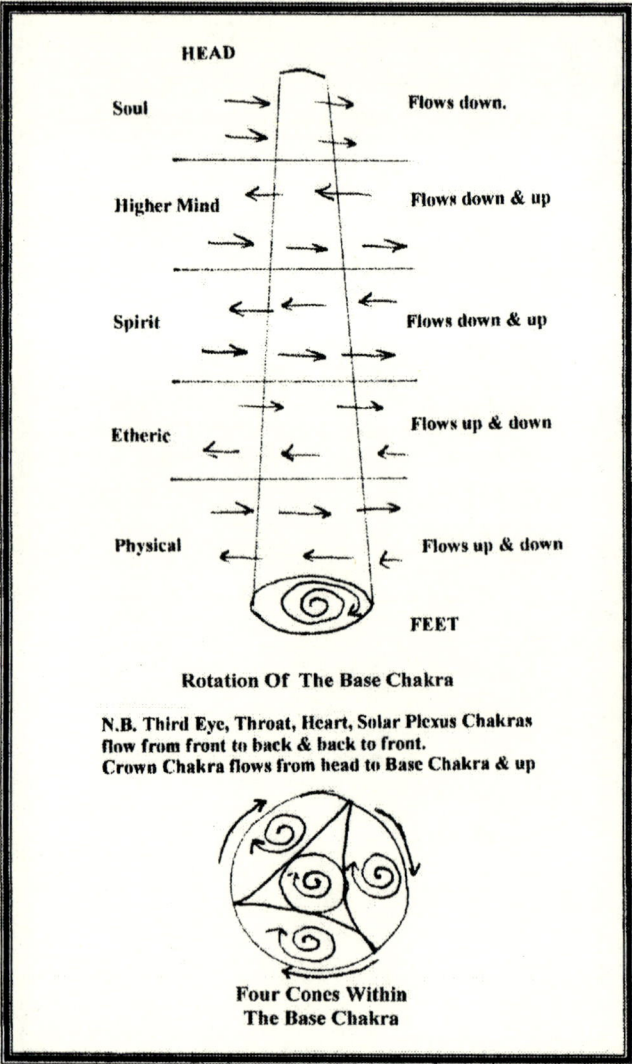

HEAD

Soul — Flows down.

Higher Mind — Flows down & up

Spirit — Flows down & up

Etheric — Flows up & down

Physical — Flows up & down

FEET

Rotation Of The Base Chakra

N.B. Third Eye, Throat, Heart, Solar Plexus Chakras flow from front to back & back to front.
Crown Chakra flows from head to Base Chakra & up

**Four Cones Within
The Base Chakra**

THE MERIDIANS

THE MERIDIANS

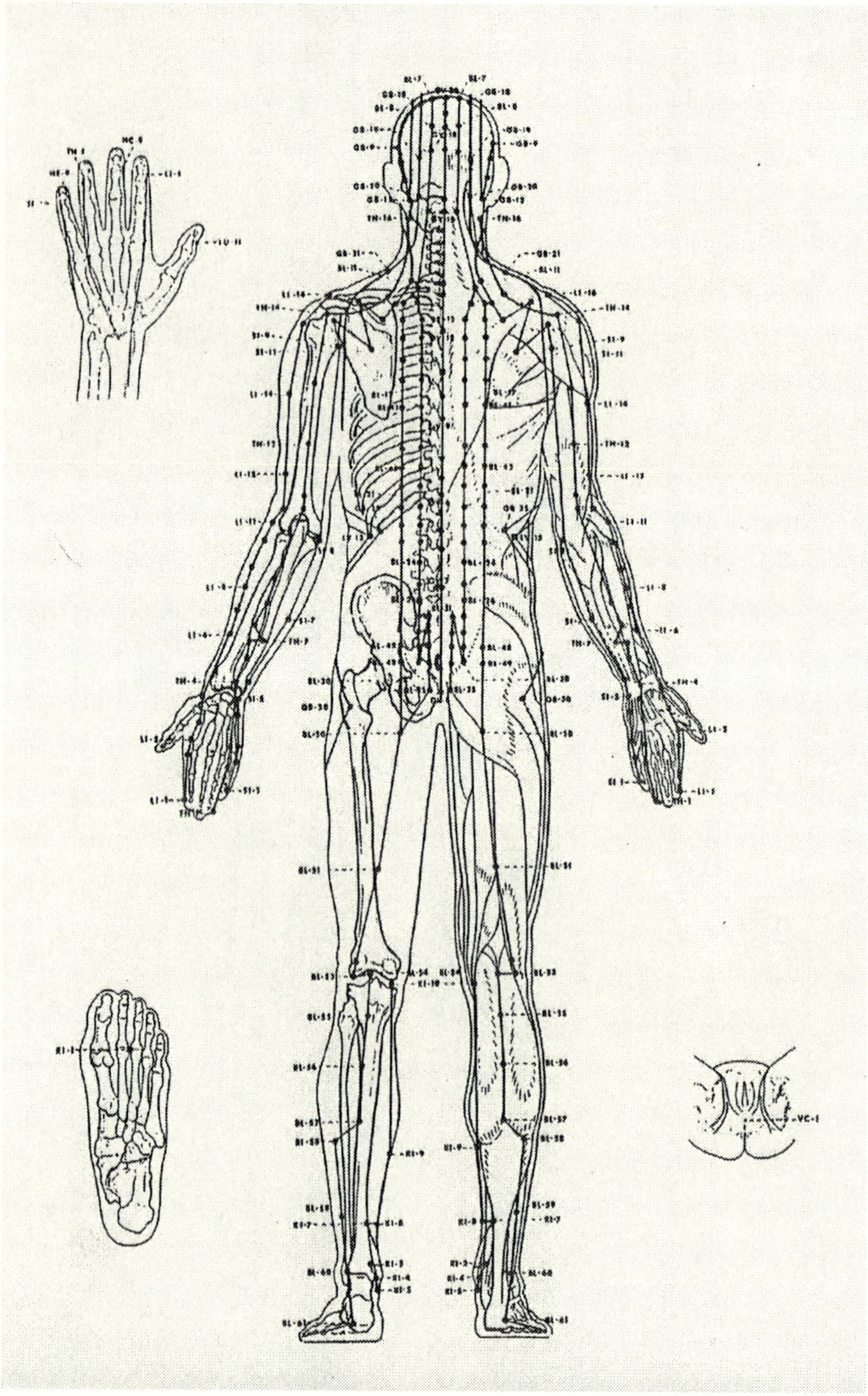

TREATMENT DIAGRAMS
FOR THE CHAKRAS & MAJOR
SYSTEMS
OF THE PHYSICAL BODY

TREATMENT TO BALANCE & HARMONIZE THE CHAKRAS

MAJOR & MINOR CHAKRAS

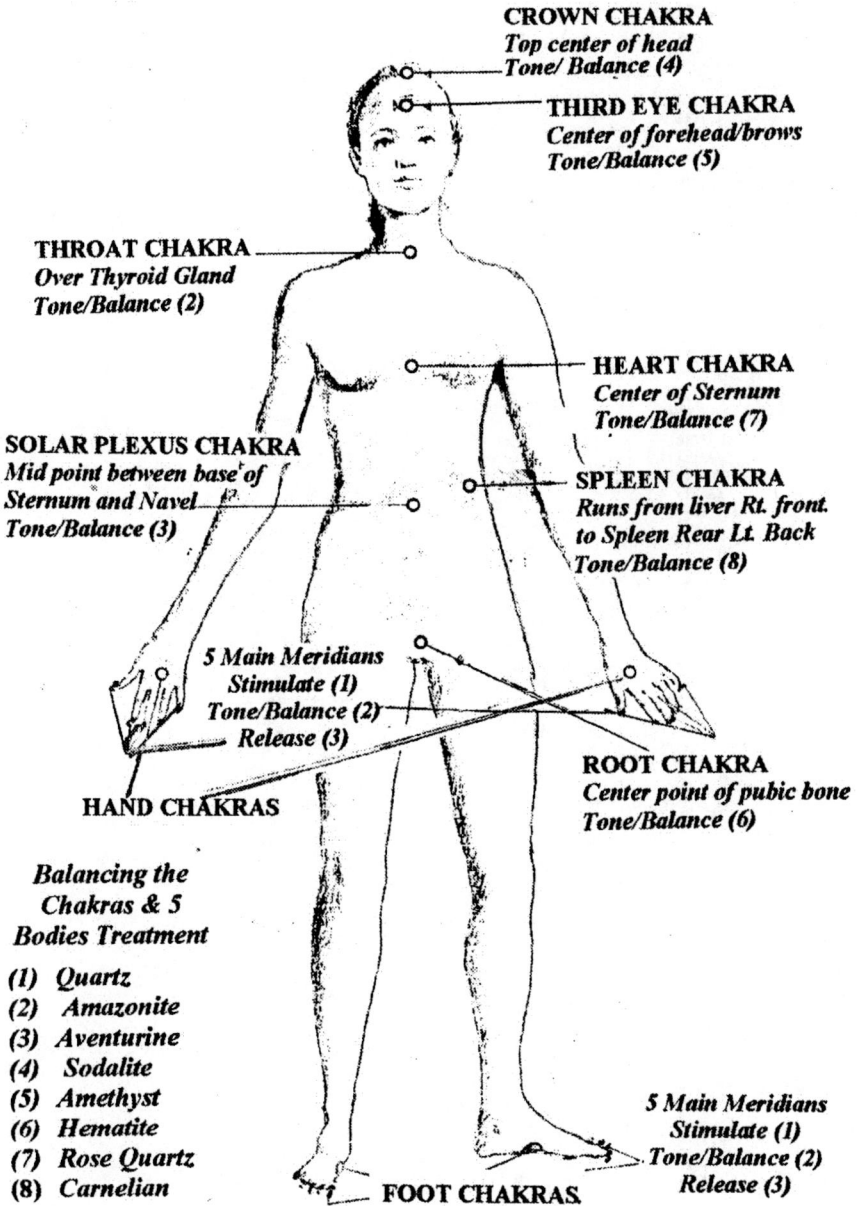

CROWN CHAKRA
Top center of head
Tone/ Balance (4)

THIRD EYE CHAKRA
Center of forehead/brows
Tone/Balance (5)

THROAT CHAKRA
Over Thyroid Gland
Tone/Balance (2)

HEART CHAKRA
Center of Sternum
Tone/Balance (7)

SOLAR PLEXUS CHAKRA
Mid point between base of
Sternum and Navel
Tone/Balance (3)

SPLEEN CHAKRA
Runs from liver Rt. front.
to Spleen Rear Lt. Back
Tone/Balance (8)

5 Main Meridians
Stimulate (1)
Tone/Balance (2)
Release (3)

ROOT CHAKRA
Center point of pubic bone
Tone/Balance (6)

HAND CHAKRAS

Balancing the
Chakras & 5
Bodies Treatment

(1) *Quartz*
(2) *Amazonite*
(3) *Aventurine*
(4) *Sodalite*
(5) *Amethyst*
(6) *Hematite*
(7) *Rose Quartz*
(8) *Carnelian*

5 Main Meridians
Stimulate (1)
Tone/Balance (2)
Release (3)

FOOT CHAKRAS.

Treatment For The Digestive System (Front)

Tension and distress can cause acid indigestion, nervous bowel syndrome and malnourishment. Emotional and mental negativity can affect the way you smell and taste which can cause you to eat the wrong foods. Using the crystals regularly on the points described below can help you change your metabolic rate, which will allow you to eat moderately and correctly eliminate waste products. A healthy body can result if this treatment is given once a week. Remember to allow for emotional and mental changes that may occur as you develop new routines.

Ingest food every two or three hours with plenty of water according to your weight. Drink herbal tea remedies such as Malva flowers with nettle to help eliminate mucous and fatty waste.

(1) Quartz (2) Carnelian (3) Aventurine

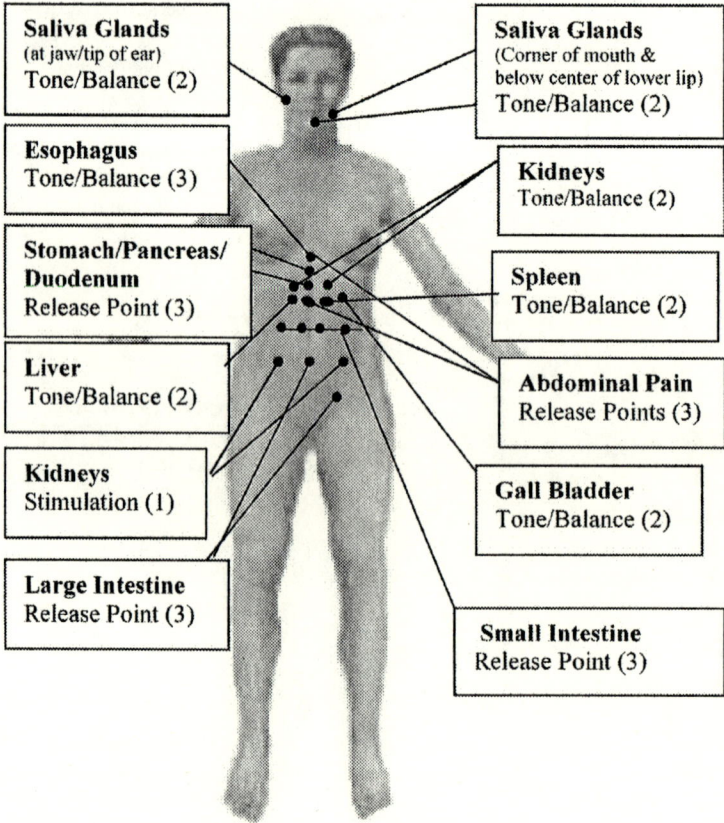

Saliva Glands
(at jaw/tip of ear)
Tone/Balance (2)

Saliva Glands
(Corner of mouth &
below center of lower lip)
Tone/Balance (2)

Esophagus
Tone/Balance (3)

Kidneys
Tone/Balance (2)

Stomach/Pancreas/
Duodenum
Release Point (3)

Spleen
Tone/Balance (2)

Liver
Tone/Balance (2)

Abdominal Pain
Release Points (3)

Kidneys
Stimulation (1)

Gall Bladder
Tone/Balance (2)

Large Intestine
Release Point (3)

Small Intestine
Release Point (3)

Treatment For The Digestive System (Front Cont.)

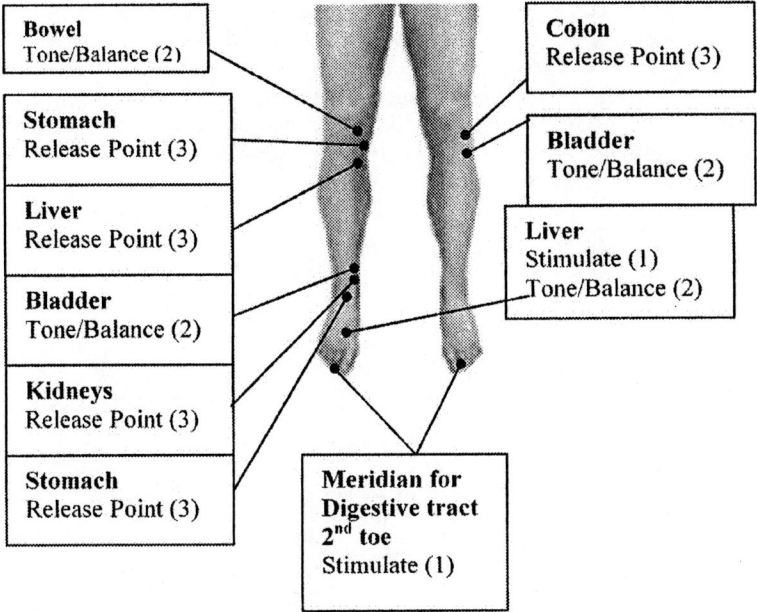

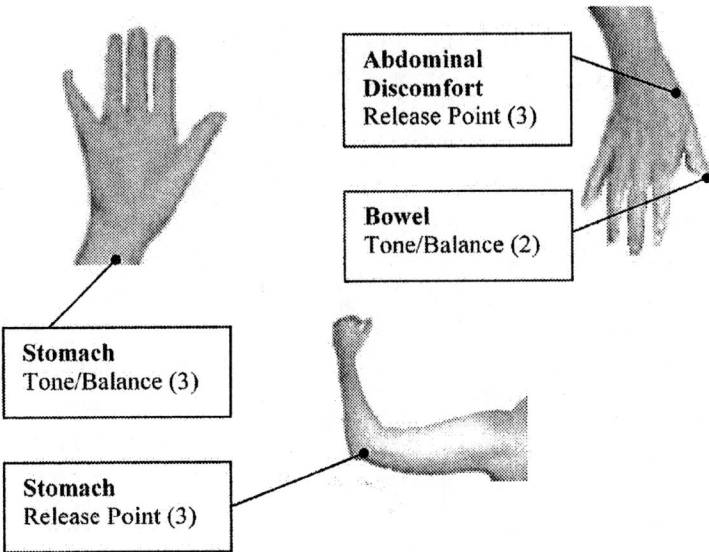

Bowel
Tone/Balance (2)

Colon
Release Point (3)

Stomach
Release Point (3)

Bladder
Tone/Balance (2)

Liver
Release Point (3)

Liver
Stimulate (1)
Tone/Balance (2)

Bladder
Tone/Balance (2)

Kidneys
Release Point (3)

Stomach
Release Point (3)

Meridian for Digestive tract
2nd toe
Stimulate (1)

Abdominal Discomfort
Release Point (3)

Bowel
Tone/Balance (2)

Stomach
Tone/Balance (3)

Stomach
Release Point (3)

Treatment for Digestive System (Back)

Working on your own back is practically impossible; however, these points shown below are ideal for individuals who find it difficult to lie on their backs for long periods while being treated. Many of these points also connect with muscular pain and discomfort. By working the back, you can open up the energies of the spine and stimulate a general rebuilding of cells, which in the long term will results in full recovery. Back treatments will be given once a week, which will allow time for the movements of energy to have its healing effect.

(1) Quartz   (2) Carnelian   (3) Aventurine

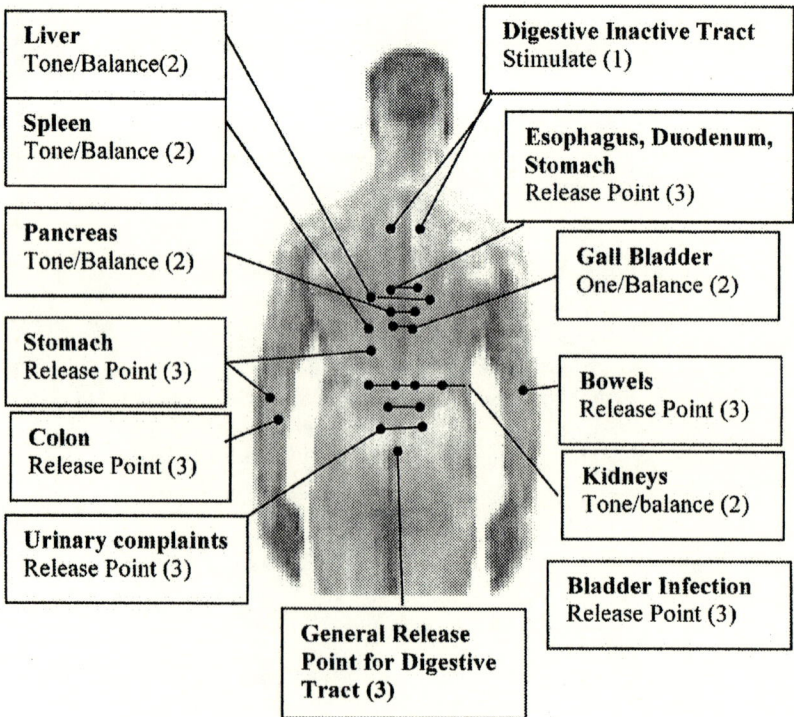

Liver
Tone/Balance(2)

Spleen
Tone/Balance (2)

Pancreas
Tone/Balance (2)

Stomach
Release Point (3)

Colon
Release Point (3)

Urinary complaints
Release Point (3)

Digestive Inactive Tract
Stimulate (1)

Esophagus, Duodenum, Stomach
Release Point (3)

Gall Bladder
One/Balance (2)

Bowels
Release Point (3)

Kidneys
Tone/balance (2)

Bladder Infection
Release Point (3)

General Release
Point for Digestive
Tract (3)

Treatment For The Digestive System (Cont.)

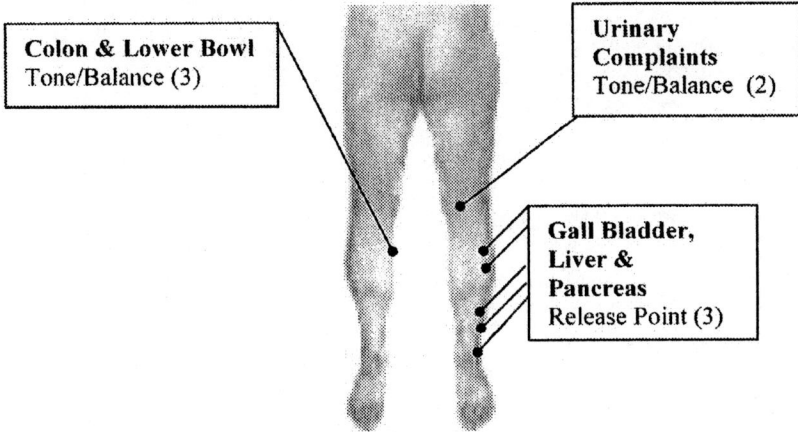

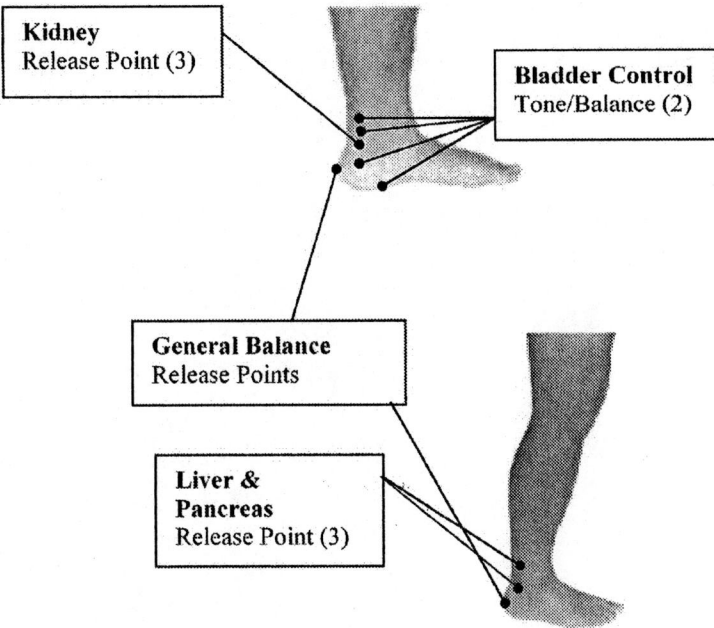

Colon & Lower Bowl
Tone/Balance (3)

**Urinary
Complaints**
Tone/Balance (2)

**Gall Bladder,
Liver &
Pancreas**
Release Point (3)

Kidney
Release Point (3)

Bladder Control
Tone/Balance (2)

General Balance
Release Points

**Liver &
Pancreas**
Release Point (3)

Treatment To Improve The Circulatory System

Being worried and anxious can prevent joy from manifesting in your life. By using the Crystals on the points shown below, you can help yourself feel more vital and develop greater strength. While your problems will not necessarily disappear, your attitude in dealing with them can change for the better. You will find yourself feeling more relaxed and capable of handling emotional stress. When blood circulates carrying the right nutriments along with oxygen to rejuvenate, healing occurs. These points should be worked once of twice a week along with deep breathing exercises from time to time. The rear or front maybe worked on at one time, but always do the hands and feet too.

A good diet with low fat and a remedy herbal tea such as Mistletoe twigs and leaves brewed cold will clear the arteries and veins of cholesterol. Nettle Tea will purify the blood and assist the liver to cleanse.

(1) Quartz (2) Amazonite (3) Rose Quartz

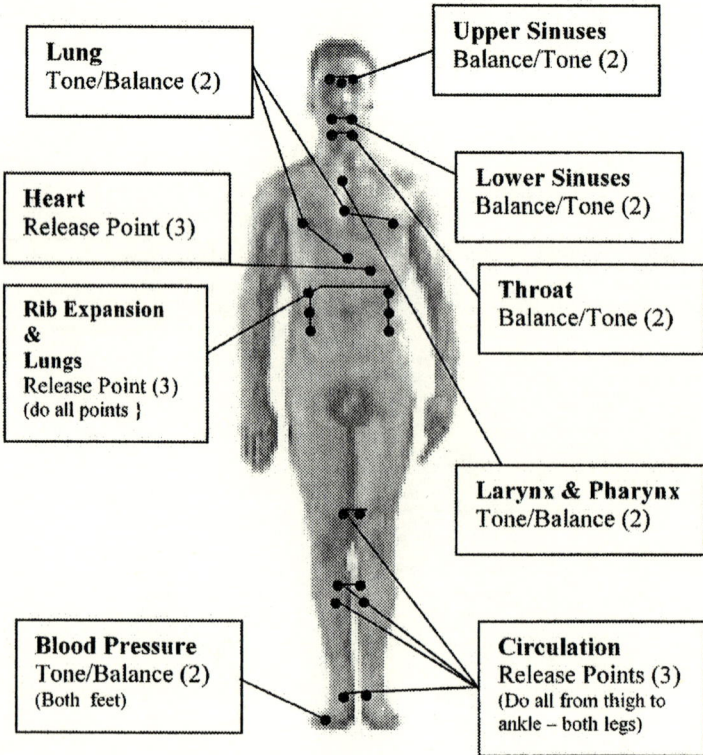

Lung
Tone/Balance (2)

Upper Sinuses
Balance/Tone (2)

Heart
Release Point (3)

Lower Sinuses
Balance/Tone (2)

**Rib Expansion
&
Lungs**
Release Point (3)
(do all points)

Throat
Balance/Tone (2)

Larynx & Pharynx
Tone/Balance (2)

Blood Pressure
Tone/Balance (2)
(Both feet)

Circulation
Release Points (3)
(Do all from thigh to
ankle – both legs)

Treatment To Improve The Circulatory System (Cont.)

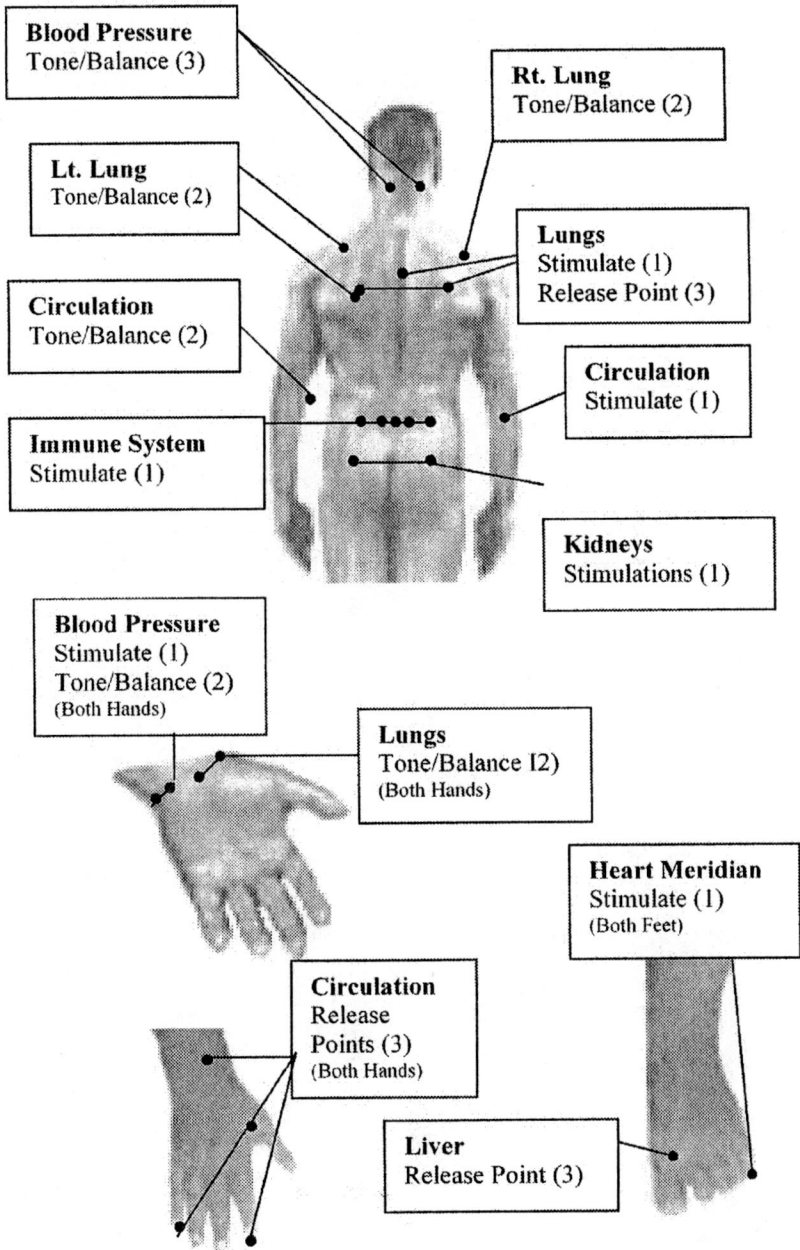

Blood Pressure
Tone/Balance (3)

Rt. Lung
Tone/Balance (2)

Lt. Lung
Tone/Balance (2)

Lungs
Stimulate (1)
Release Point (3)

Circulation
Tone/Balance (2)

Circulation
Stimulate (1)

Immune System
Stimulate (1)

Kidneys
Stimulations (1)

Blood Pressure
Stimulate (1)
Tone/Balance (2)
(Both Hands)

Lungs
Tone/Balance I2)
(Both Hands)

Heart Meridian
Stimulate (1)
(Both Feet)

Circulation
Release
Points (3)
(Both Hands)

Liver
Release Point (3)

Treatment for Harmonizing The Nervous System (Front)

From early childhood, we are trained to think and react with caution, fear, pain, anger and guilt, along with excitement, anticipation, joy, love and pleasure. Both negative and positive attitudes bring emotional responses that cause us to over-react. When this occurs, the Nervous System becomes overloaded. Tension brought on by control issues confines us. Life becomes an endless cycle of suffering. It is important to relax the nerves throughout the body. By using Crystals on the points shown below, you can stimulate, tone and balance the nerve endings, which will allow relaxation and healing to occur.

(1) Quartz (2) Sodalite (3) Amethyst

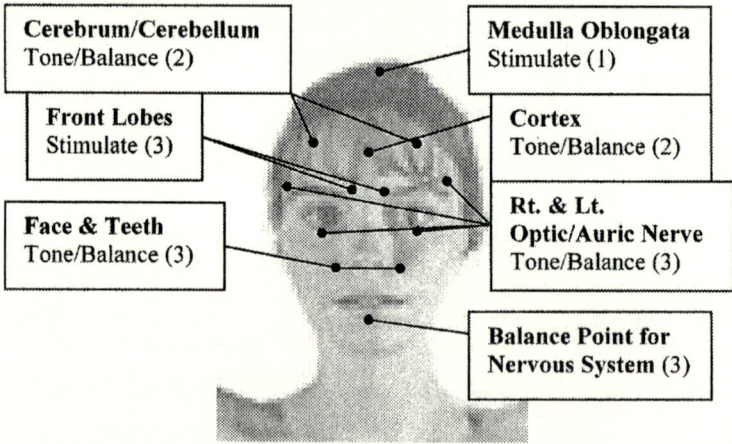

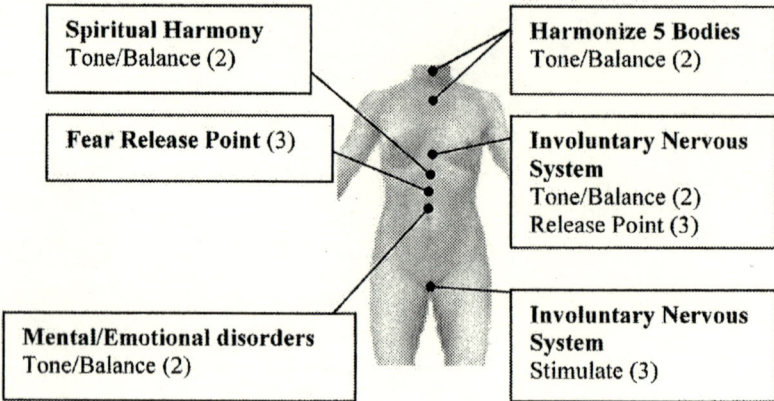

Cerebrum/Cerebellum
Tone/Balance (2)

Medulla Oblongata
Stimulate (1)

Front Lobes
Stimulate (3)

Cortex
Tone/Balance (2)

Face & Teeth
Tone/Balance (3)

Rt. & Lt.
Optic/Auric Nerve
Tone/Balance (3)

Balance Point for
Nervous System (3)

Spiritual Harmony
Tone/Balance (2)

Harmonize 5 Bodies
Tone/Balance (2)

Fear Release Point (3)

Involuntary Nervous
System
Tone/Balance (2)
Release Point (3)

Mental/Emotional disorders
Tone/Balance (2)

Involuntary Nervous
System
Stimulate (3)

Treatment for Harmonizing The Nervous System (Front Cont.))

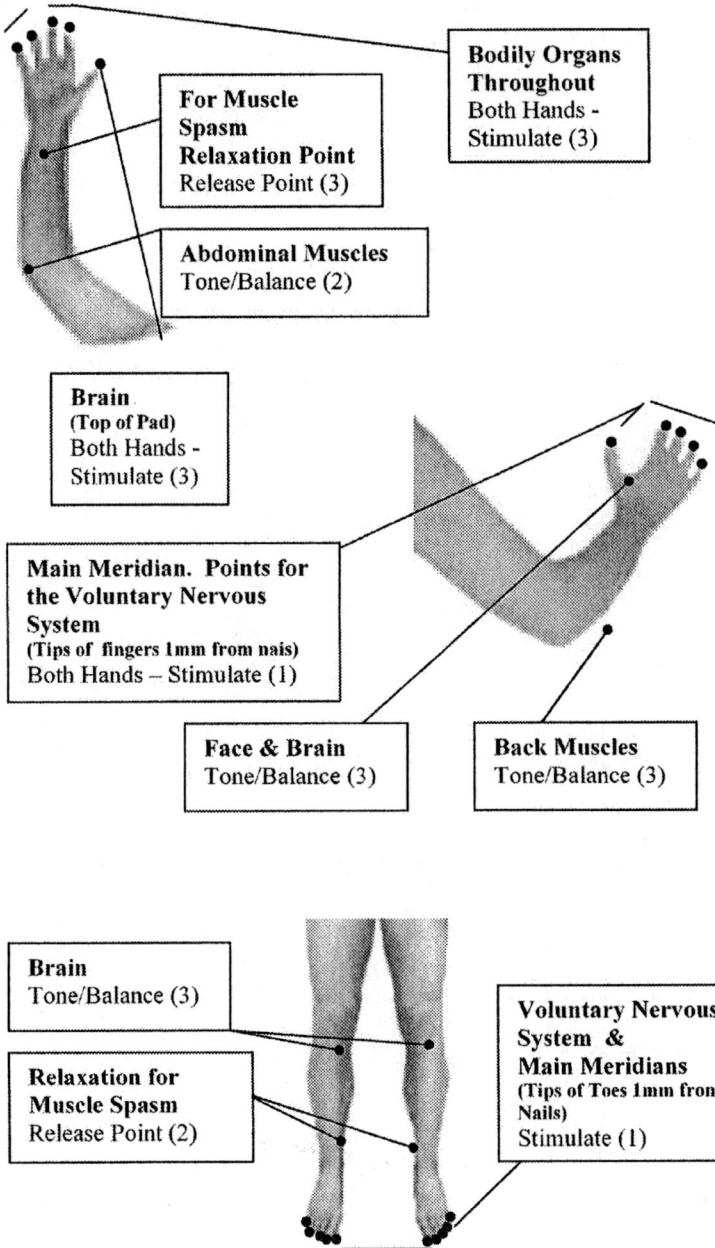

Bodily Organs Throughout
Both Hands - Stimulate (3)

For Muscle Spasm Relaxation Point
Release Point (3)

Abdominal Muscles
Tone/Balance (2)

Brain
(Top of Pad)
Both Hands - Stimulate (3)

Main Meridian. Points for the Voluntary Nervous System
(Tips of fingers 1mm from nais)
Both Hands – Stimulate (1)

Face & Brain
Tone/Balance (3)

Back Muscles
Tone/Balance (3)

Brain
Tone/Balance (3)

Relaxation for Muscle Spasm
Release Point (2)

Voluntary Nervous System & Main Meridians
(Tips of Toes 1mm from Nails)
Stimulate (1)

Treatment To Relax The Nervous System (Back)

Working the back of the body will help to erase fears from shock and anxiety which has usually been coded into the rear cells of the body. Physical events where an individual is dealing with the unknown or unexpected surprise actions, often result in nervousness and irritability. These individuals are usually walking around with a heightened sense of psychometry (psychic sense of feeling) and often will over-react to everything they hear.

(1) Quartz (2) Sodalite (3) Amethyst

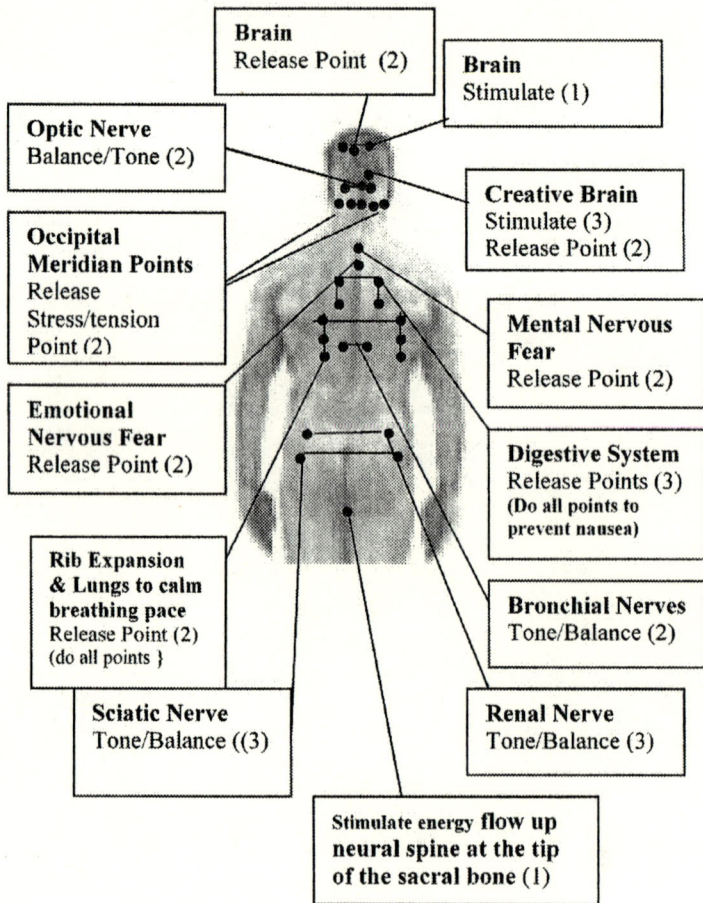

Brain Release Point (2)

Brain Stimulate (1)

Optic Nerve Balance/Tone (2)

Creative Brain Stimulate (3) Release Point (2)

Occipital Meridian Points Release Stress/tension Point (2)

Mental Nervous Fear Release Point (2)

Emotional Nervous Fear Release Point (2)

Digestive System Release Points (3) **(Do all points to prevent nausea)**

Rib Expansion & Lungs to calm breathing pace Release Point (2) (do all points }

Bronchial Nerves Tone/Balance (2)

Sciatic Nerve Tone/Balance ((3)

Renal Nerve Tone/Balance (3)

Stimulate energy flow up neural spine at the tip of the sacral bone (1)

Treatment To Improve The Glandular System

Our various glands within the body are vital to our survival. They help us rebuild, revitalize and rejuvenate ourselves. Each gland produces enzymes that are important to bodily operations. Without them, your body ceases to function. Keeping your glands working productively can help you maintain a healthy body. If you are already healthy, then give yourself a fine tune up once a month. If you have health problems, you should work these points every other day. General well being will be obtained over a length of time, though some individuals report instant changes in specific areas of self. For many diseases and minor complaints, it is always advisable to spend time working these points anyway.

(1) Quartz (2) Carnelian (3) Aventurine (4) Amazonite

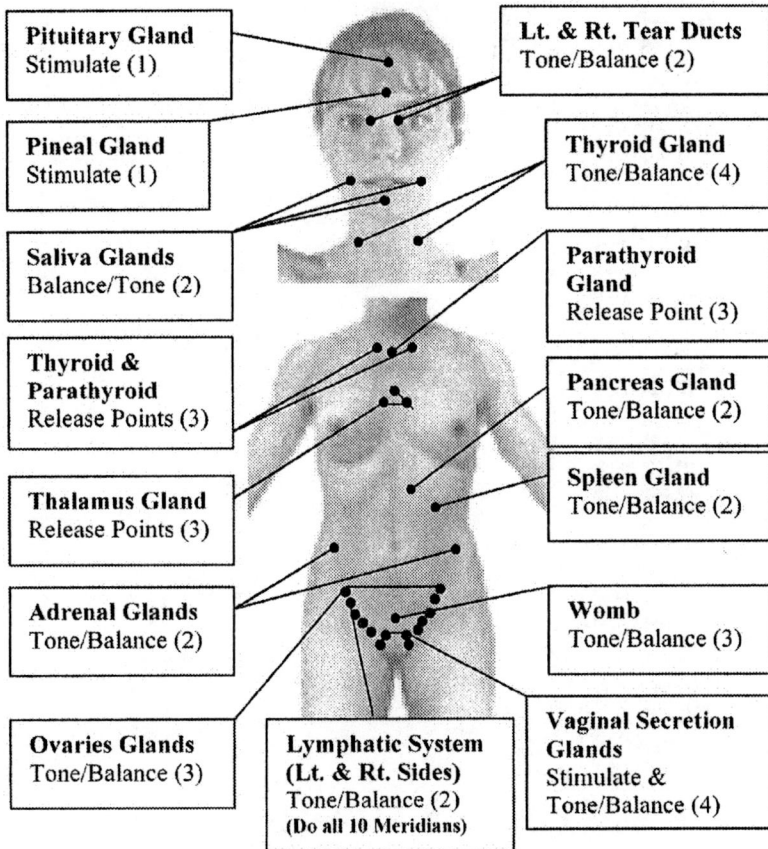

Pituitary Gland Stimulate (1)

Lt. & Rt. Tear Ducts Tone/Balance (2)

Pineal Gland Stimulate (1)

Thyroid Gland Tone/Balance (4)

Saliva Glands Balance/Tone (2)

Parathyroid Gland Release Point (3)

Thyroid & Parathyroid Release Points (3)

Pancreas Gland Tone/Balance (2)

Thalamus Gland Release Points (3)

Spleen Gland Tone/Balance (2)

Adrenal Glands Tone/Balance (2)

Womb Tone/Balance (3)

Ovaries Glands Tone/Balance (3)

Lymphatic System (Lt. & Rt. Sides) Tone/Balance (2) **(Do all 10 Meridians)**

Vaginal Secretion Glands Stimulate & Tone/Balance (4)

Treatment To Improve The Glandular System (Cont.)

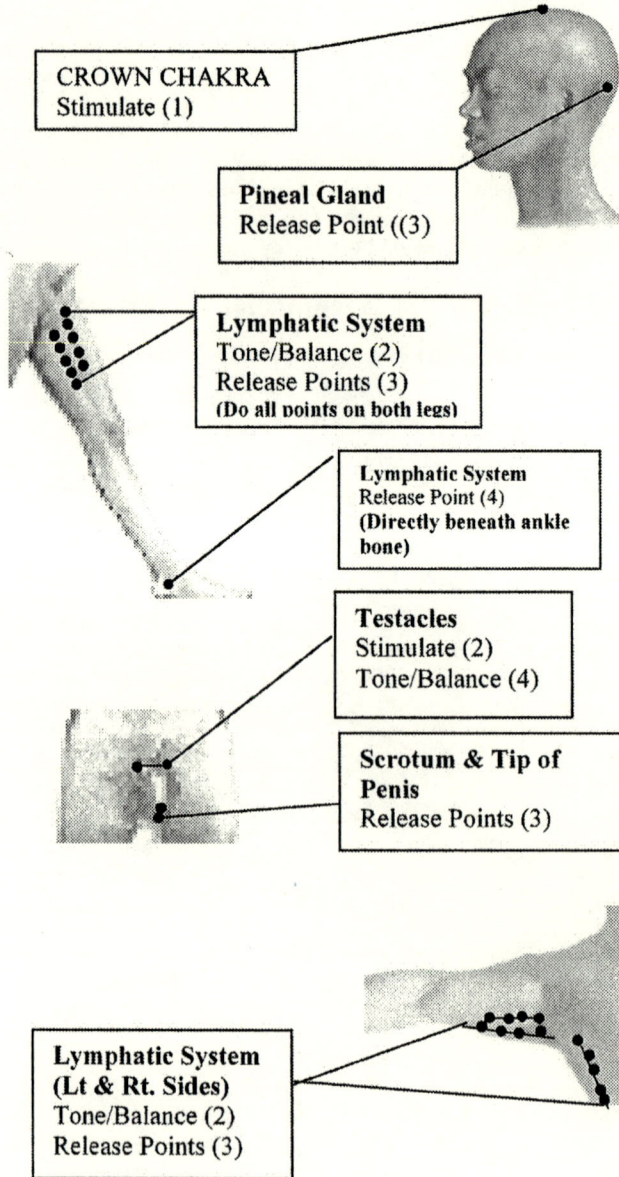

CROWN CHAKRA
Stimulate (1)

Pineal Gland
Release Point ((3)

Lymphatic System
Tone/Balance (2)
Release Points (3)
(Do all points on both legs)

Lymphatic System
Release Point (4)
(Directly beneath ankle bone)

Testacles
Stimulate (2)
Tone/Balance (4)

Scrotum & Tip of Penis
Release Points (3)

Lymphatic System (Lt & Rt. Sides)
Tone/Balance (2)
Release Points (3)

GENERAL TREATMENTS
FOR AILMENTS

Treatment for Stress Reduction

Whether you are hurrying to work, or worrying about housework, there is always some level of stress. The points below are to help you prevent stress. Quite simply begin your day by spending ten minutes working the points. When you begin your day's activities, you will find yourself in a happier frame of mind. If you are constantly stressed, however, working these points before bedtime will relax you enough to dream out your anxiety and give you a comfortable night.

(1) Quartz (4) Sodalite (2) Hematite (5) Amethyst (6) Rose Quartz

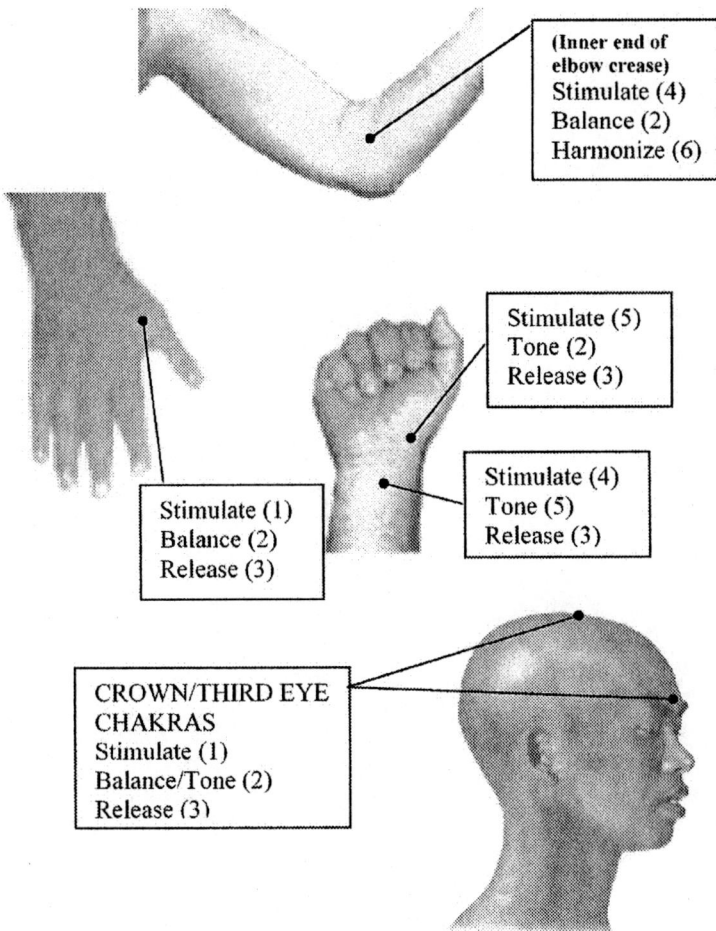

(Inner end of elbow crease)
Stimulate (4)
Balance (2)
Harmonize (6)

Stimulate (5)
Tone (2)
Release (3)

Stimulate (4)
Tone (5)
Release (3)

Stimulate (1)
Balance (2)
Release (3)

CROWN/THIRD EYE CHAKRAS
Stimulate (1)
Balance/Tone (2)
Release (3)

Treatment For Throat Infections

If you have a throat infection, you are probably suppressing something you want to say. By working the points shown below, you will allow blocks in the Throat Chakra to move and you can then bring up any issues that need to be solved. General aches in the jaw and throat are often the result of resistance to truth received or given in an argument along with an emotional need to cry. Be prepared to vent and release old issues. Just one or two treatments over a few days will allow rapid healing to occur. Remember that a good old-fashioned gargle will also help, along with eating the right foods.

(1) Sodalite (2) Rose Quartz (3) Carnelian

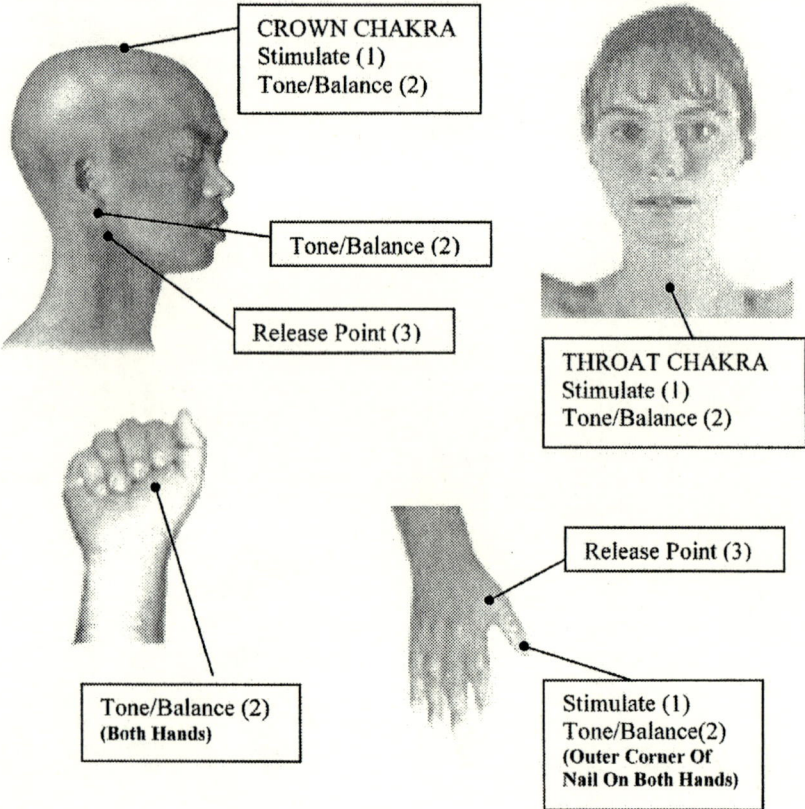

CROWN CHAKRA
Stimulate (1)
Tone/Balance (2)

Tone/Balance (2)

Release Point (3)

THROAT CHAKRA
Stimulate (1)
Tone/Balance (2)

Tone/Balance (2)
(Both Hands)

Release Point (3)

Stimulate (1)
Tone/Balance(2)
**(Outer Corner Of
Nail On Both Hands)**

Treatment For Migraine/Headaches

If you have a headache or, even worse, a migraine, then you are emotionally and mentally at war with yourself and the rest of the world. Your constant worrying about performance and the results have caused many blocks in your body, and your head is telling you to take a break and relax. Take time out to release negative beliefs and emotional trauma that you have insisted upon relying on. Remember your history is only an experience and new experiences are exciting and interesting. Plan a new outlook and let the pain go.

(1) Amethyst   (2) Hematite   (3) Aventurine

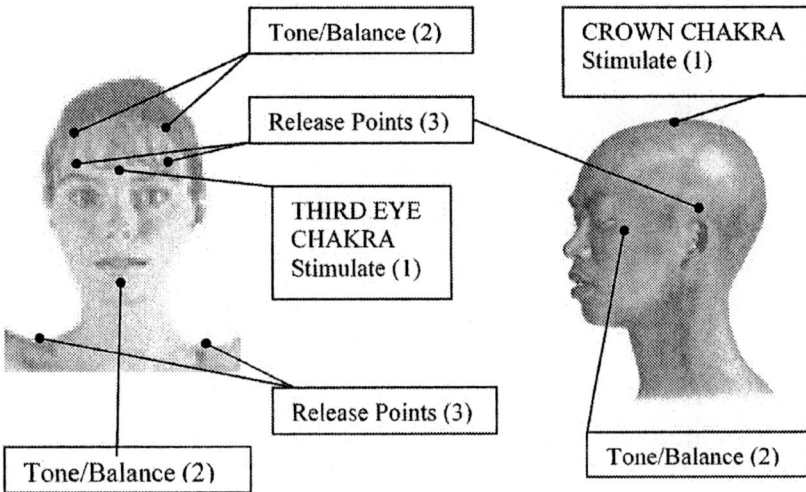

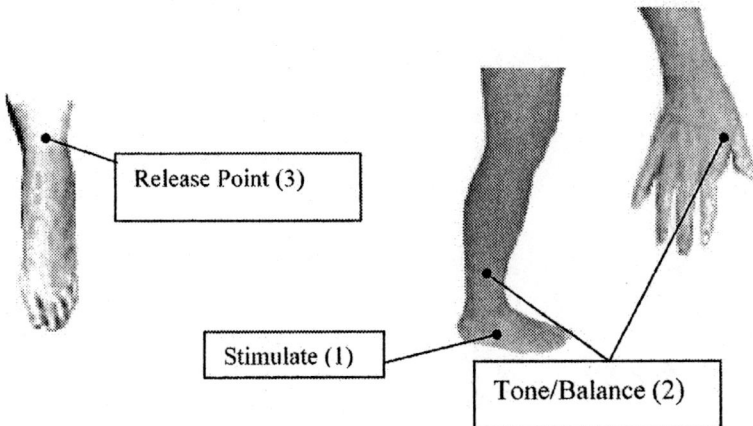

Tone/Balance (2)

CROWN CHAKRA
Stimulate (1)

Release Points (3)

THIRD EYE
CHAKRA
Stimulate (1)

Release Points (3)

Tone/Balance (2)

Tone/Balance (2)

Release Point (3)

Stimulate (1)

Tone/Balance (2)

Treatment For Hay Fever/Sinus/Allergies

If you are suffering with these or any other similar complaints, then you most assuredly have subliminal memories associated with smells and tastes from your very early childhood. The smell of cooked bread may have an unhappy connotation. Fortunately, we do not need to directly face most of these deeply buried memories. With Crystal Acupuncture[sm] applied to the points shown below, you can eliminate these memories on a cellular level. Expect to dream out the fears with anger and pain of those years and awaken to happy days ahead, being free of your allergies etc. Be sure to continue with your prescribed medication and advice until you feel you no longer need them.

(1) Sodalite (2) Rose Quartz (3) Aventurine (4) Carnelian

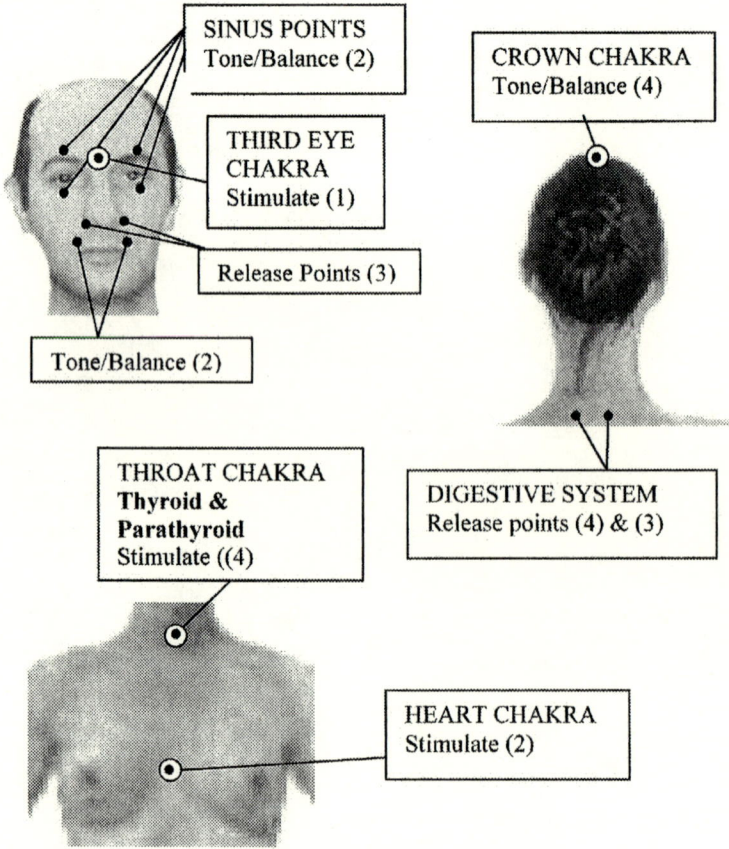

SINUS POINTS
Tone/Balance (2)

CROWN CHAKRA
Tone/Balance (4)

THIRD EYE
CHAKRA
Stimulate (1)

Release Points (3)

Tone/Balance (2)

THROAT CHAKRA
Thyroid &
Parathyroid
Stimulate ((4)

DIGESTIVE SYSTEM
Release points (4) & (3)

HEART CHAKRA
Stimulate (2)

Treatment For Hay Fever/Sinus/Allergies (Cont.)

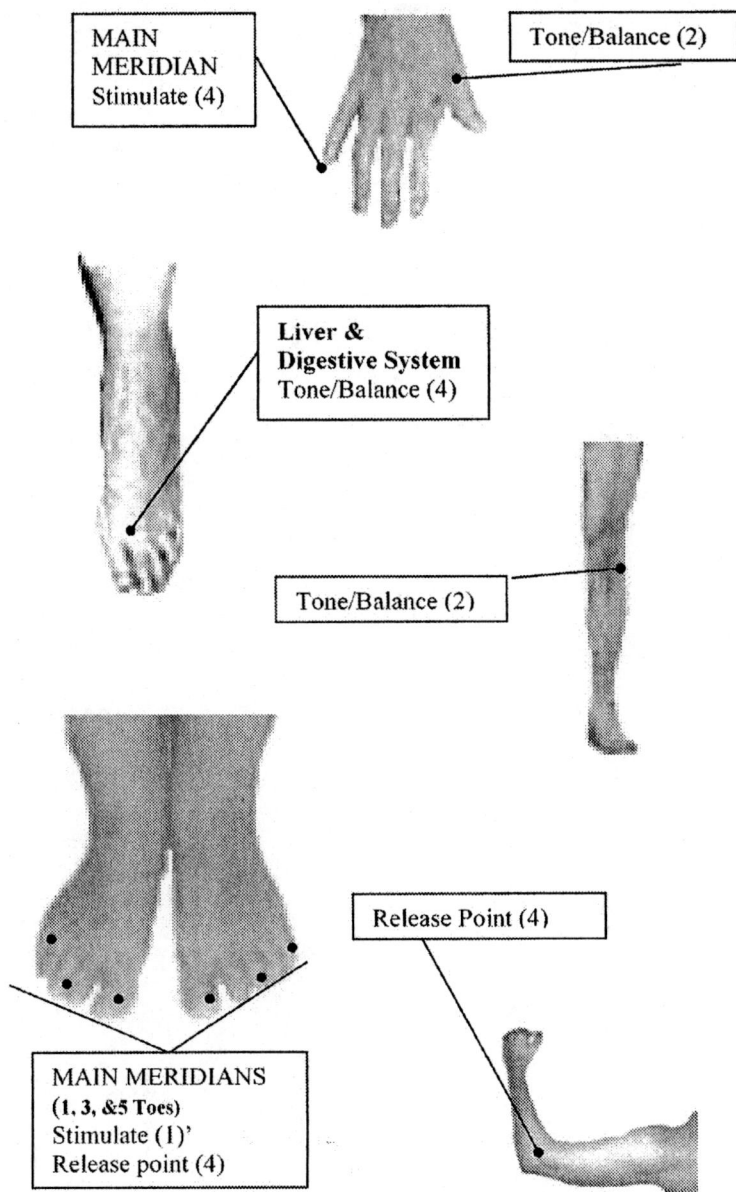

MAIN
MERIDIAN
Stimulate (4)

Tone/Balance (2)

**Liver &
Digestive System**
Tone/Balance (4)

Tone/Balance (2)

Release Point (4)

MAIN MERIDIANS
(1, 3, &5 Toes)
Stimulate (1)'
Release point (4)

Dr. Margaret Rogers Van Coops

Treatment For Earache & Hearing Loss

There are three parts to the ears: the inner, middle and outer. If you have an infection, then you should continue regular medical treatment along with daily treatment of the Crystal Acupuncture[sm] points below.

If you find yourself suffering with hearing loss, tin-panning, or dizziness, consult a physician. Once you have received advice, work the points shown below, twice a week. Take time for healing to occur between treatments along with release of fear, pain, anger and guilt. These might be why you are having loss of hearing. In some cases, tin-panning of the middle ear is caused by nervous awareness, where super hearing of every little sound, including dead sound, becomes annoying. Expect to dream a lot while working on these points.

(1) Quartz (2) Carnelian (3) Hematite (4) Aventurine

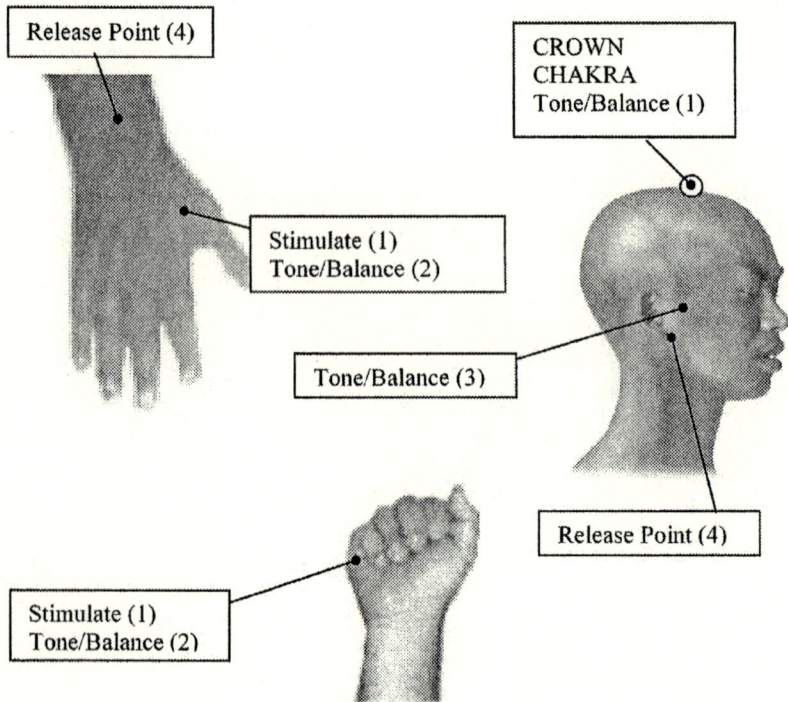

Release Point (4)

CROWN CHAKRA Tone/Balance (1)

Stimulate (1) Tone/Balance (2)

Tone/Balance (3)

Release Point (4)

Stimulate (1) Tone/Balance (2)

60

Treatment for Eye Troubles

Regular check-ups are important along with health care. Eyes are very important and should be checked regularly. Working with the crystal acupuncture points below you may wish to focus on improvement of vision and your perceptions in the way you see your life and that of others. Regular treatments will also help you to improve your psychic sense of clairvoyance. If you are suffering with cataracts or eye infections, then along with medical treatment, you might like to place cucumber or chamomile tea bags on your eyes while working the points.

(1) Quartz (2) Carnelian (3) Hematite (4) Aventurine

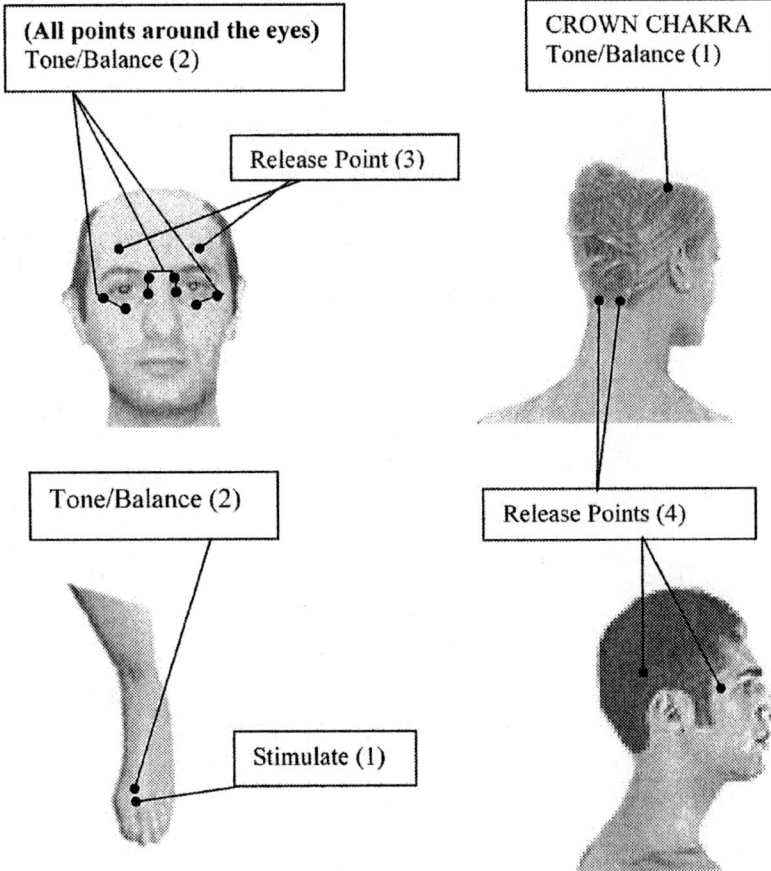

(All points around the eyes)
Tone/Balance (2)

Release Point (3)

CROWN CHAKRA
Tone/Balance (1)

Tone/Balance (2)

Release Points (4)

Stimulate (1)

Treatment for Neck Problems

Generally, neck problems are caused by stress and tension. The head is held in a fixed position while reacting to all five senses. This kind of intense strain often occurs during working or studying hours. However, those who see themselves as over-burdened with responsibility, and who insist on carrying their burden despite opportunities to delegate may also find themselves locked in the back of the neck. By working these points, one can release fear of failure and stimulate enjoyment of the five senses. Creative pursuits should be encouraged, along with light conversation.

(1) Sodalite (2) Amazonite (3) Aventurine (4) Rose Quartz

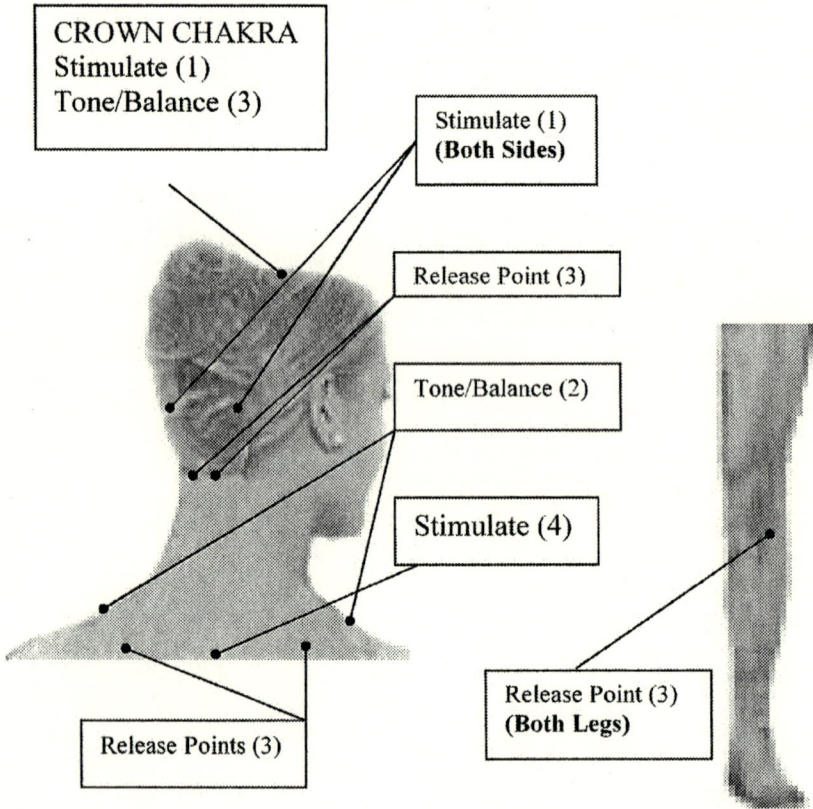

CROWN CHAKRA
Stimulate (1)
Tone/Balance (3)

Stimulate (1)
(Both Sides)

Release Point (3)

Tone/Balance (2)

Stimulate (4)

Release Point (3)
(Both Legs)

Release Points (3)

Treatment for Neck Problems (Cont.)

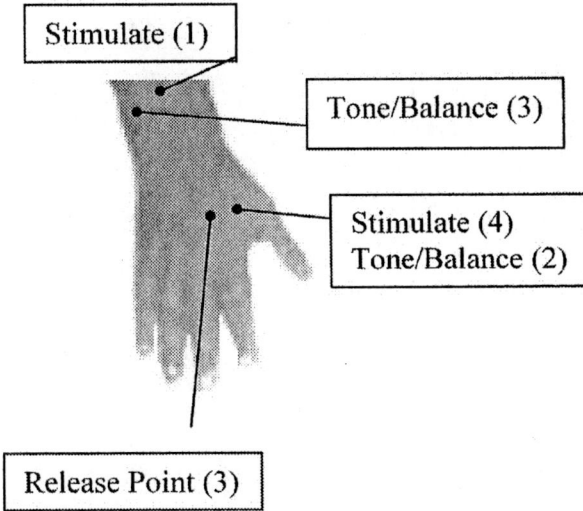

Stimulate (1)

Tone/Balance (3)

Stimulate (4)
Tone/Balance (2)

Release Point (3)

(Do all points on both hands)

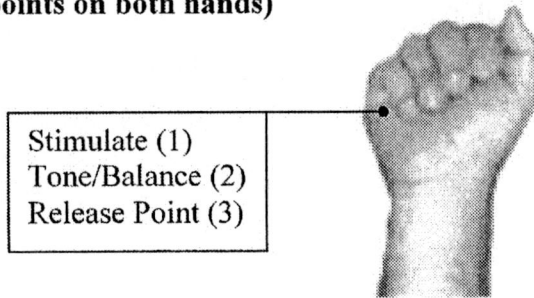

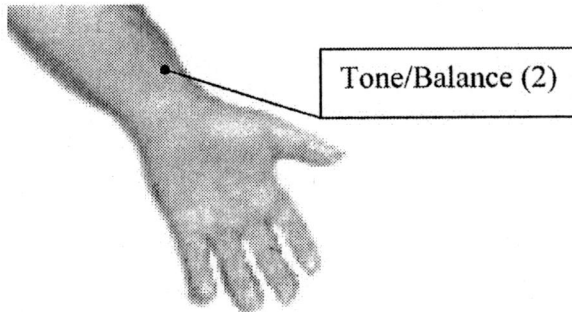

Stimulate (1)
Tone/Balance (2)
Release Point (3)

Tone/Balance (2)

Treatment For Asthma/Bronchitis

The lungs are vital to our life's quality as well as continuance. If we cannot breathe, of course, we cannot exist, but every inhalation also has a direct line into the deep subconscious where all memories of this life are stored. As toddlers, we learn to play and have fun. As teenagers, we learn the values of discipline. Often these disciplines create restrictive habits that prevent us from having fun. Lung disorders directly reflect lack of joy in life. Usually, these conditions accompany heart palpitations or other more serious symptoms. If you have any negative symptoms connected to respiration, consult a physician. Crystal Acupuncture[sm] will enhance medical treatment and assist you to overcome any resentment and/or resistance you may have to changes that will allow joy back into your life. Once you let yourself be happy, lung complaints, along with fear, pain, anger and guilt, should clear up

(1) Hematite   (2) Rose Quartz   (3) Amazonite

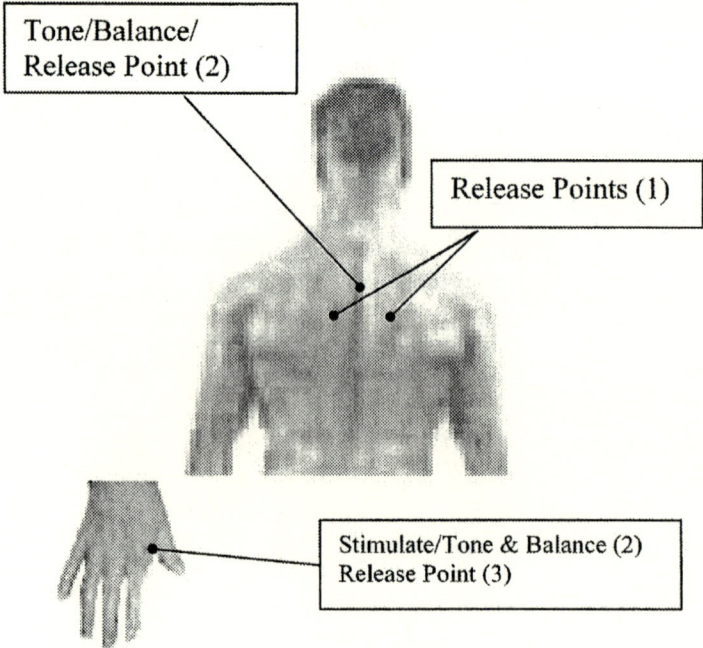

Tone/Balance/
Release Point (2)

Release Points (1)

Stimulate/Tone & Balance (2)
Release Point (3)

Treatment For Asthma/Bronchitis (Cont.)

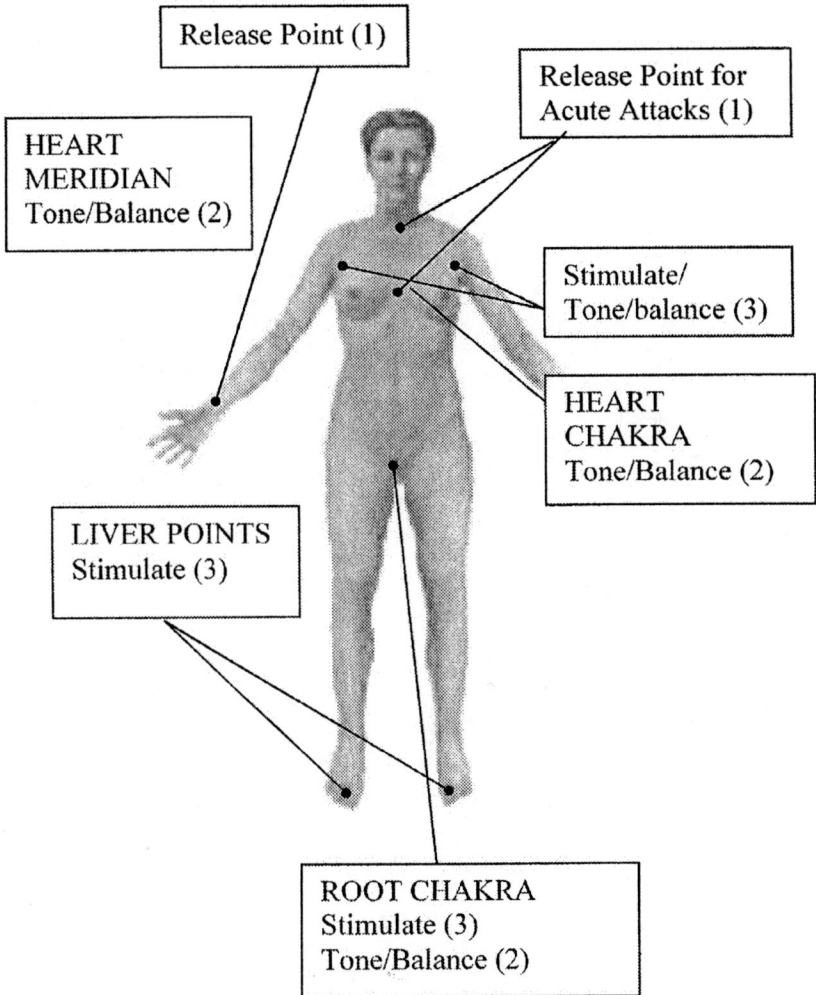

Release Point (1)

Release Point for
Acute Attacks (1)

HEART
MERIDIAN
Tone/Balance (2)

Stimulate/
Tone/balance (3)

HEART
CHAKRA
Tone/Balance (2)

LIVER POINTS
Stimulate (3)

ROOT CHAKRA
Stimulate (3)
Tone/Balance (2)

Treatment For Back Pain
(Rheumatism, Arthritis, Strain, Stiffness)

Back pain can originate from many different causes. Rheumatism, Arthritis, and bone deformity are generally associated with anger and fear held over many years. Those with these conditions should work the Nervous System and Digestive System after working the Acu Points shown below. Physical exercise and good nutrition will also help the body to heal. If you have hurt yourself through an accident or a fall, release the fear and shock of the event by first working the Nervous System and then following up with the Acu points below. Consult a Physician or a Chiropractor also for treatment of chronic conditions.

(1) Quartz (2) Rose Quartz (3) Sodalite (4) Hematite
(5) Amethyst (6) Carnelian

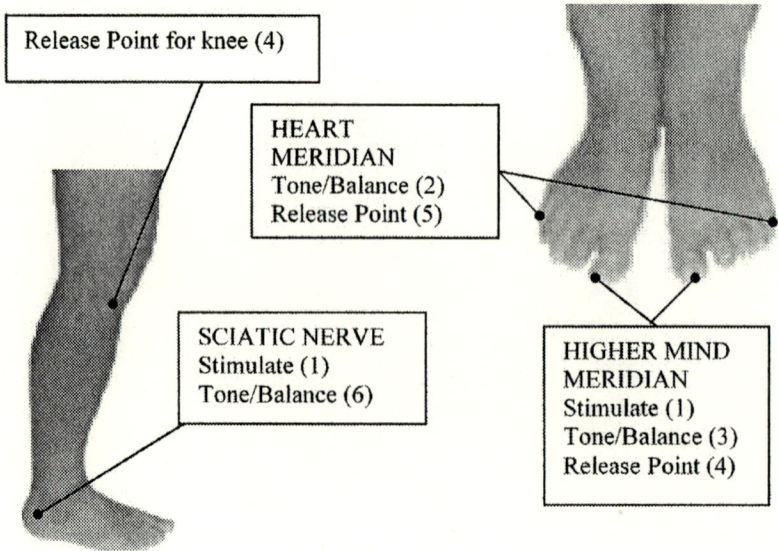

Release Point for knee (4)

HEART
MERIDIAN
Tone/Balance (2)
Release Point (5)

SCIATIC NERVE
Stimulate (1)
Tone/Balance (6)

HIGHER MIND
MERIDIAN
Stimulate (1)
Tone/Balance (3)
Release Point (4)

Treatment For Back Pain (Cont.)
(Rheumatism, Arthritis, Strain, Stiffness)

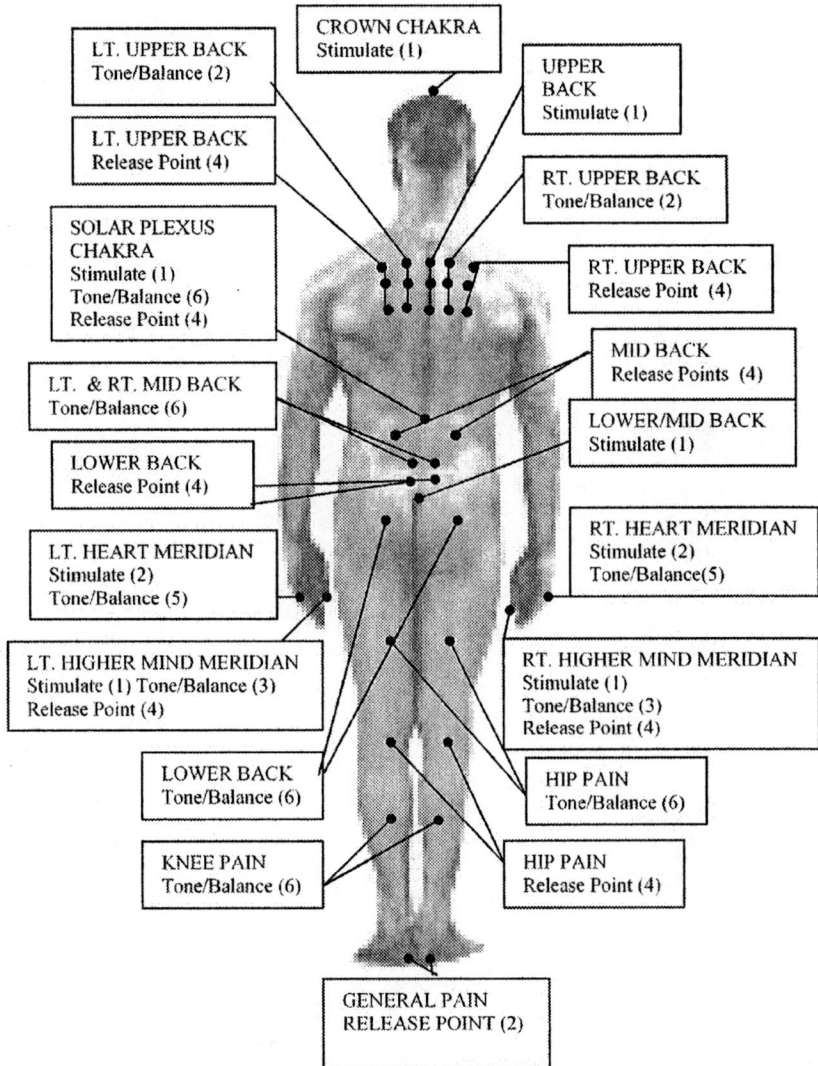

CROWN CHAKRA
Stimulate (1)

LT. UPPER BACK
Tone/Balance (2)

UPPER
BACK
Stimulate (1)

LT. UPPER BACK
Release Point (4)

RT. UPPER BACK
Tone/Balance (2)

SOLAR PLEXUS
CHAKRA
Stimulate (1)
Tone/Balance (6)
Release Point (4)

RT. UPPER BACK
Release Point (4)

MID BACK
Release Points (4)

LT. & RT. MID BACK
Tone/Balance (6)

LOWER/MID BACK
Stimulate (1)

LOWER BACK
Release Point (4)

RT. HEART MERIDIAN
Stimulate (2)
Tone/Balance(5)

LT. HEART MERIDIAN
Stimulate (2)
Tone/Balance (5)

LT. HIGHER MIND MERIDIAN
Stimulate (1) Tone/Balance (3)
Release Point (4)

RT. HIGHER MIND MERIDIAN
Stimulate (1)
Tone/Balance (3)
Release Point (4)

LOWER BACK
Tone/Balance (6)

HIP PAIN
Tone/Balance (6)

KNEE PAIN
Tone/Balance (6)

HIP PAIN
Release Point (4)

GENERAL PAIN
RELEASE POINT (2)

Treatment for General Aches and Pains

If stiffness with general myalgia is the problem, then work the Acu Points for the Nervous, Digestive and Glandular Systems first before working with the Acu points shown below. It is most likely that you are suffering from a deep-seated childhood inferiority complex with control issues. It is always advisable to seek counsel. Every individual case is unique. These aches and pains that seem to move around the body, are signs that your energies in the Physical, Etheric and Spirit Bodies are blocked. Working the Acu Points shown will disperse these blocks. Expect to dream out your childhood fears.

Before beginning this treatment, spend time contemplating surrender and embracing a new style of life with a new point of view.

(1) Quartz (2) Carnelian (3) Aventurine

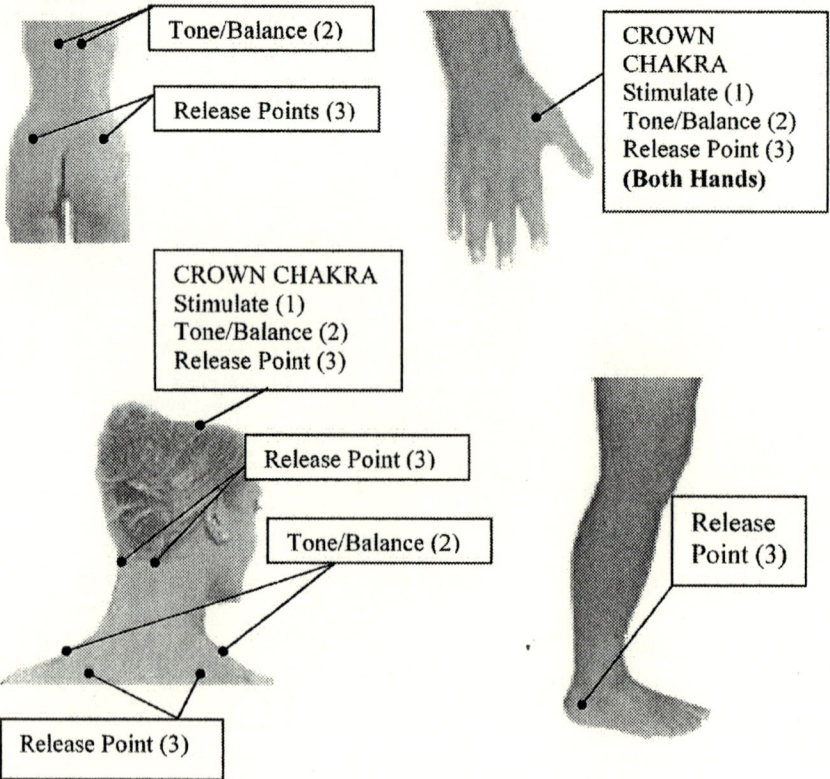

Tone/Balance (2)

Release Points (3)

CROWN CHAKRA
Stimulate (1)
Tone/Balance (2)
Release Point (3)
(Both Hands)

CROWN CHAKRA
Stimulate (1)
Tone/Balance (2)
Release Point (3)

Release Point (3)

Tone/Balance (2)

Release Point (3)

Release Point (3)

Treatment for Reproductive Problems In Women
Menstruation, Menopause, Hot Flushes, Fertility

If you have been trying to have a baby without success, it is important to look inward to discover your innermost fears. Lack of confidence about motherhood will often cause blocks in ovulation, along with blocks in the fallopian tubes and/or womb. These blocks can cause a back flow of energy that will prevent pregnancy or cause deformity. If menstruation is the problem, the Glandular System should also be worked, paying special attention to the Crown Chakra and the Pituitary Gland, which controls the state of all the other glands in the body. For Menopause/hot flushes, the Nervous System, Circulation System and the Chakras as well as the Acu points below should also be worked. Allow one week between treatments for changes to occur between treatments and enjoy dreaming out your fear, pain, anger, guilt and loneliness. Invite love into your life and be happy being a woman.

(1) Rose Quartz (2) Carnelian (3) Amazonite (4) Amethyst

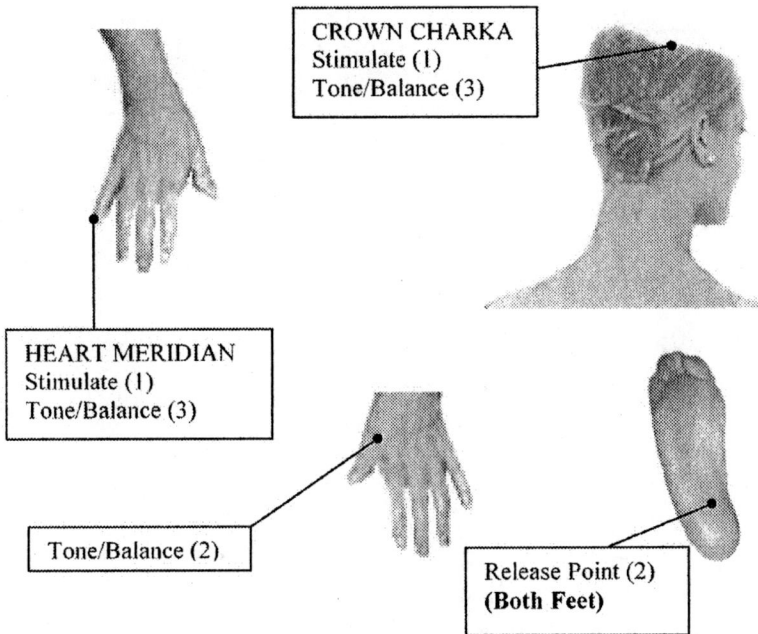

CROWN CHARKA
Stimulate (1)
Tone/Balance (3)

HEART MERIDIAN
Stimulate (1)
Tone/Balance (3)

Tone/Balance (2)

Release Point (2)
(Both Feet)

Treatment for Reproductive Problems In Women
Menstruation, Menopause, Hot Flushes, Fertility (Cont.)

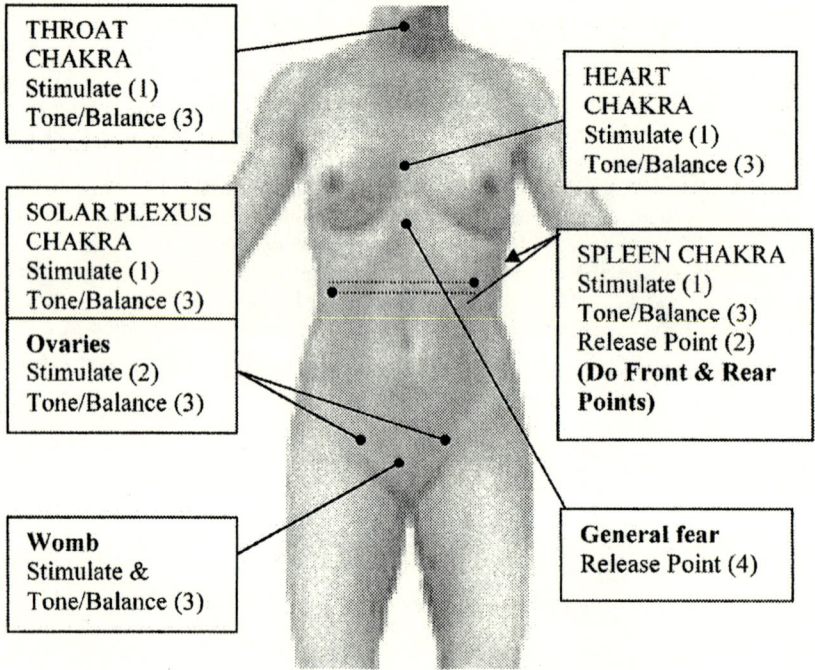

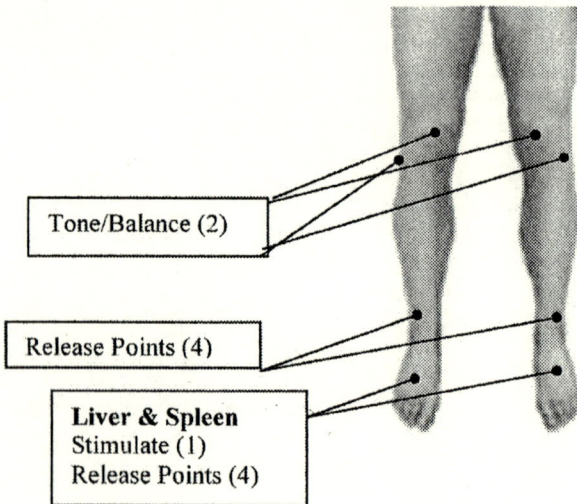

THROAT
CHAKRA
Stimulate (1)
Tone/Balance (3)

HEART
CHAKRA
Stimulate (1)
Tone/Balance (3)

SOLAR PLEXUS
CHAKRA
Stimulate (1)
Tone/Balance (3)

Ovaries
Stimulate (2)
Tone/Balance (3)

SPLEEN CHAKRA
Stimulate (1)
Tone/Balance (3)
Release Point (2)
**(Do Front & Rear
Points)**

Womb
Stimulate &
Tone/Balance (3)

General fear
Release Point (4)

Tone/Balance (2)

Release Points (4)

Liver & Spleen
Stimulate (1)
Release Points (4)

Treatment For Hot Flushes With Panic Attacks & Sexual Dysfunction For Men

It is not unusual for men above 30 years old to find themselves having panic attacks while under stress combined with hot flashes that create a great deal of physical perspiration with redness of skin. Often these conditions are likely to occur while dealing with the opposite sex or an older man. Whether beginning or currently involved you will find times when certain events in your life will automatically trigger subconscious nervous memories, resulting in this uncomfortable state. For older men, the mid-life crisis can disturb the metabolic rate. During this time, the Liver, Pancreas and Spleen will be under constant strain to find a new level of bio-chemical balance. While the mind may be willing, physical sexual activities often become impossible. These points must be done every day, until positive results are consistent and then weekly, thereafter.

(1) Carnelian (2) Amethyst (3) Hematite (4) Sodalite (5) Rose Quartz

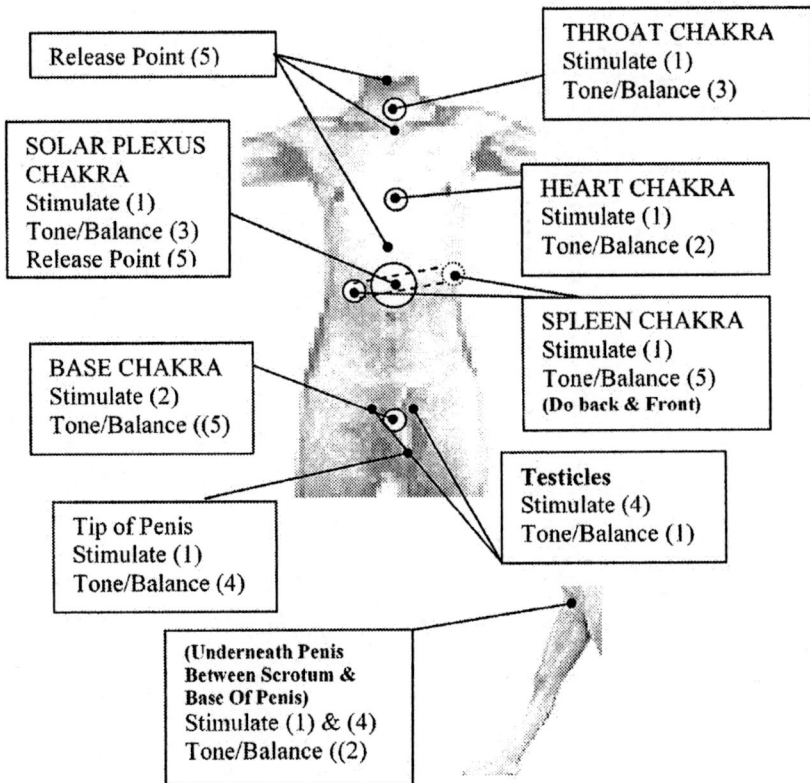

Release Point (5)

THROAT CHAKRA
Stimulate (1)
Tone/Balance (3)

SOLAR PLEXUS CHAKRA
Stimulate (1)
Tone/Balance (3)
Release Point (5)

HEART CHAKRA
Stimulate (1)
Tone/Balance (2)

SPLEEN CHAKRA
Stimulate (1)
Tone/Balance (5)
(Do back & Front)

BASE CHAKRA
Stimulate (2)
Tone/Balance ((5)

Testicles
Stimulate (4)
Tone/Balance (1)

Tip of Penis
Stimulate (1)
Tone/Balance (4)

(Underneath Penis
Between Scrotum &
Base Of Penis)
Stimulate (1) & (4)
Tone/Balance ((2)

Treatment For Hot Flushes With Panic Attacks & Sexual Dysfunction For Men (cont.)

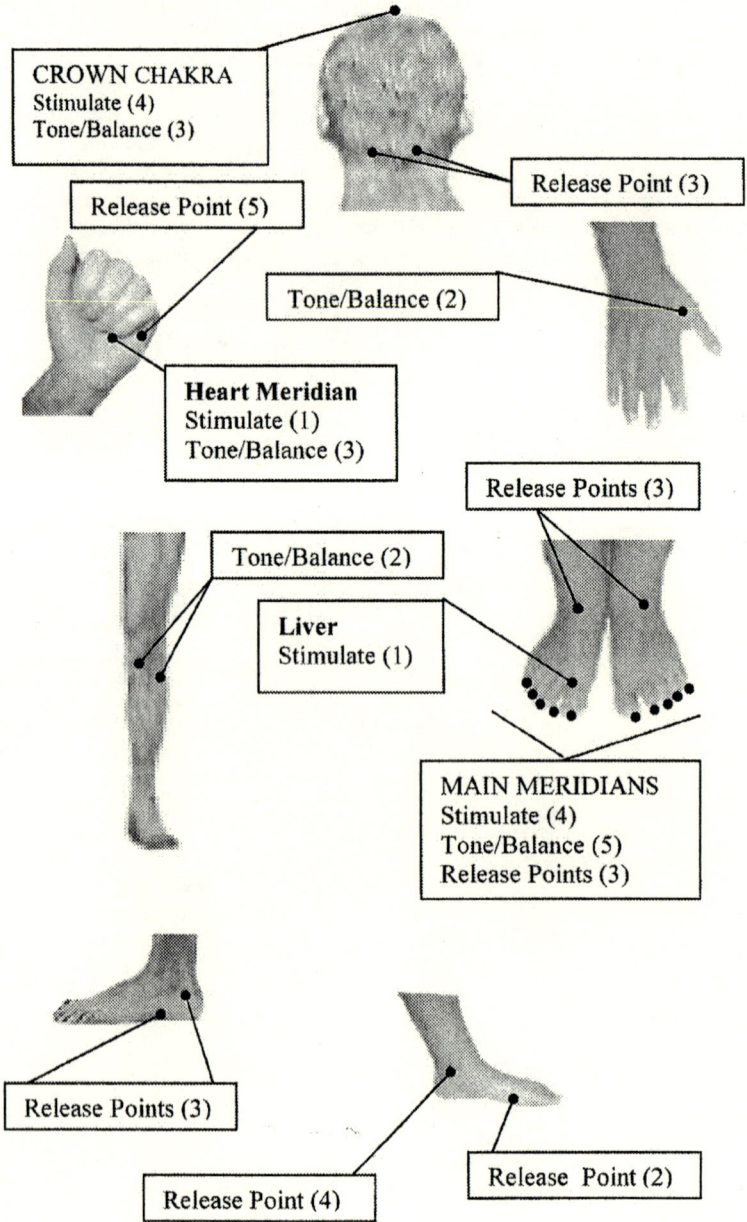

CROWN CHAKRA
Stimulate (4)
Tone/Balance (3)

Release Point (3)

Release Point (5)

Tone/Balance (2)

Heart Meridian
Stimulate (1)
Tone/Balance (3)

Release Points (3)

Tone/Balance (2)

Liver
Stimulate (1)

MAIN MERIDIANS
Stimulate (4)
Tone/Balance (5)
Release Points (3)

Release Points (3)

Release Point (4)

Release Point (2)

Treatment For Dental Extractions, Inflamed Gums & Mouth.

The mouth is the most sensitive part of your body. As a baby, you touched everything to your lips or on your tongue. During those years, you made many impressions that you have now long forgotten on a conscious level. The mouth lies within the energy of the Throat Chakra. Dental work will press your buttons and bring up forgotten reactions from childhood. Use your Crystals to remove shock and harmonize any abnormal reactions you may notice. It would also be helpful to work the Nervous System.

(1) Amethyst (2) Hematite (3) Aventurine

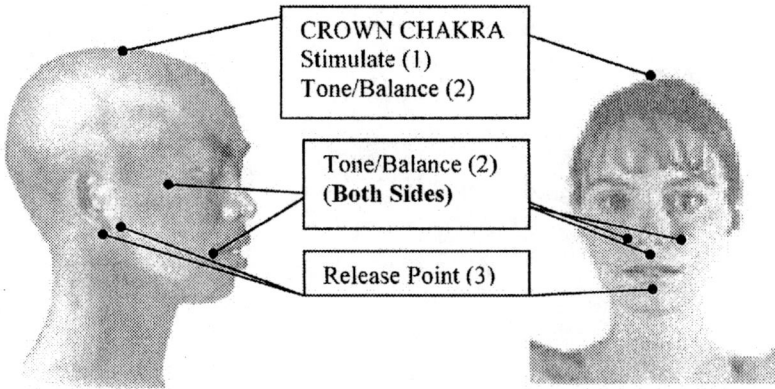

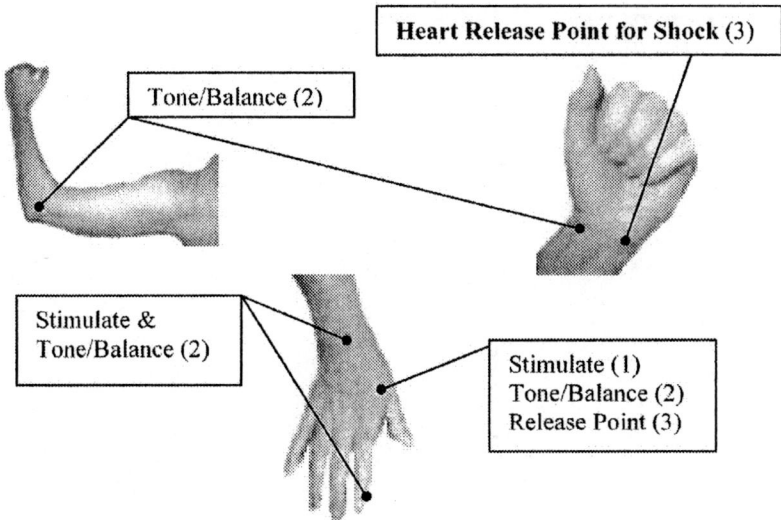

CROWN CHAKRA
Stimulate (1)
Tone/Balance (2)

Tone/Balance (2)
(Both Sides)

Release Point (3)

Heart Release Point for Shock (3)

Tone/Balance (2)

Stimulate &
Tone/Balance (2)

Stimulate (1)
Tone/Balance (2)
Release Point (3)

Treatment for Flu, Cold & Cough

No one likes to get sick, but the truth is that you are quite simply telling yourself that it is time for a break to make a change in your life. Perhaps you have been working too hard, or running your energies ragged with children and family life. Whatever the cause, your body is saying, "Enough's enough!" It is time to go to bed and heal. Be sure to seek medical advice and then find a comfortable position where you can rebuild all your Chakras (See Chakra balancing). Work with the crystals to move energy around your head, neck and lungs with the Acu points shown below. Then put the light out and sleep. Dream away all your fears, phobias, angers and frustrations and allow yourself to rejuvenate. Within a few days you should be bright and alert again with the added bonus of a new point of view that will help you change your attitude and way of life.

Note: It would also be helpful to work the Nervous System Acu points.

(1) Hematite   (2) Pink   (3) Amazonite

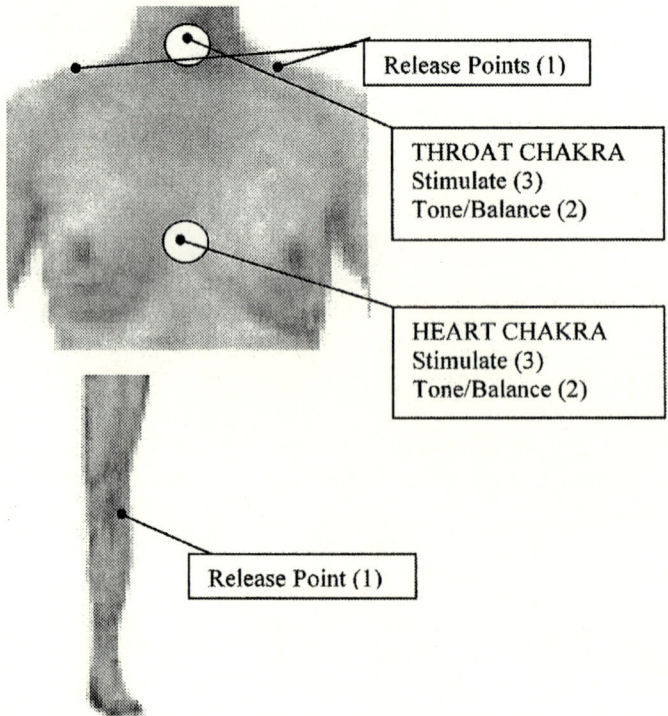

Release Points (1)

THROAT CHAKRA
Stimulate (3)
Tone/Balance (2)

HEART CHAKRA
Stimulate (3)
Tone/Balance (2)

Release Point (1)

Treatment for Flu, Cold & Cough (cont.)

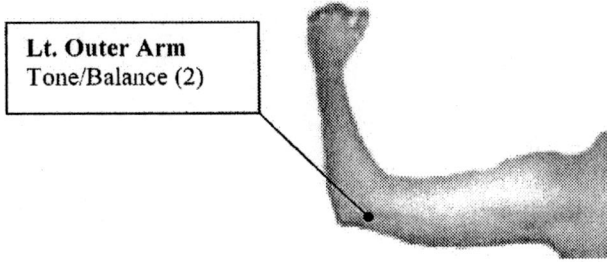

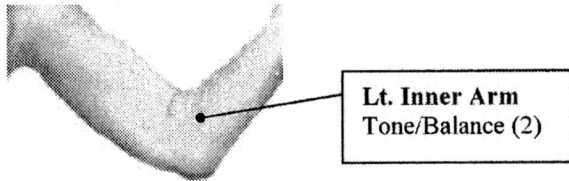

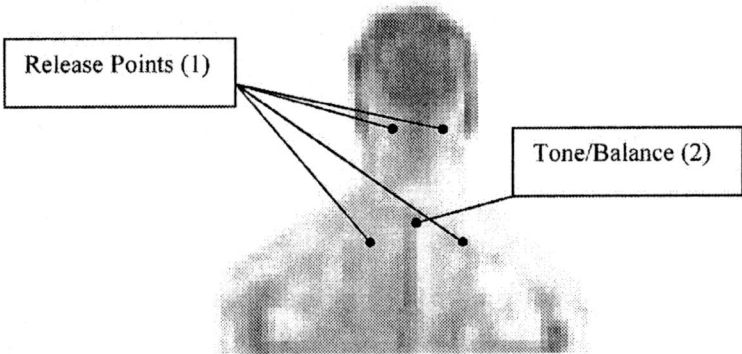

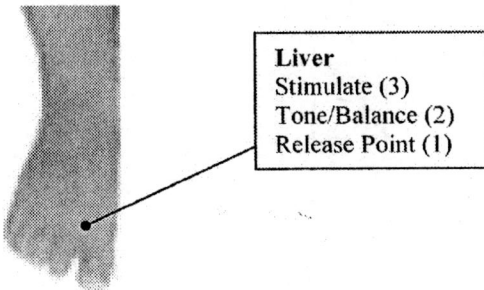

Lt. Outer Arm
Tone/Balance (2)

Lt. Inner Arm
Tone/Balance (2)

Release Points (1)

Tone/Balance (2)

Liver
Stimulate (3)
Tone/Balance (2)
Release Point (1)

Treatment To Lessen Anxiety & Fear

Any kind of fear or phobia is the result of the mind telling the heart what to feel. Real fear is the result of incidents that have caused emotional, mental and physical anxiety, such as rape or a car accident. A phobia is an accumulation of ideas creating an obsession resulting in a state of panic, such as the fear of flying, although one has never been in a plane. Work all the Chakras with strong emphasis on the rotation of the Hematite to tone and balance. If you are in extreme fear and panic, work the Nervous System. When extreme phobias and fears control a person's life to the point of having no life outside the home, it is advisable to seek medical and psychological advice.

Stimulate, tone and release all Main Meridian points on tip of hands or feet. Stimulate, tone and balance every Chakra with each crystal.

Amethyst (1) Aventurine (2) Hematite (3)

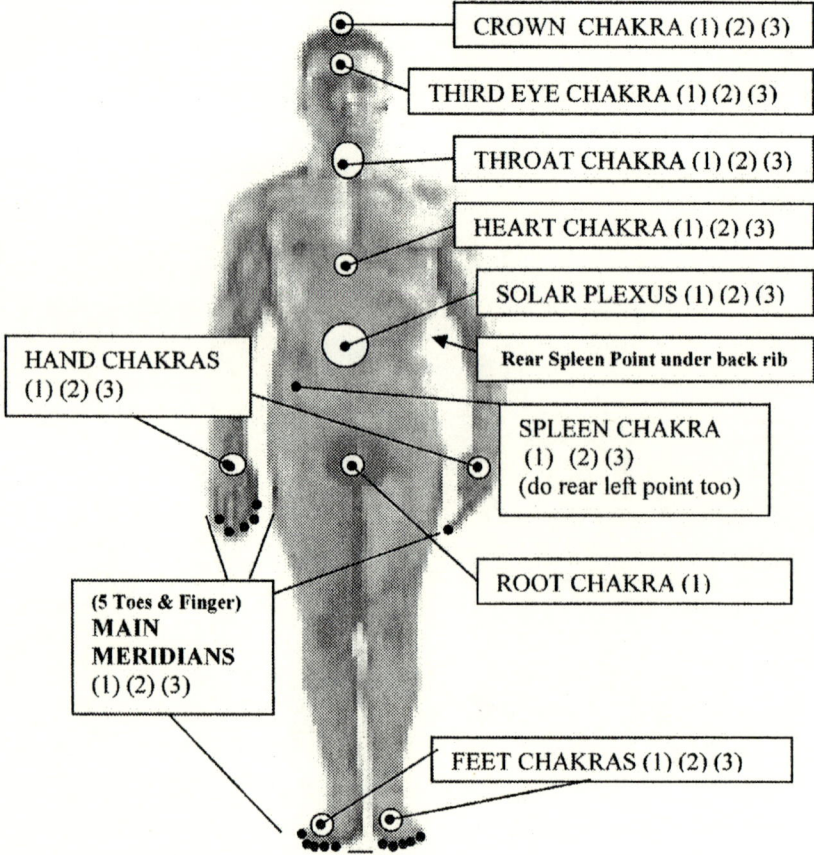

CROWN CHAKRA (1) (2) (3)

THIRD EYE CHAKRA (1) (2) (3)

THROAT CHAKRA (1) (2) (3)

HEART CHAKRA (1) (2) (3)

SOLAR PLEXUS (1) (2) (3)

HAND CHAKRAS (1) (2) (3)

Rear Spleen Point under back rib

SPLEEN CHAKRA (1) (2) (3) (do rear left point too)

ROOT CHAKRA (1)

(5 Toes & Finger) **MAIN MERIDIANS** (1) (2) (3)

FEET CHAKRAS (1) (2) (3)

Treatment for Skin (Neuro Dermatitis) & General Allergic Reactions

Generally, my experience with clients has shown me that blocked expression in a person's Spirit Body causes 90% of skin conditions. Creativity, passion and zeal for life are blocked. These people are often afraid of their own power and become inhibited and restricted by their own ideas about themselves. They rarely trust themselves with giant leaps towards change, but will instead; seek a support system that will keep them hanging on to a problem. The Acu Points shown below will work directly on the liver, and the Nervous and Circulatory Systems. (See diagrams.) However, it would be advisable to work the Digestive System (see diagram) from time to time. Seek a Counselor and Nutritionist to help speed up the healing process.

(1) Amethyst   (2) Hematite   (3) Aventurine   (4) Carnelian

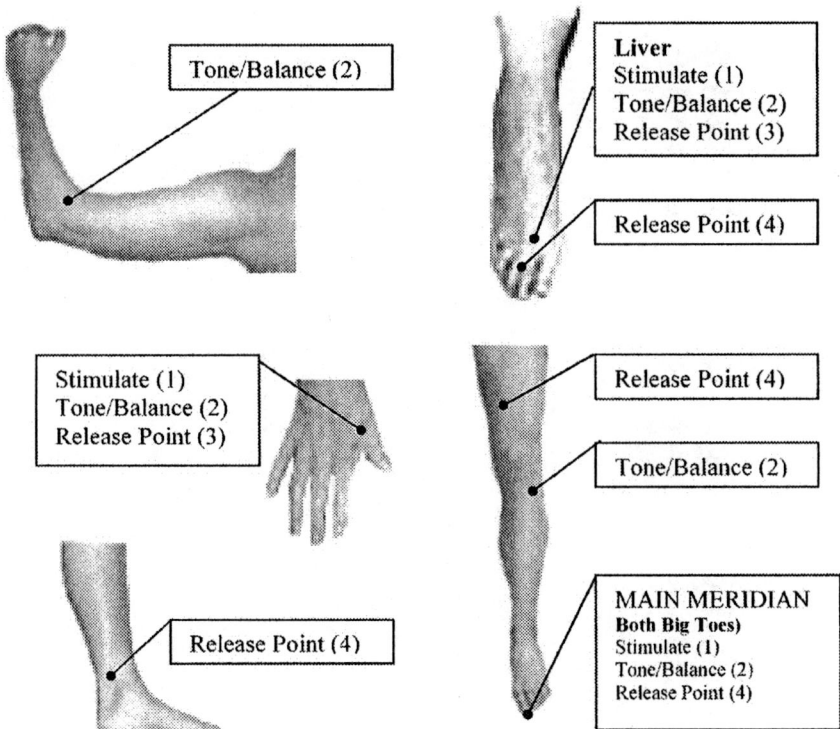

Tone/Balance (2)

Liver
Stimulate (1)
Tone/Balance (2)
Release Point (3)

Release Point (4)

Stimulate (1)
Tone/Balance (2)
Release Point (3)

Release Point (4)

Tone/Balance (2)

Release Point (4)

MAIN MERIDIAN
Both Big Toes)
Stimulate (1)
Tone/Balance (2)
Release Point (4)

Dr. Margaret Rogers Van Coops

Treatment To Aid Appetite Control

Our perceptions of the world affect us from moment to moment. If we do not react in a positive light, then we seek a comforter. Often, that comforter is food. Over-eating is as bad as under-eating. Either way, the body is in emotional pain and discomfort. My primary research has shown me that childhood guilt is often the cause. Food becomes a way to punish oneself by either starving or bloating. The Acu points shown below are trigger points that will allow this guilt and any need to punish self to immediately release along with emotional expression. Even when one is seriously ill and does not feel like eating, these points will help the sufferer to keep something in the stomach. A Chakra Balancing (Page 17) should be a follow up to this treatment. Consult a nutritionist to obtain a good diet to follow treatment.

(1)Quartz (2) Sodalite (3) Amazonite (4) Aventurine (5) Carnelian

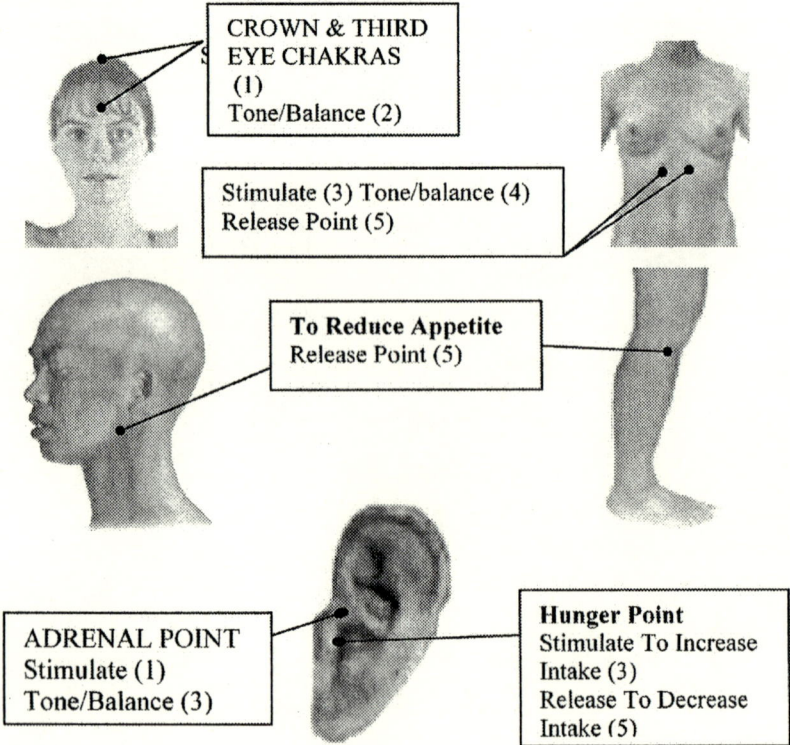

CROWN & THIRD EYE CHAKRAS (1) Tone/Balance (2)

Stimulate (3) Tone/balance (4) Release Point (5)

To Reduce Appetite Release Point (5)

ADRENAL POINT Stimulate (1) Tone/Balance (3)

Hunger Point Stimulate To Increase Intake (3) Release To Decrease Intake (5)

78

Treatment To Aid Appetite Control (Cont.)

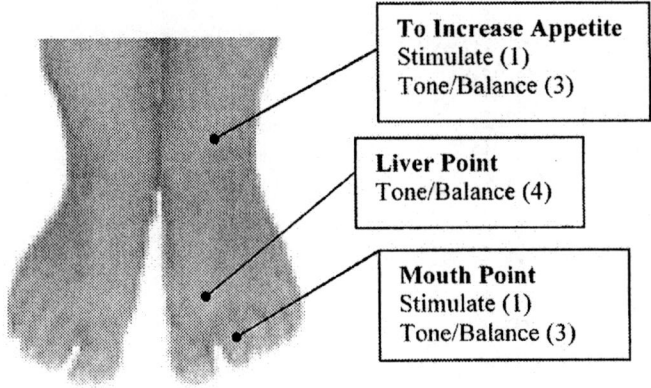

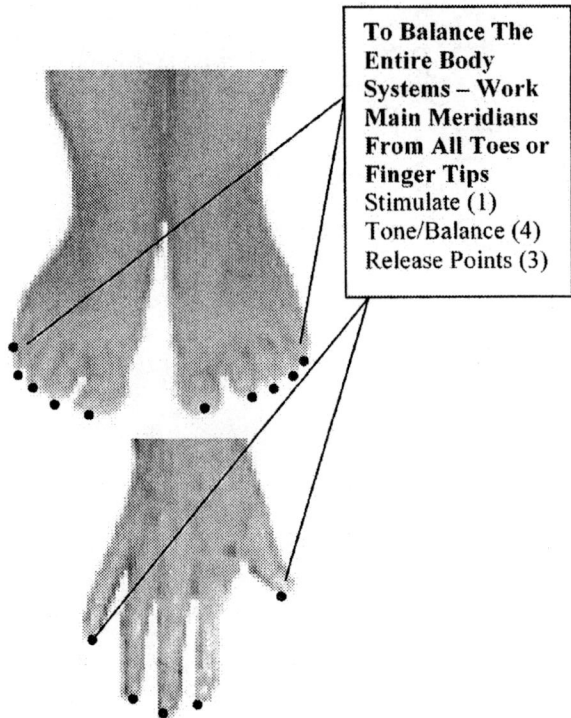

To Increase Appetite
Stimulate (1)
Tone/Balance (3)

Liver Point
Tone/Balance (4)

Mouth Point
Stimulate (1)
Tone/Balance (3)

To Balance The Entire Body Systems – Work Main Meridians From All Toes or Finger Tips
Stimulate (1)
Tone/Balance (4)
Release Points (3)

Treatment To Prevent Baldness & Thinning Hair

While one cannot escape genetic coding, one can prevent certain traits from manifesting too quickly. Thin hair does not necessarily have to fall out, as most believe. By feeding the roots of the hair with a good balanced diet and keeping a good blood flow to the scalp, hair can grow abundantly. The Acu points below are trigger points to help the five bodies to harmonize. You can also help yourself by balancing The Chakras and by working the Digestive System once a week. (See Diagram Page.) Massage to the scalp with Rosemary oil diluted in base oil will also help the hair follicles to function more efficiently. Expect to dream out fear, pain, anger, guilt, isolation and abandonment when working this way. Do stress points first.

(1) Quartz (2) Amazonite (3) Sodalite (4) Aventurine

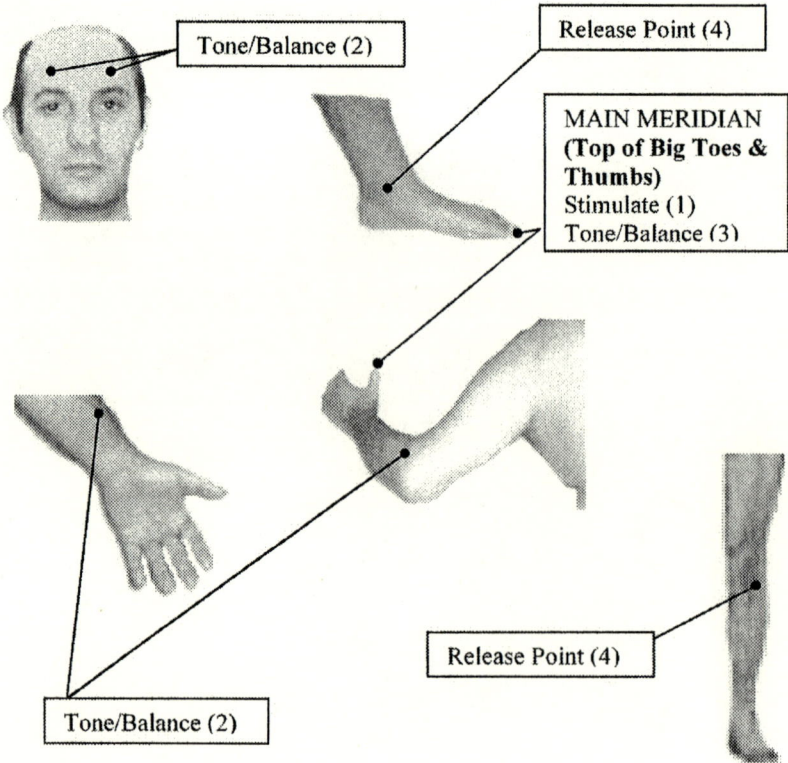

Tone/Balance (2)

Release Point (4)

MAIN MERIDIAN
(Top of Big Toes & Thumbs)
Stimulate (1)
Tone/Balance (3)

Release Point (4)

Tone/Balance (2)

Treatment for Diabetes

Diabetes has a direct link into martyrdom and anger. My research with this condition has shown that the Spleen Chakra is continually out of balance, which affects the liver, pancreas and spleen. The body does not get a good supply of energy in this area. The Adrenal Glands are constantly dumping adrenaline into the blood, speeding up the heart and sending the whole body into a panic. A diabetic's biggest fear is being out of control or of being controlled by others. Surrender is the key word! Let the body be what it needs to be. The Acu points shown below will allow the body to return to normal and to balance the brain by bringing it into a more relaxed frame of mind. Do this treatment daily in coordination with medical advice and medication. If this condition is treated early enough, the body can return to normal, preventing the need for insulin.

Within each of the Main Chakras lie the important glands of the body. By balancing the Chakras, these glands will begin to work productively. Pay special attention to the Crown Chakra and the Pituitary Gland, which controls all the other glands in the body.

**(1) Quartz (2) Amazonite (3) Rose Quartz
(4) Carnelian (5) Hematite**

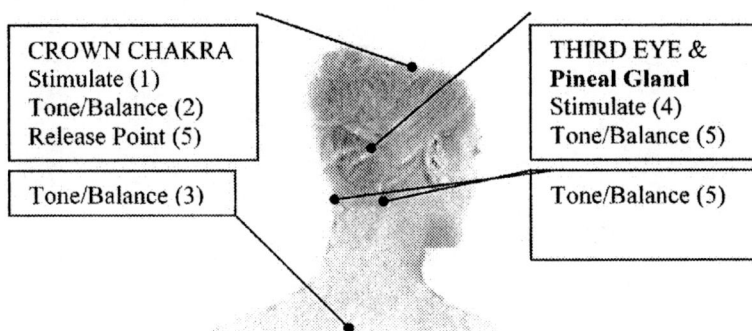

CROWN CHAKRA
Stimulate (1)
Tone/Balance (2)
Release Point (5)

THIRD EYE &
Pineal Gland
Stimulate (4)
Tone/Balance (5)

Tone/Balance (3)

Tone/Balance (5)

Treatment for Diabetes (Cont.)

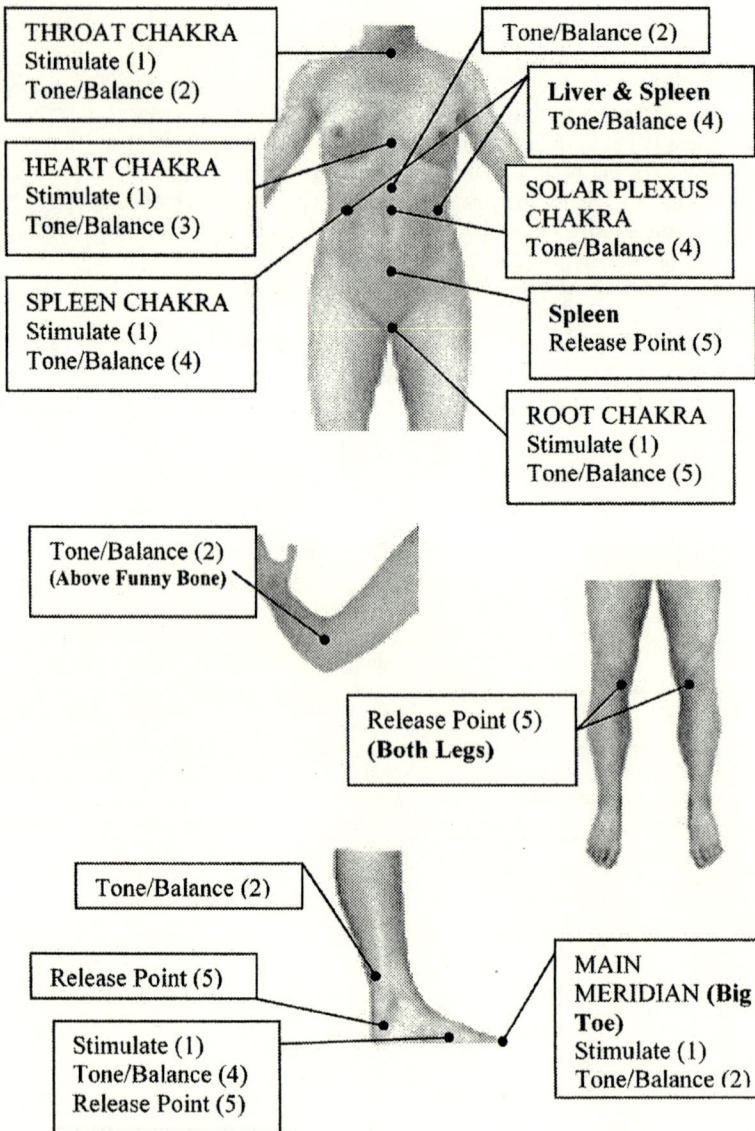

THROAT CHAKRA
Stimulate (1)
Tone/Balance (2)

Tone/Balance (2)

Liver & Spleen
Tone/Balance (4)

HEART CHAKRA
Stimulate (1)
Tone/Balance (3)

SOLAR PLEXUS
CHAKRA
Tone/Balance (4)

SPLEEN CHAKRA
Stimulate (1)
Tone/Balance (4)

Spleen
Release Point (5)

ROOT CHAKRA
Stimulate (1)
Tone/Balance (5)

Tone/Balance (2)
(Above Funny Bone)

Release Point (5)
(Both Legs)

Tone/Balance (2)

Release Point (5)

MAIN
MERIDIAN **(Big
Toe)**
Stimulate (1)
Tone/Balance (2)

Stimulate (1)
Tone/Balance (4)
Release Point (5)

Treatment For Addiction With Smoking, Alcohol & Food

Any addiction, however mild, is a sign of fear from rejection. Every day we meet different people with their own points of view, most of which have nothing to do with us. Yet, we constantly try to fit in and please the entire population of the world. This is a grandiose idea. No one can be that important! Along with this need to be a *People-Pleaser* is the fear of failure. The more one tries to be a *Pleaser*, the less one seems to be appreciated, hence, the need for an addiction. "Old habits die hard," so they say, which justifies continuing the habit. If you really want to quit, then the Acu points shown below will help you, but do find a counselor and support system to keep you on your road to recovery. Most importantly, remember to have God in your life, so that your Spirit Body can rebuild and help the Etheric and Physical Bodies to recover.

Do the Acu points for stress first and then follow up often throughout the day by doing the points listed below.

(1) Quartz (2) Sodalite (3) Amazonite (4) Hematite   (5) Carnelian

POINTS FOR DRUG/SMOKE ABUSE TO CALM & RELEASE TOXINS

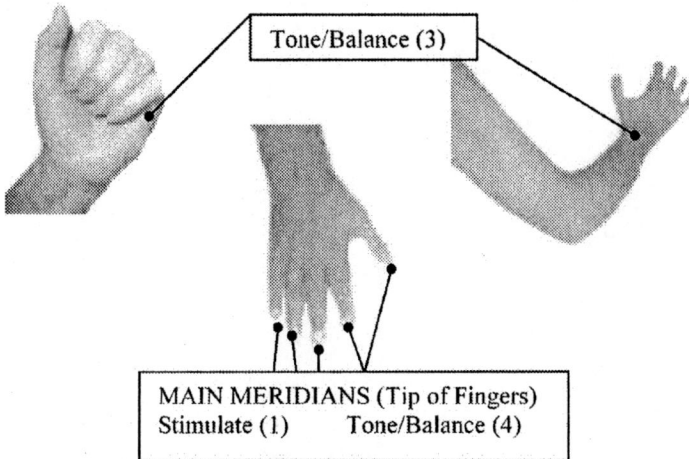

Tone/Balance (3)

MAIN MERIDIANS (Tip of Fingers)
Stimulate (1)   Tone/Balance (4)

Treatment For Addiction With Smoking, Alcohol & Food (Cont.)

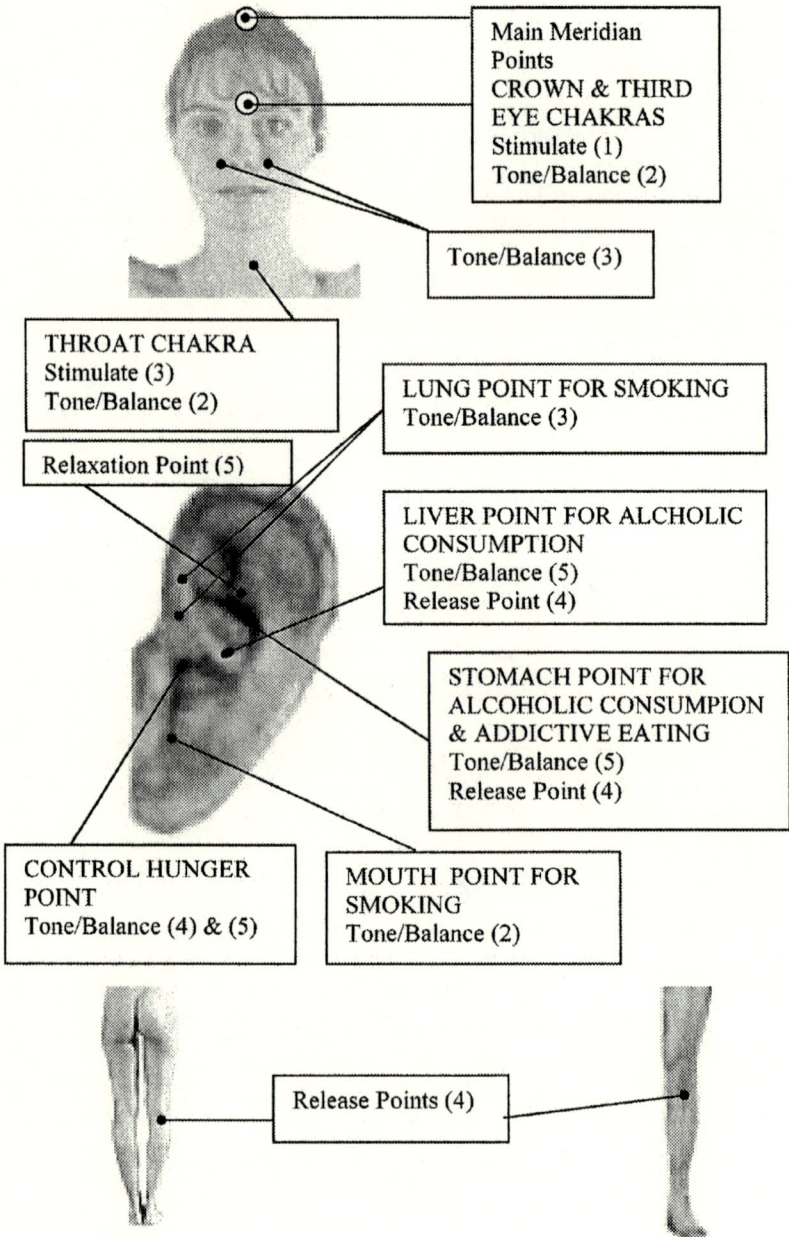

Main Meridian
Points
CROWN & THIRD
EYE CHAKRAS
Stimulate (1)
Tone/Balance (2)

Tone/Balance (3)

THROAT CHAKRA
Stimulate (3)
Tone/Balance (2)

LUNG POINT FOR SMOKING
Tone/Balance (3)

Relaxation Point (5)

LIVER POINT FOR ALCHOLIC
CONSUMPTION
Tone/Balance (5)
Release Point (4)

STOMACH POINT FOR
ALCOHOLIC CONSUMPION
& ADDICTIVE EATING
Tone/Balance (5)
Release Point (4)

CONTROL HUNGER
POINT
Tone/Balance (4) & (5)

MOUTH POINT FOR
SMOKING
Tone/Balance (2)

Release Points (4)

Treatment to Ease & Retard Epilepsy

During research projects concerning the mind, I have discovered time and again that fear of one's existence in this world rears it head. There are many ways one can be afraid of life. Epilepsy is just one manifestation. We are all entitled to our existence in which we take up space and have an effect on others. During pregnancy, each child–to-be absorbs his/her mother's fearful experiences in life. By the time of birth, the child is full of fear, though it has yet still to understand. If the mother is exceptionally fearful during the pregnancy, then the child's Spirit is not able to flow creatively. During the first 5-6 years of life, a child will manifest fears that with nurturing will be automatically overcome. A lack of touch and love results in a fear of life. Panic attacks result with a lack of breath and constant mucus. Balancing of the Left and Right Hemispheres of the brain is important as well as keeping the main meridians open. Continually rebuild the Chakras and seek confidence and encouragement from a qualified counselor. This treatment, though sufficient on its own, is also complementary to medication and medical care. With a doctor's approval, medication may be reduced. For severe attacks, treat head and hands immediately.

(1) Sodalite (2) Hematite (3) Carnelian (4) Amethyst

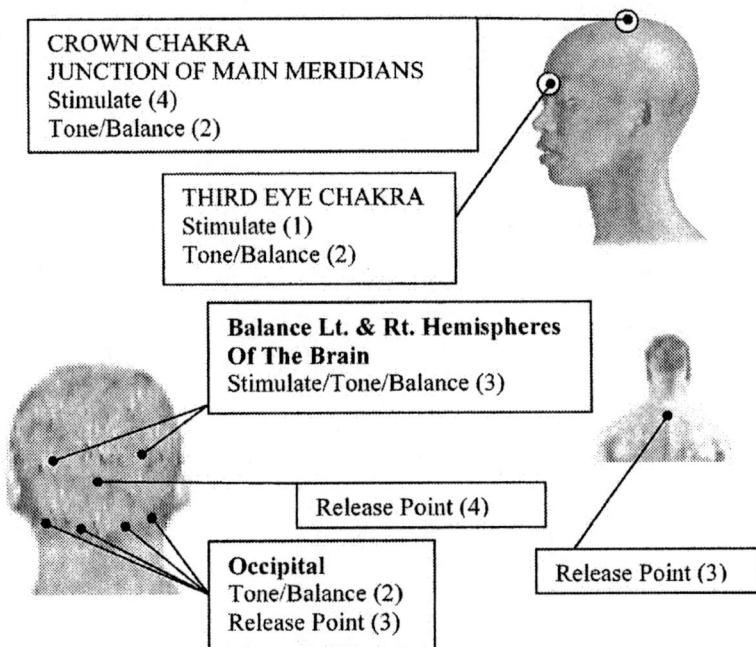

CROWN CHAKRA
JUNCTION OF MAIN MERIDIANS
Stimulate (4)
Tone/Balance (2)

THIRD EYE CHAKRA
Stimulate (1)
Tone/Balance (2)

Balance Lt. & Rt. Hemispheres Of The Brain
Stimulate/Tone/Balance (3)

Release Point (4)

Occipital
Tone/Balance (2)
Release Point (3)

Release Point (3)

Treatment To Ease & Retard Epilepsy (Cont.)

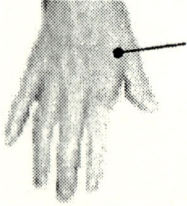

Stimulate (1)
Tone/Balance (2)
Release Point (4)

Tone/Balance (2)
Release Point (3)

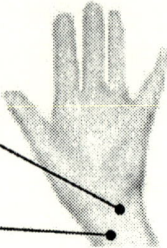

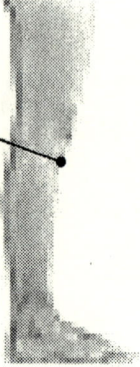

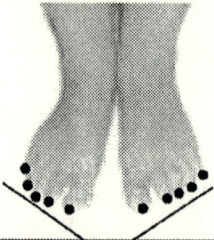

Tone/Balance (2)
Release point (3)

Liver
Tone/Balance (3)
Release Point (4)

Tone/Balance (2)
Release Point (3)

ALL MAIN MERIDIANS
Stimulate (1)
Tone/Balance (2)
Release Point (3)

Treatment For Fluid Retention
(Swollen Feet & Kidney Balance)

First, consult a Physician. Drink plenty of water. Treat Circulatory System if swelling is severe. (See Diagram Page.)

There are many medical reasons for fluid retention. However, my research has led me to discover that, no matter what the medical reason is, there is an imbalance between the emotions and the physical activities occurring in one's life. The Etheric Body is often loaded with false beliefs about the purpose of one's life. Individuals are often under the misguided belief that they are not worthy to receive anything worth having. They settle for second best and make do with next to nothing. Look at your life and give yourself a break. The Acu points illustrated will harmonize the five bodies and help the physical body rebuild itself. Do this treatment daily.

(1) Quartz (2) Sodalite (3) Amethyst (4) Rose Quartz
(5) Carnelian (6) Aventurine

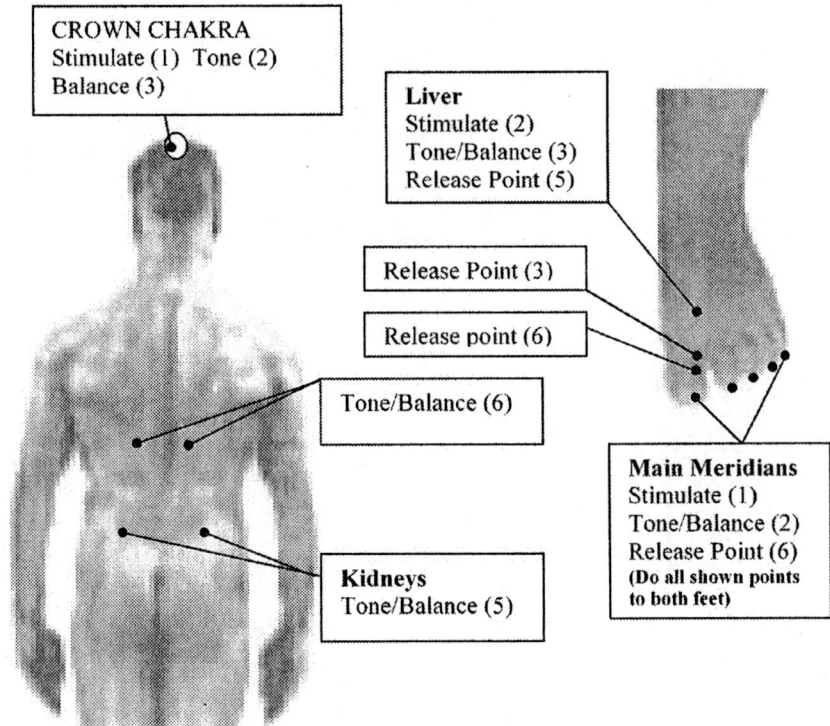

CROWN CHAKRA
Stimulate (1) Tone (2)
Balance (3)

Liver
Stimulate (2)
Tone/Balance (3)
Release Point (5)

Release Point (3)

Release point (6)

Tone/Balance (6)

Main Meridians
Stimulate (1)
Tone/Balance (2)
Release Point (6)
(Do all shown points to both feet)

Kidneys
Tone/Balance (5)

Treatment For Fluid Retention (Cont.)
(Swollen Feet & Kidney Balance)

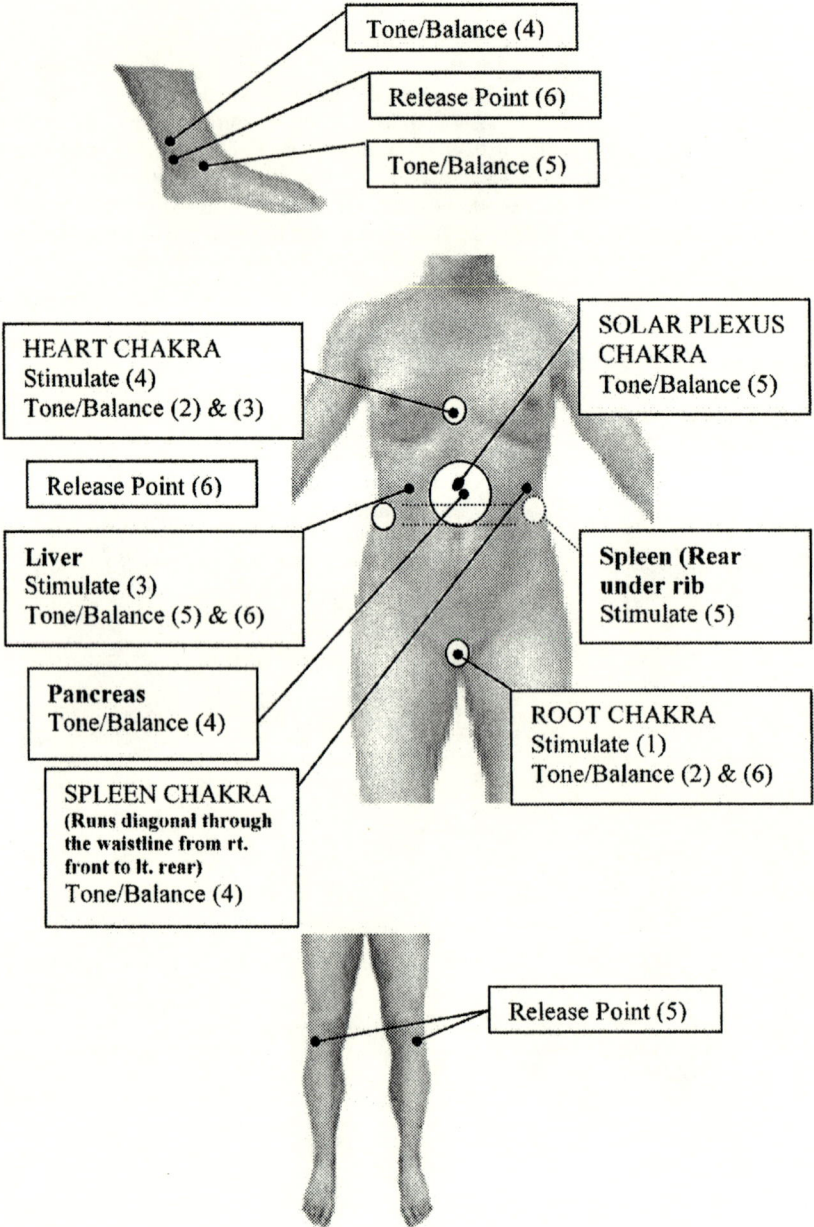

Tone/Balance (4)

Release Point (6)

Tone/Balance (5)

HEART CHAKRA
Stimulate (4)
Tone/Balance (2) & (3)

SOLAR PLEXUS CHAKRA
Tone/Balance (5)

Release Point (6)

Liver
Stimulate (3)
Tone/Balance (5) & (6)

Spleen (Rear under rib
Stimulate (5)

Pancreas
Tone/Balance (4)

ROOT CHAKRA
Stimulate (1)
Tone/Balance (2) & (6)

SPLEEN CHAKRA
(Runs diagonal through the waistline from rt. front to lt. rear)
Tone/Balance (4)

Release Point (5)

Treatment To Ease Hemorrhoids, Rectum & Bowel Problems.

If you have any of these complaints, first consult a Physician and obtain medication if necessary. Once you are on the program, begin working on yourself with the Acu Points shown below. Despite childbirth (chief cause of Hemorrhoids) in women, and general constipation or diarrhea in many individuals, the real reason for discomfort in the lower digestive tract is generally caused by a low level of self-esteem, self-worth and self-value. Individuals are often stubborn and fixed in their habits, which in turn affects the flow of the Five Bodies and the rotation of the Chakras. By working the Acu Points shown below, you can open up to healing and a change in outlook that will lead you to a better way of life.

Always consult with a Nutritionist or obtain medical advice and seek emotional and mental guidance from a counselor or psychologist or Metaphysiotherapist.

(1) Quartz (2) Carnelian (3) Amethyst (4) Aventurine

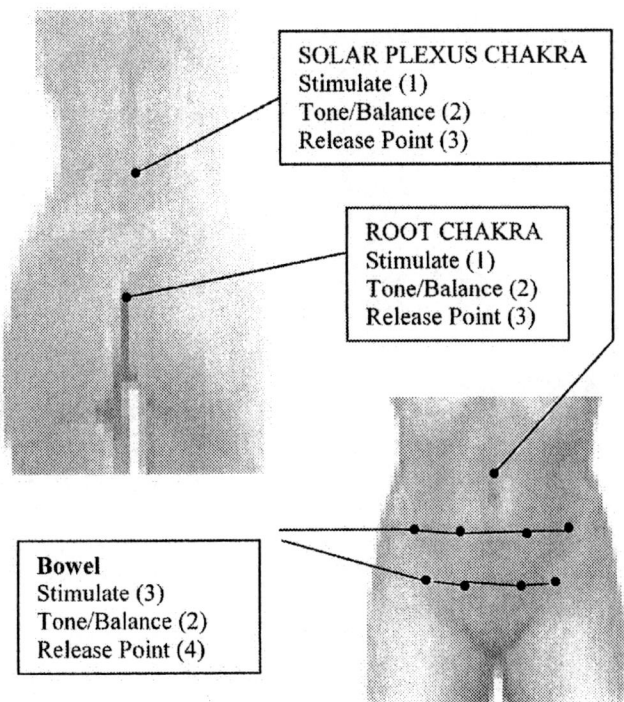

SOLAR PLEXUS CHAKRA
Stimulate (1)
Tone/Balance (2)
Release Point (3)

ROOT CHAKRA
Stimulate (1)
Tone/Balance (2)
Release Point (3)

Bowel
Stimulate (3)
Tone/Balance (2)
Release Point (4)

Treatment To Ease Hemorrhoids, Rectum & Bowel Problems (Cont.)

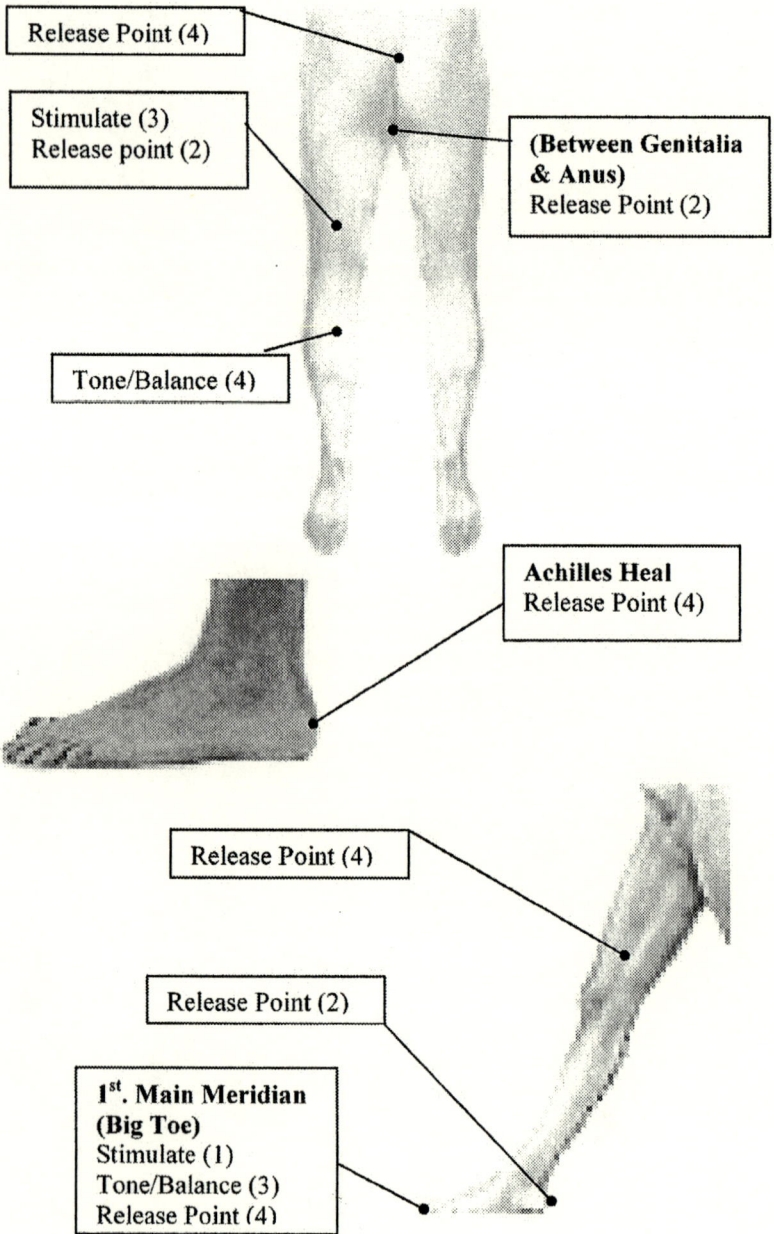

Release Point (4)

Stimulate (3)
Release point (2)

(Between Genitalia & Anus)
Release Point (2)

Tone/Balance (4)

Achilles Heal
Release Point (4)

Release Point (4)

Release Point (2)

**1st. Main Meridian
(Big Toe)**
Stimulate (1)
Tone/Balance (3)
Release Point (4)

To Reduce Cellulite & Weight On Hips, Thighs & Legs.

There is no single known cure for completely erasing cellulite and excess weight. However, with help from a good balanced diet and plenty of exercise, you can help yourself with Crystal Acupuncture^{sm}. The Acu Points shown below will help you keep your main meridians open and flowing freely. Address issues about self-protection with a Counselor or Physician. As you continue to work the Acu Points, feminine and masculine energies within the body will harmonize. Women who gain weight in the buttocks and thighs are generally too masculine, having to control the lives of those around them as well as their own. Men who gain weight in the abdomen are usually dealing with too much female energy. They are often argumentative and stubborn, causing their partner to pamper them even more, thus keeping them in a feminine mode. A daily treatment in the morning will result in a better attitude throughout the day. A treatment each night will help you dream away fears of change, which will result in a more positive you and a reduction in weight.

(1) Rose Quartz (2) Carnelian (3) Aventurine

For Whole Body

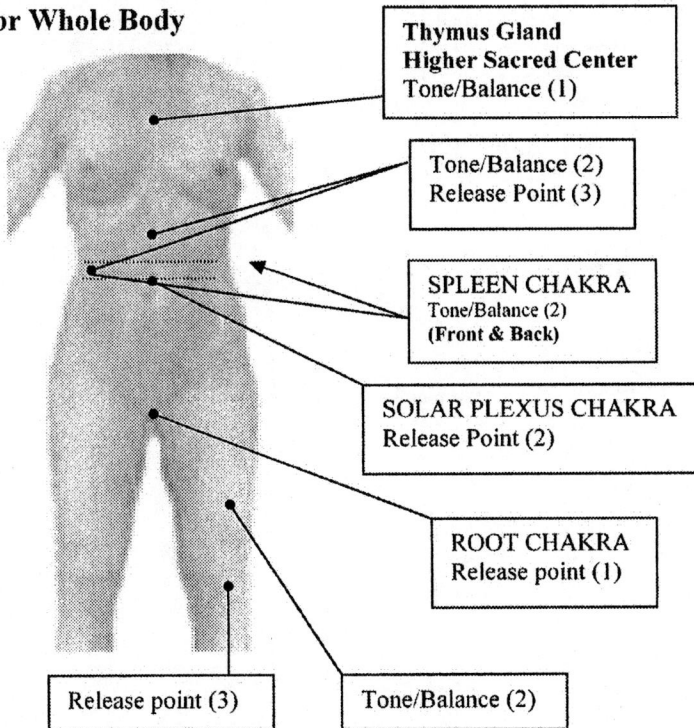

Thymus Gland
Higher Sacred Center
Tone/Balance (1)

Tone/Balance (2)
Release Point (3)

SPLEEN CHAKRA
Tone/Balance (2)
(Front & Back)

SOLAR PLEXUS CHAKRA
Release Point (2)

ROOT CHAKRA
Release point (1)

Release point (3)

Tone/Balance (2)

To Reduce Cellulite & Weight On Hips, Thighs & Legs (Cont.)

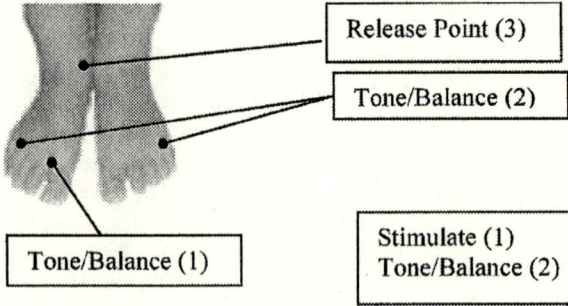

Release Point (3)

Tone/Balance (2)

Tone/Balance (1)

For Heavy Legs

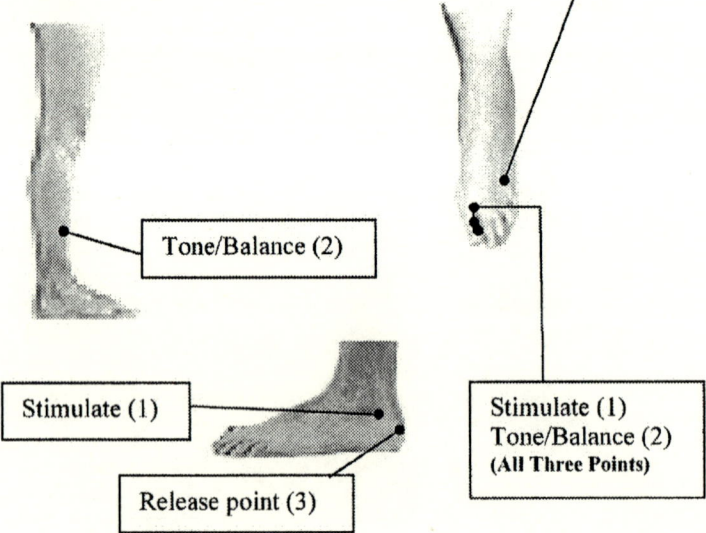

Stimulate (1)
Tone/Balance (2)

Tone/Balance (2)

Stimulate (1)

Stimulate (1)
Tone/Balance (2)
(All Three Points)

Release point (3)

For Heavy Thighs

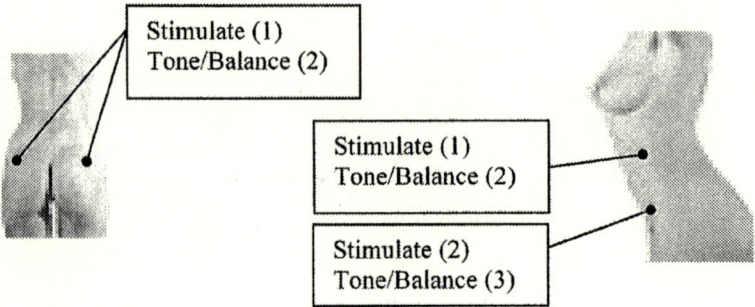

Stimulate (1)
Tone/Balance (2)

Stimulate (1)
Tone/Balance (2)

Stimulate (2)
Tone/Balance (3)

Treatment for Snoring, Sleep Apnea & Insomnia

Any form of sleep discomfort is from a need to control. If you sleep easily, but wake up tired, then you have worried yourself too much all night with dreams evolving around your problems. If, you sleep deeply, unaware of your snoring, then you are probably dealing with a physical deformity, such as a deviated septum, which does not allow you to breathe freely. Surgery will correct this condition. However, if you wake yourself up with loud snorts, then you are giving yourself panic attacks that affect your heart each time you hear the snort. You simply frighten yourself to death. Sleep Apnea is dangerous and needs medical attention. If you are unable to fall asleep each night, then you are afraid of success. You hide it well by focusing on the fear of failure. Whatever your condition, the Acu Point shown will have a profound effect. You will find yourself sleeping well if you treat yourself before retiring. Balance the Chakras (see Chakra Diagram) to erase fear and anxiety if you feel more than one of these symptoms.

(1) Amethyst (2) Sodalite (3) Aventurine (4) Rose Quartz (5) Hematite

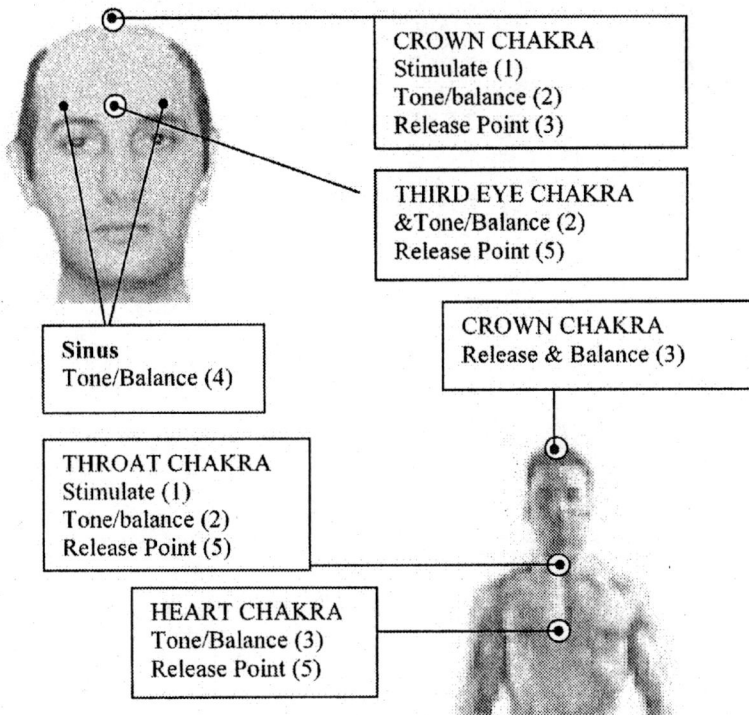

CROWN CHAKRA
Stimulate (1)
Tone/balance (2)
Release Point (3)

THIRD EYE CHAKRA
&Tone/Balance (2)
Release Point (5)

CROWN CHAKRA
Release & Balance (3)

Sinus
Tone/Balance (4)

THROAT CHAKRA
Stimulate (1)
Tone/balance (2)
Release Point (5)

HEART CHAKRA
Tone/Balance (3)
Release Point (5)

Treatment For Snoring, Sleep Apnea & Insomnia (Cont.)

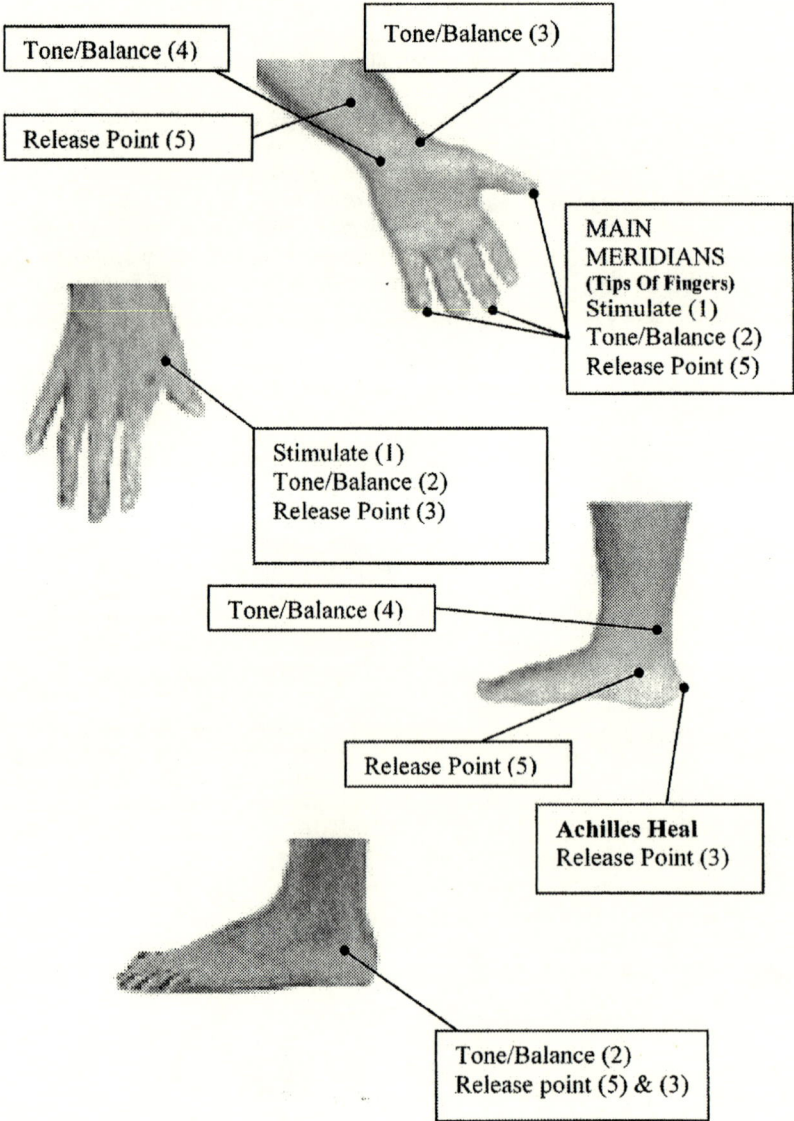

Tone/Balance (4)

Tone/Balance (3)

Release Point (5)

MAIN
MERIDIANS
(Tips Of Fingers)
Stimulate (1)
Tone/Balance (2)
Release Point (5)

Stimulate (1)
Tone/Balance (2)
Release Point (3)

Tone/Balance (4)

Release Point (5)

Achilles Heal
Release Point (3)

Tone/Balance (2)
Release point (5) & (3)

Treatment To Improve A Deficient Immune System

My research has proven that a deficiency in the Immune System always arises when a person is in stress or distress. No matter what you may be going through in your life, if the Immune System is down, you will be vulnerable to every virus, bacteria etc. in existence. Therefore, it is important to focus on the Main Meridians and Chakras to keep them balanced, as well as keeping the Circulatory, Nervous, Digestive and Glandular Systems flowing. (See Diagram Pages.) In cases of more serious complaints such as HIV or Leukemia, the points for all systems must be worked upon daily. Below are the Acu Points shown to help stimulate, tone and balance the Immune System. These points should also be done daily for less serious complaints.

(1) Quartz (2) Sodalite (3) Amazonite (4) Hematite

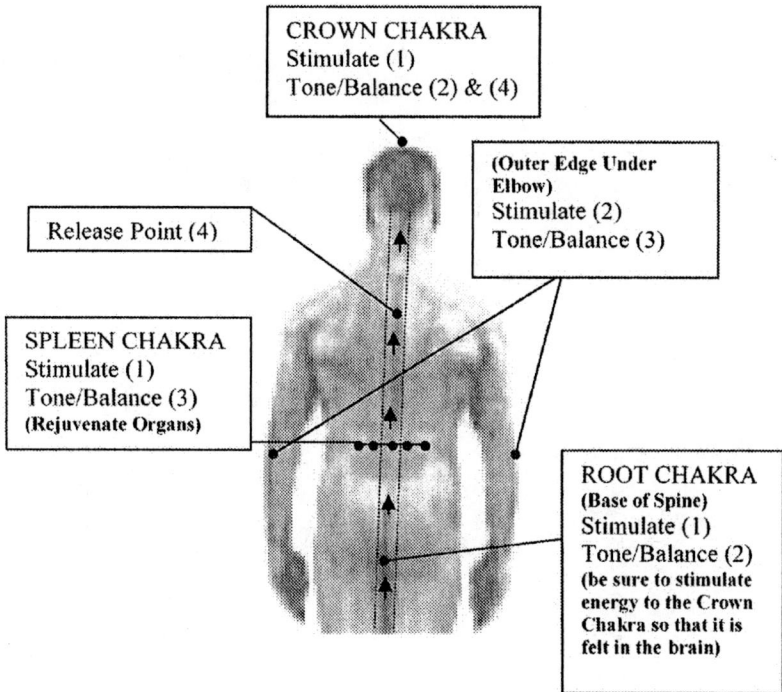

CROWN CHAKRA
Stimulate (1)
Tone/Balance (2) & (4)

(Outer Edge Under Elbow)
Stimulate (2)
Tone/Balance (3)

Release Point (4)

SPLEEN CHAKRA
Stimulate (1)
Tone/Balance (3)
(Rejuvenate Organs)

ROOT CHAKRA
(Base of Spine)
Stimulate (1)
Tone/Balance (2)
(be sure to stimulate energy to the Crown Chakra so that it is felt in the brain)

Treatment To Improve A Deficient Immune System (Cont.)

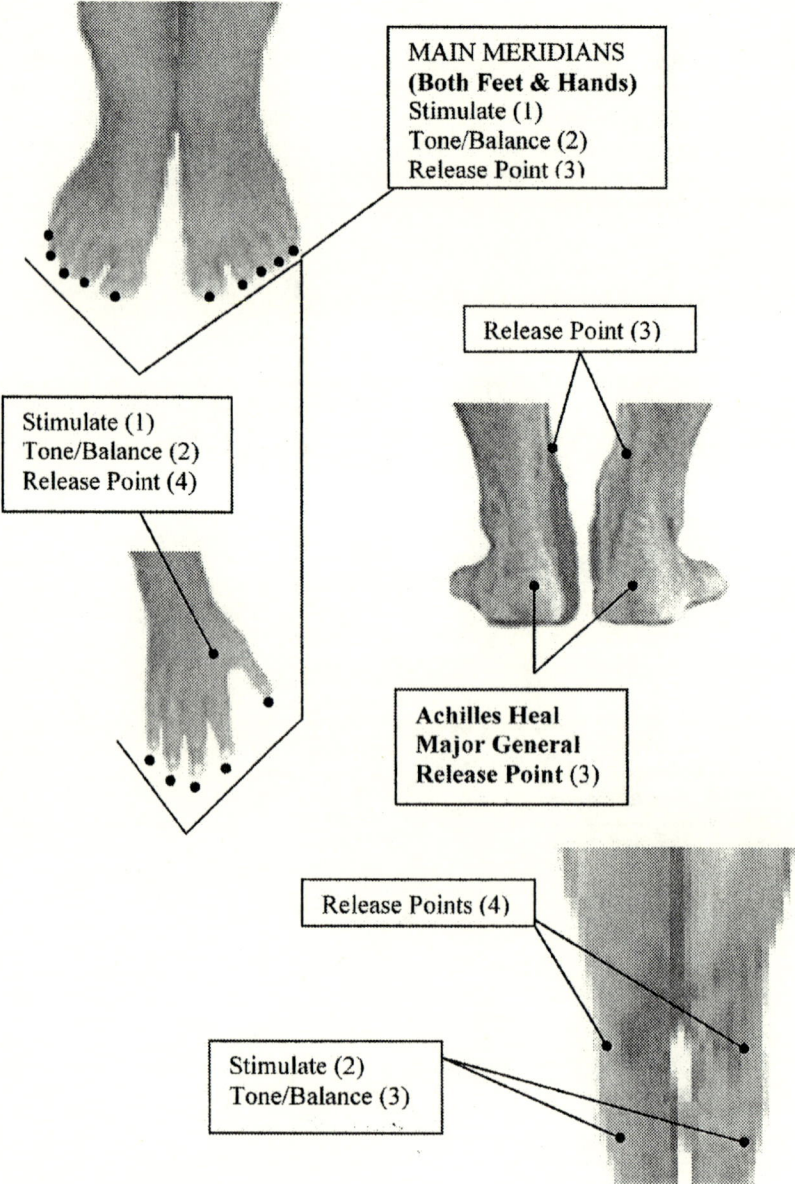

MAIN MERIDIANS
(Both Feet & Hands)
Stimulate (1)
Tone/Balance (2)
Release Point (3)

Release Point (3)

Stimulate (1)
Tone/Balance (2)
Release Point (4)

**Achilles Heal
Major General
Release Point** (3)

Release Points (4)

Stimulate (2)
Tone/Balance (3)

Treatment To Improve memory

Whether we are young or old, there are times when we forget what we would like to remember. The conscious mind is very selective. It only remembers things that are relative to the moment. The subconscious mind stores *all* experiences in picture form, which when shuffled around and presented to the conscious mind, controls the outcome. These two parts of your mind often disagree, bringing up negativity in the form of fear and pain, along with anger and guilt. Without the third part of your mind, the *deep subconscious*, otherwise known as your spiritual awareness, you would not grow. By stimulating, toning and balancing the meridians that feed the brain, you can improve your memory and focus more diligently. Emotionally, you will find yourself better stimulated towards beliefs of success, rather than those of failure.

(1) Sodalite (2) Amazonite (3) Amethyst

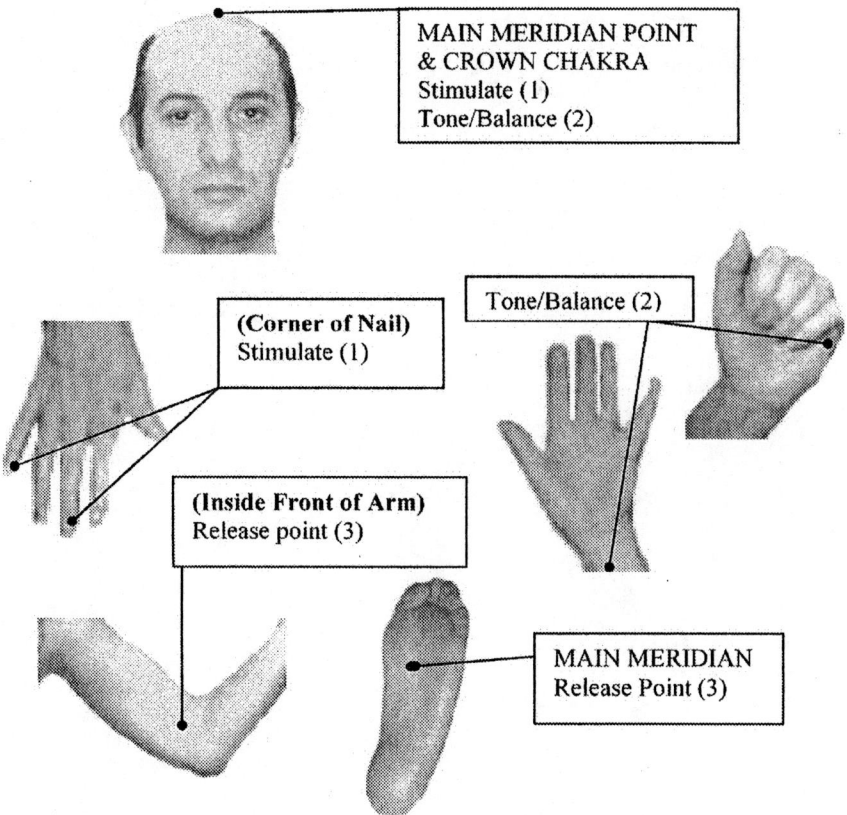

MAIN MERIDIAN POINT
& CROWN CHAKRA
Stimulate (1)
Tone/Balance (2)

(Corner of Nail)
Stimulate (1)

Tone/Balance (2)

(Inside Front of Arm)
Release point (3)

MAIN MERIDIAN
Release Point (3)

Treatment For Depression

When the Physical, Etheric and Spirit Bodies are loaded with negativity, depression hits hard. Moving energy around the main meridians breaks up the blocks, which in turn releases a deluge of old mindsets, emotions and spiritual revelations. By working the Acu points shown here, each cell in your body will release old habits. Slowly but surely, you will find yourself climbing up out of the darkness into the light. Remember, your Spirit Guardian Angels are around you, so allow them to help you. Also, remember to allow God into your life. God does hear your prayers and does answer them, though it may not be in the form that you expect. So, let go and let happen. Be prepared to deal with many dreams as you eliminate negativity. Points are included to help you balance the enzymes of the brain to harmonize your serotonin and dopamine levels along with your pituitary and pineal glands.

(1) Quartz (2) Amazonite (3) Sodalite (4) Hematite (5) Carnelian

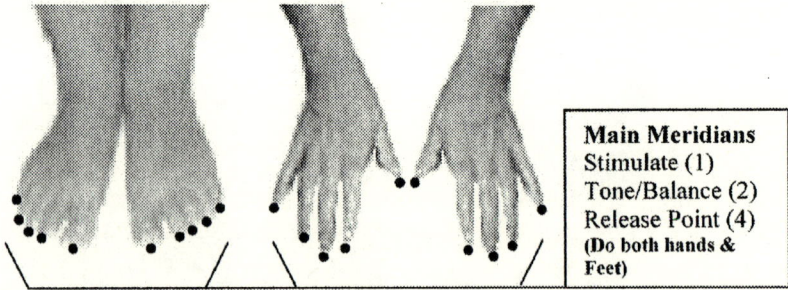

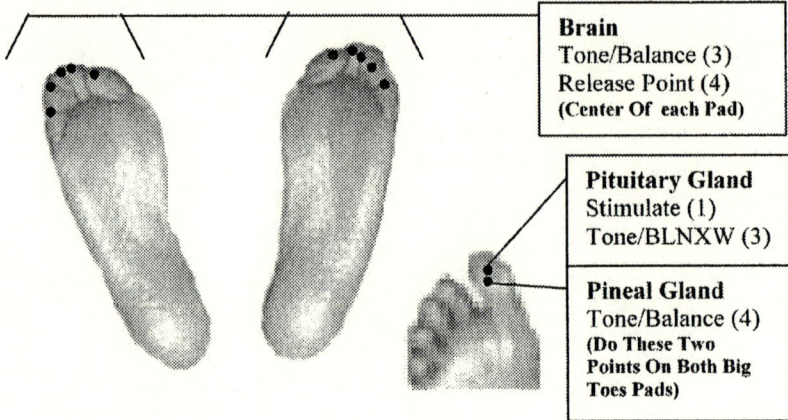

Main Meridians
Stimulate (1)
Tone/Balance (2)
Release Point (4)
(Do both hands & Feet)

Brain
Tone/Balance (3)
Release Point (4)
(Center Of each Pad)

Pituitary Gland
Stimulate (1)
Tone/BLNXW (3)

Pineal Gland
Tone/Balance (4)
(Do These Two Points On Both Big Toes Pads)

Treatment For Depression (Cont.)

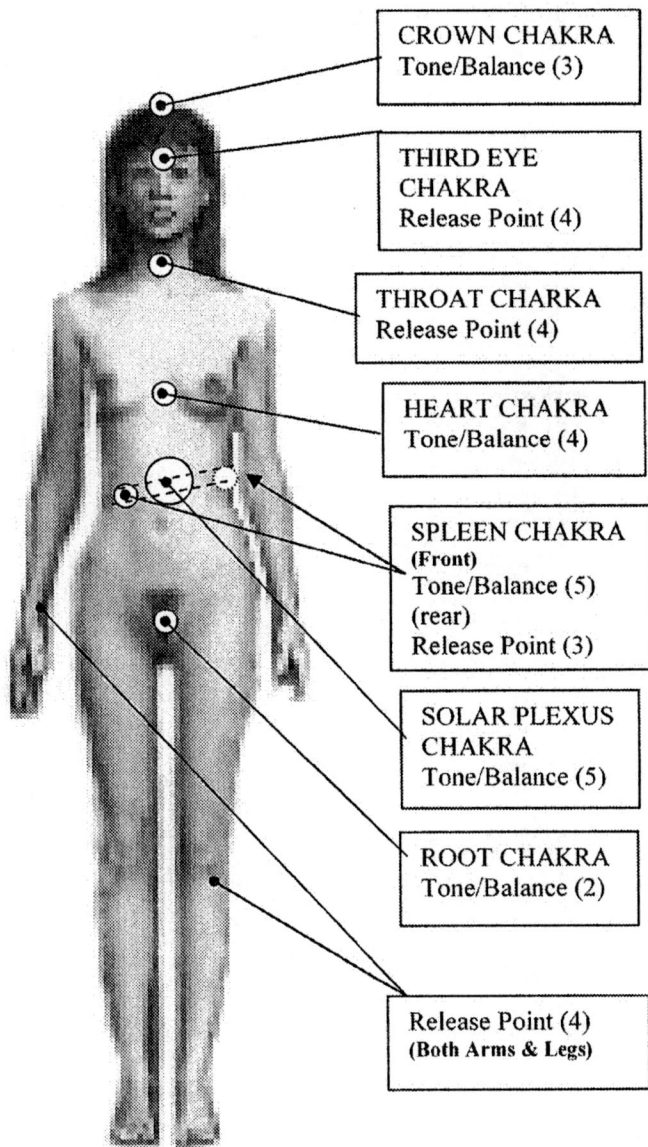

CROWN CHAKRA
Tone/Balance (3)

THIRD EYE
CHAKRA
Release Point (4)

THROAT CHARKA
Release Point (4)

HEART CHAKRA
Tone/Balance (4)

SPLEEN CHAKRA
(Front)
Tone/Balance (5)
(rear)
Release Point (3)

SOLAR PLEXUS
CHAKRA
Tone/Balance (5)

ROOT CHAKRA
Tone/Balance (2)

Release Point (4)
(Both Arms & Legs)

For Beauty Treatment To Tone Up The Face & Smooth Wrinkles

You have heard the saying "Beauty is skin deep." Real Beauty lies within. Each time you screw your face up into a negative expression, you program negativity in each cell of your face, as well as the body. Also, your eyes reflect the state of your mood. They are "The mirror image of your Soul." By working the Acu points shown below, you will help yourself to release negativity from all the tiny muscles of your face. In time, you will appear younger and more vital as you learn to develop a more positive attitude. You can work these points as often as you like, but remember that each time you do the treatment you will dream out your negativity and have reactions to stimuli that will test your attitude along with your emotions.

(1) Amazonite (2) Carnelian

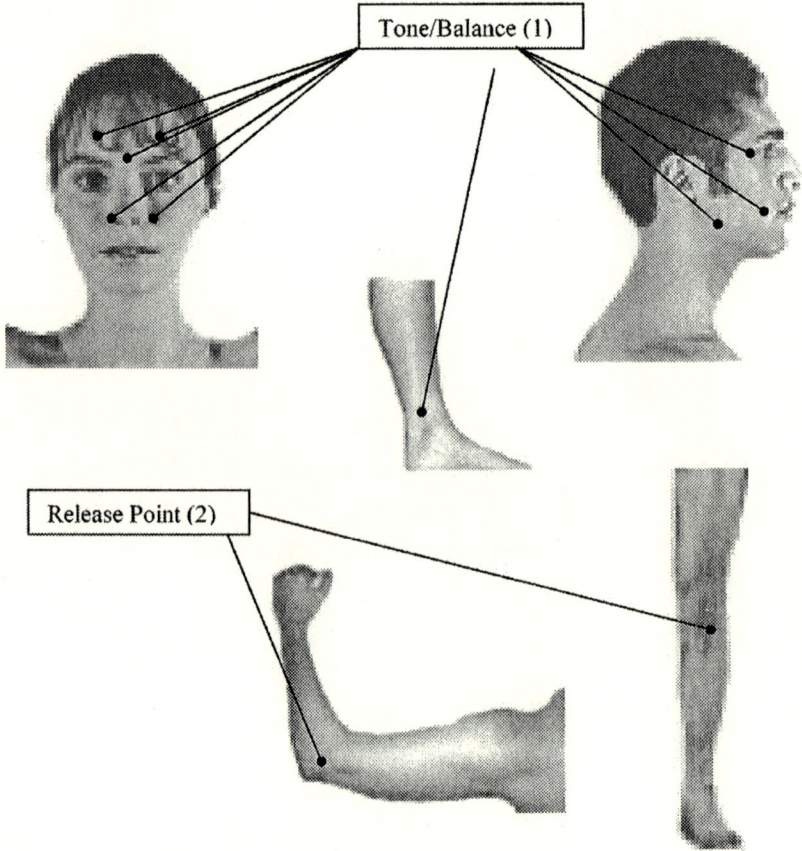

Tone/Balance (1)

Release Point (2)

CRYSTAL ACUPUNCTURE^{SM} POINTS

DIAGRAMS
FOR HEALING THE
ENTIRE BODY

Main Crystal Acupuncture Points Of The Feet

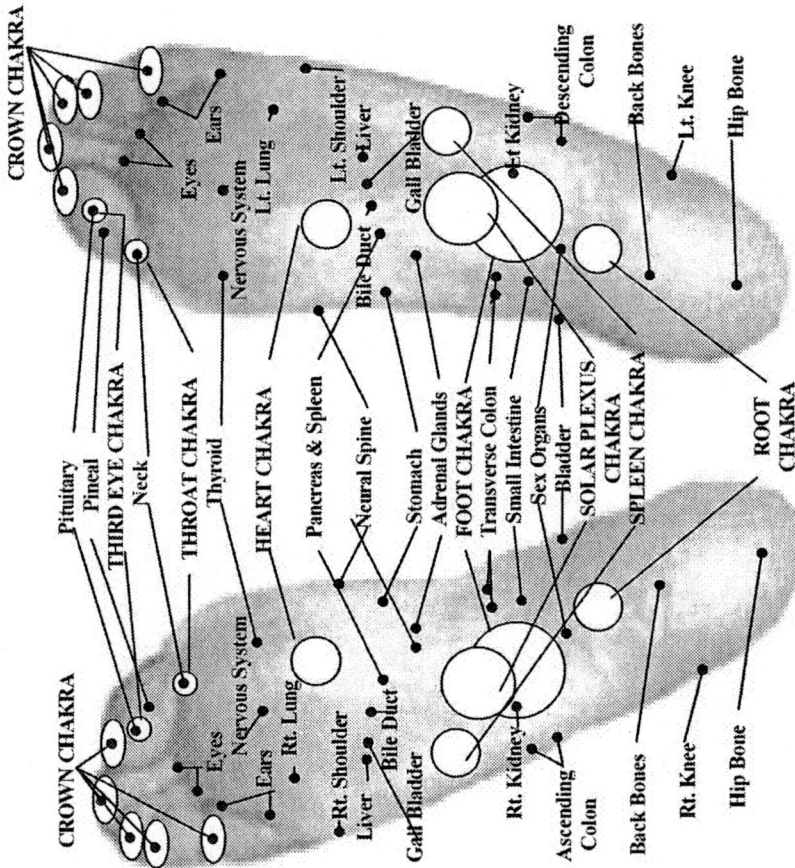

If you are unable to reach or treat the body, then work the points of the feet instead. Reflexology together with Aromatherapy is a good combination with the Crystal Acupuncture[sm]. Select the crystal of your choice to stimulate, tone and balance the Acu Point that you have selected. You may interchange your crystals according to your inspiration. Often your own Psychic senses will tell you instantly which crystals to use. However, if you are stuck, turn to the page that is relevant to the condition you are treating and select those crystals that are shown. Remember the feet have small Chakras that need balancing. Send all negativity into the Earth by visualizing it in the form of dark oil leaking out into the ground.

Diagram labels:

CROWN CHAKRA

Ears
Eyes
Nervous System
Lt. Lung
Lt. Shoulder
Liver
Gall Bladder
Rt Kidney
Descending Colon
Back Bones
Lt. Knee
Hip Bone
Bile Duct

Pituitary
Pineal
THIRD EYE CHAKRA
Neck
THROAT CHAKRA
Thyroid
HEART CHAKRA
Pancreas & Spleen
Neural Spine
Stomach
Adrenal Glands
FOOT CHAKRA
Transverse Colon
Small Intestine
Sex Organs
Bladder
SOLAR PLEXUS CHAKRA
SPLEEN CHAKRA
ROOT CHAKRA

CROWN CHAKRA
Eyes
Ears
Nervous System
Rt. Lung
Rt. Shoulder
Bile Duct
Liver
Gall Bladder
Rt. Kidney
Ascending Colon
Back Bones
Rt. Knee
Hip Bone

103

Main Crystal Acupuncture℠ Points Of The Hands

If you are unable to reach/treat the body or feet, then work the points of the hands instead. Reflexology with Aromatherapy is good in combination with the Crystal Acupuncture℠. Massage the hands and then select the Crystals of your choice to stimulate, then tone and balance the Acu Points that you have selected. You may interchange your crystals according to your inspiration. Often your own Psychic senses will tell you instantly which crystals to use. However, if you are stuck, then try the Crystal Acupuncture℠ Points of the Ear.

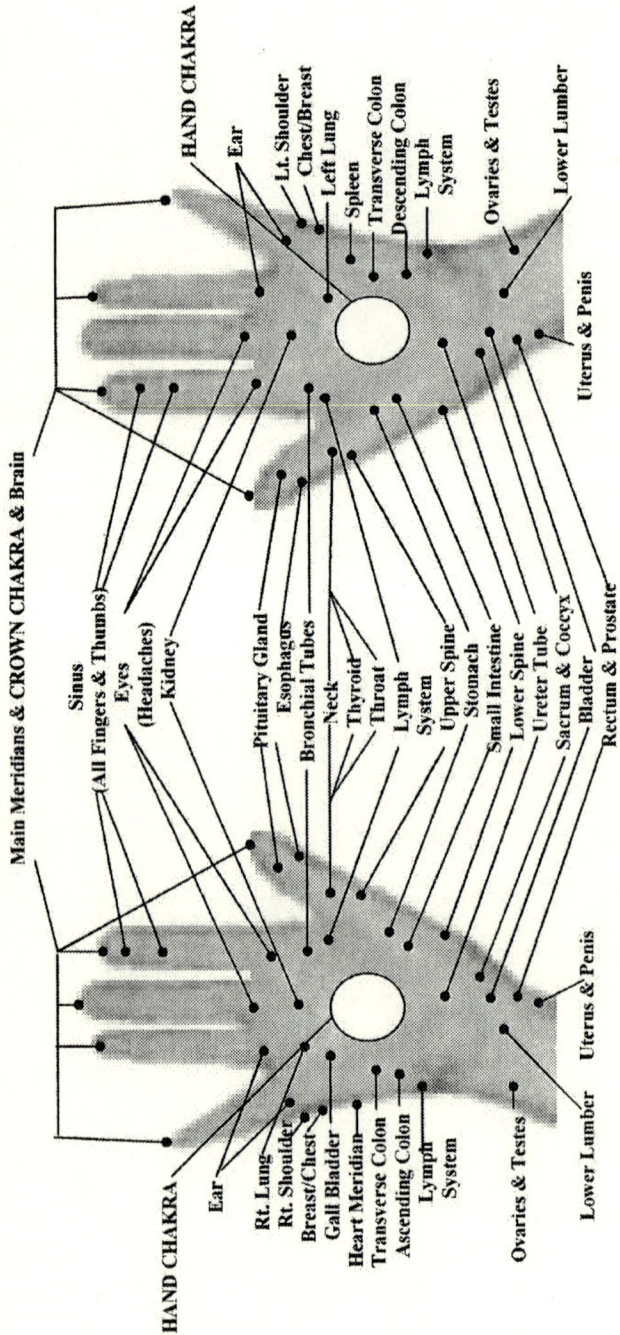

HAND CHAKRA
Ear
Lt. Shoulder
Chest/Breast
Left Lung
Spleen
Transverse Colon
Descending Colon
Lymph System
Ovaries & Testes
Lower Lumber
Uterus & Penis

Main Meridians & CROWN CHAKRA & Brain
Sinus
Eyes (All Fingers & Thumbs)
(Headaches)
Kidney
Pituitary Gland
Esophagus
Bronchial Tubes
Neck
Thyroid
Throat
Lymph System
Upper Spine
Stomach
Small Intestine
Lower Spine
Ureter Tube
Sacrum & Coccyx
Bladder
Rectum & Prostate
Uterus & Penis
Lower Lumber
Ovaries & Testes

HAND CHAKRA
Ear
Rt. Lung
Rt. Shoulder
Breast/Chest
Gall Bladder
Heart Meridian
Transverse Colon
Ascending Colon
Lymph System

104

Crystal Acupuncture Points Of The Ear

In the event that you are unable to work on any part of the body, feet or hands, then the ears are a good place to start. As in the feet, select the crystals of your choice, or turn to the relevant pages for pre-selected crystals and apply them to the Acu Point. Stimulate, then tone and balance accordingly.

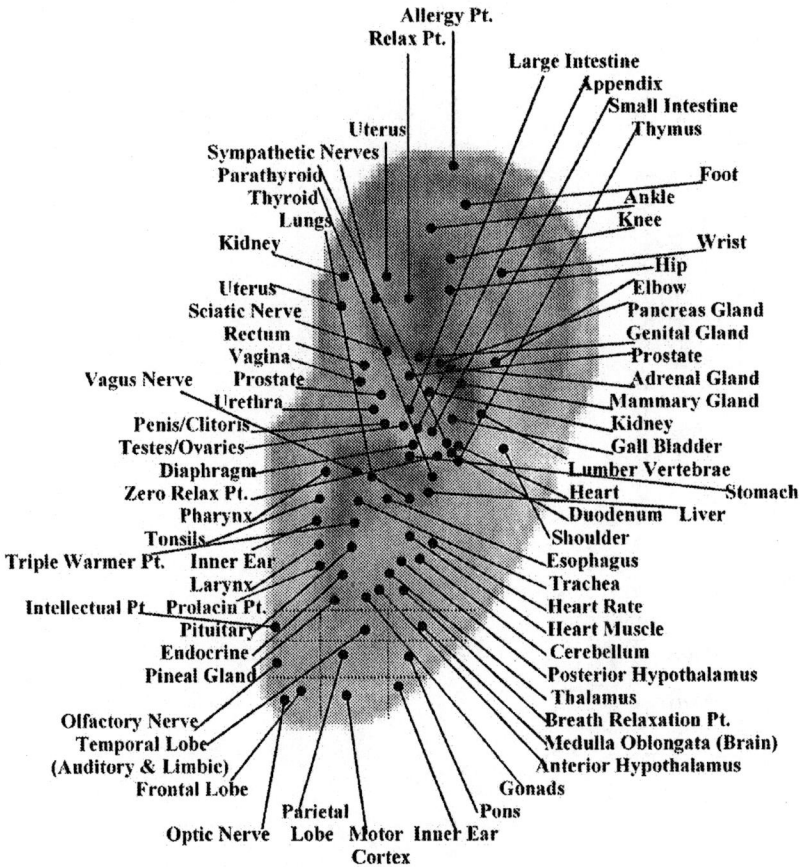

105

NEW CRYSTAL STONES FOR THE TREATMENT OF SPECIFIC DISEASES

New Crystal Stones

Now that you have become familiar with the basic Crystal Acupuncture^{sm} Crystals, it is time to introduce you to some other crystals that I myself like to work with. While I stress once again that there is no rule as to which stone you always use, it is important to understand the healing properties of each stone before using them. Listed below are more stones that are mentioned through the rest of the book.

Agate:
(Various colors of agate cause various changes in many dimensions)
- **Balancer of the Five Bodies.**
- **Spiritual harmonizer of the Major and Minor Chakras.**
- **Stimulates awareness of negativity and a need to release.**
- **Cleanses the Etheric Body of negativity.**
- **Awakens the Spirit Body with physical signs of psychic development.**
- **Strengthens visual and visionary capabilities.**
- **Links the mind and emotions to Spirit Guides.**
- **Stimulates development of creative talents.**
- **General physical healing stone for the entire body.**

Aqua Aura Quartz:
(Manmade crystal – laboratory bonded gold to quartz)
- **Clears negative from the Chakras by stimulating the cones to rotate faster**
- **Uplifts the five senses and transforms the auric vibration.**
- **Improves the ability to retain knowledge. Study is made easy.**
- **Stimulates an awareness of psychic connections to Spirit Guides and God.**
- **Improves awareness of personality and characteristic traits.**
- **Stimulates an awareness of Higher Self divine consciousness.**
- **Aids in the development of the psychic skills as a channel.**
- **Creates an awareness of the Power of Spirit to manifest.**
- **Improves the circulation and the heart functions.**

- **Purifies and sanctifies forgiveness and acceptance of self on all levels in all Five Bodies.**

Blue Lace Agate:
- **Creates powerful healing for the Throat Chakra by releasing negative history through vocal expression.**
- **Stimulates a refined quality of lightness of being.**
- **Inspires inner wisdom to become conscious.**
- **Harmonizes the Higher-Self Chakras (Crown, Third Eye &Throat) with the Lower-Self Chakras (Solar Plexus, Spleen and Base).**
- **Aids the healing of bone diseases and strengthens the skeletal structure.**
- **Moderates the balance of calcium and other minerals throughout the body.**
- **Improves the digestion and Endocrine Glands.**
- **Controls fluid retention, especially around the brain.**
- **Opens and expands energy along all meridians.**

Blue Russian Quartz /Siberian Blue Quartz:
(Manmade in a laboratory in Russia by mixing cobalt with Quartz.)
- **Activates Throat and Third Eye Chakras**
- **Influences the development of psychic abilities with increased visions.**
- **Assists an individual to awaken to new thoughts and overcome limited mindsets and beliefs.**
- **Creates a change in perception of this world.**
- **Expands the mind into acceptance through sight to perceive true realities.**
- **Heals the thyroid and parathyroid, throat, neck, base of the skull, upper lungs and upper arms, stomach and skin.**
- **Using this stone brings The Higher Self consciousness into this earthly world of existence.**
- **Manifests energy into form, which can result in a clearing and healing miracle.**
- **Brings love from the heart through words of wisdom expressing greater truths that brings peace of mind and heart.**
- **Helps those near death to pass over easily.**

Calcite:
- This natural amplifier aids in helping the mind to remember spiritual experiences such as astral traveling.
- An aid in harmonizing the conscious, sub-conscious and deep-subconscious parts of the mind to connect with Spirit Guides.
- Stimulates the mind to have total recall.
- Assists the Spirit Body's physical experiences in the Spirit World to be remembered as a Physical Body experience.
- Establishes a link for healing and a need to perfect one's way of life.
- Polarizes and activates all the Chakras to cleanse and rebuild without negativity.
- Excellent crystal for stimulating the Crown Chakra and connecting to God and Spirit Guides.
- Is an effective generator and stimulant that can cause the physical growth of new cells throughout the Physical Body.
- Extremely effective in rejuvenating the Liver, Spleen, Pancreas, kidneys and adrenal glands within the Spleen Chakra.

Citrine:
- Powerfully transmutes and dissipates negative energy.
- The user finds the ability to manifest better business abilities, acquiring wealth and a positive status in life.
- Opens and energizes the Solar Plexus Chakra, directing personal power, creativity and intelligent decisiveness.
- Stimulates potency in the reproductive organs.
- Activates the Third Eye Chakra.
- Awakens the Higher Self purpose into the Lower Self consciousness.
- Is an aid in developing a connection with Spirit Master Teachers.
- Removes negativity and old history patterns from the Base Chakra, allowing a wonderful sense of well being to manifest.
- Gives a new perspective on relationships, which can become harmonious and supportive.
- Aligns the 5 bodies and lifts an individual's vibration through the Crown Chakra.

Fluorite:
(Various colors have a different vibration)
- **Balances disorganized and disruptive growth, creating new cells.**
- **Initiates a change of mind from chaos to organization.**
- **Helps to create detachment in situations involving strong negative emotions.**
- **Increases the ability to concentrate and study easily.**
- **Helps individuals to converse without fear or judgment.**
- **Encourages expectations of health in balance with mind, body and spirit consciousness.**
- **Builds up the Immune System.**
- **Helps in the assistance of treating the mentally unstable.**
- **Reduces the swellings and tumors of the body.**
- **Strengthens bones and body tissue.**

Green Russian Quartz (rare)
(Often manmade in a laboratory in Russia by mixing Chromium with Quartz.)
- **Activates the Heart Chakra to release negative emotions.**
- **Stimulates love to pour from the Higher Self into the Lower Self.**
- **Transforms negative cells into positive ones that rebuild and repair the body's systems.**
- **Stimulates consciousness to consider others.**
- **Protects from negative emotional outpourings from others.**
- **Creates strong healing energy throughout the blood circulatory system.**
- **Stimulates a need to find one's personal journey.**
- **Aids in the release of negatively obtained possessions that cause suffering.**
- **Provides protection from Earthbound Spirits.**

Howlite:
- **Creates moods of calmness.**
- **Stimulates conversations that express true emotions.**
- **Provides the confidence to reason, observe and practice patience.**

- Assist the mind to retain memory.
- Used to confront insecurities and to erase fear of the unknown.
- Eliminates pain, stress, rage and feelings of abandonment.
- Helpful in entering into a state of reflection and change.
- Can be used to focus and stimulate new growth in various areas of the body.
- Builds Character and personality.
- Connects the conscious mind with the deep-subconscious mind to awaken inner truths.

Jade:
- Awakens dreams and stimulates action to manifest those dreams in practical ways.
- It assists individuals to sleep well and to release negativity through dreaming.
- Assists a healer to sense and transform negativity into positive energy.
- The use of this stone can result in apparent magical happenings, manifesting the unexpected.
- Dysfunctional relatives can find harmonious relationships by using this stone to transform attitudes.
- Physically, this stone heals the skeletal system, strengthening bones and ligaments, while removing pain, smoothing tissue and reducing scars.
- Harmonizes the mind, body and Spirit and awakens a sense of purpose.
- Instills resourcefulness, self-assuredness, self-reliance and self-sufficiency.
- Strengthens male reproduction organs.

Lapis Lazuli:
- Creates an open mind to greater spiritual awareness.
- Harmonizes the conscious, subconscious and deep-subconscious minds.
- Releases old history in favor of new discoveries.
- Enhances the wisdom of the sage in daily conversations that manifest the teacher.

- **Activates and energizes the Throat and Third Eye Chakras creating an awareness of visions and realizations.**
- **Develops the Psychic Senses.**
- **Reinforces knowledge and expands reason.**
- **Assists in expanding and developing creative skills.**
- **Helps in meditations to overcome depression and focus on Ascension.**
- **Physically aids the body to heal the throat, thymus, immune system, and to generate new red cells of the blood.**
- **Disperses mental fears i.e. insomnia, vertigo and dizziness caused by panic.**

Magnetite:
- **Aligns the Major and Minor chakras.**
- **Harmonizes the Five Bodies and regenerates the Aura.**
- **Opens up the Meridians and stimulates a release of negativity from the Etheric Body.**
- **Stimulates passion and desire for new experiences.**
- **Spiritual awareness is heightened with the use of this stone.**
- **Grounds hysteria, fear and anxiety, allowing a calm state to manifest.**
- **Allows a healer to ground negativity while giving a treatment.**
- **Stimulates personal power in the face of adversities.**
- **Practice with this stone can develop remote viewing.**
- **Raises personal appeal and attractiveness from the Heart Chakra.**
- **Physically rejuvenates bone, hair, blood vessels, skin, general tissue and bone cells.**

Malachite:
- **Transforms energy, creating a change in life patterns.**
- **Creates receptivity to new spiritual evolutionary ideas.**
- **Clears and activates all cones in all The Major Chakras.**
- **Creates acceptance of self and personal responsibility for happiness.**
- **Helps to create strong bonds with friends and family.**
- **Allows a total release of negative unconscious memories.**
- **Stimulates a release of negative irrational emotions.**

- **Provides personal insight into the nature and cause of a disease.**
- **Can be used to focus on aspirations and goals.**
- **Can be used as a protection from psychic attack and verbal abuse.**
- **Physically strengthens RNA/DNA and tissue cells throughout the body.**

Moldavite:
(Not of this world - ancient meteorite)
- **Stimulates the basic DNA strands to restructure.**
- **Creates a transformation of energy from cell to cell.**
- **Useful in meditation to gain out-of-body experiences.**
- **Opens up the mind to Universal Consciousness and personal connections to The Oneness and God.**
- **Draws Universal light patterns of creativity into form.**
- **Expands Psychic senses beyond the norm.**
- **Awakens the Higher Self into physical consciousness.**
- **Develops communication with Spirit Guides and dead loved ones.**

Moss Agate:
- **Connects the Spirit's life force to the Earth and to embodiment.**
- **Awakens senses of physical connections to all creatures on earth.**
- **Harmonizes energies of the Physical Body with all forms created on Earth.**
- **Helps in improving self-esteem, worth and value.**
- **Creates a positive outlook and life and an awareness of all things beautiful.**
- **Physically aids with eye disorders, dehydration conditions, elimination of toxins and the reduction of fungus growth.**
- **Stimulates the Digestive System to function productively.**
- **Generates energy to stimulate the Glandular System to balance and produce a good metabolic reaction.**
- **Aids in clearing skin disorders.**
- **Calms the nerves and harmonizes the emotions.**
- **Frees the mind of mental stress.**

Rainbow Quartz:
- **Stimulates and expands the Aura generating powerful healing.**
- **Awakens awareness to the lightness of being.**
- **Releases negativity from the Major Chakras.**
- **Opens up awareness of the psychic senses in creative modes.**
- **Stimulates an outpouring of love.**
- **Infuses the colors of the rainbow into the Five Bodies creating a transformation of personal power.**
- **Develops a clear channel for receiving healing from Spirit Guides.**
- **Can be used for absent healing.**
- **Stimulates the Glandular System – especially the Pituitary Gland.**
- **Regenerates the mind and lifts depression.**

Red Jasper:
- **Reveals mental and emotional obstacles that block truth.**
- **Increases perception and stimulates the desire to find solutions to problems.**
- **Provides an excellent tool for remembering dreams.**
- **Stimulates the Third Eye Chakra to discover visions.**
- **Helps the conscious mind to remember important aspects of dreams upon waking.**
- **Also helpful for returning into the dream state and repeat it for further insight.**
- **Allows old memories to rise into the conscious mind for re-evaluation and, if necessary, elimination.**
- **Produces a sense of responsibility for one's personal situations.**
- **Inspires new ideas that are motivated into action and to manifest results.**
- **Physically aids in the healing of all organs within the Spleen Chakra.**
- **Returns the sense of smell and taste by clearing the sinuses.**
- **Balances the mineral contents of the Physical Body.**

Ruby/Raspberry Quartz:
(Manmade in a laboratory in Russia by mixing Titanium, Silver and Gold with Quartz.)

- **Synthesizes the Main Chakras – a musical vibration that heals.**
- **Lifts the Physical form out of misery and pain.**
- **Prevents suicidal tendencies.**
- **Awakens positive attitudes to life.**
- **Connects the conscious mind with the awareness of The Oneness and God.**
- **Releases fear, phobias and paranoia**
- **Releases anger and guilt and aids in the evolution beyond the "Stage of Loss".**
- **Transforms auric emanations of energy into a state of calm.**
- **Stimulates growth in patience and endurance.**
- **Helps in focusing on Ascension and connections with Spirit Guides.**

Titanium Quartz:
- **Radically moves energy around the Five Bodies causing an enormous shift.**
- **Generates a force field of protection.**
- **Lifts depression and transforms emotions into joy.**
- **Develops a state of psychic awareness instantly.**
- **Brings ancient childhood emotional trauma to the surface to be released.**
- **Brings old memories of mental trauma to the surface to be instantly released.**
- **Generates a sense of relief and freedom.**
- **Connects the Lower Self to the Higher Self and harmonizes the two.**
- **Best used with individuals who are ready for big changes.**
- **Attitudes, emotions and actions are immediately transformed into a new state of reality.**

Zebra Jasper:
- **Creates a true sense of nurturing with unconditional love abounding.**
- **Loosens fixed energy at the base of the skull.**

- **Stimulates a need to be free of earthly conditioning.**
- **Allows the release of emotional and mental negativity absorbed in childhood.**
- **Creates a balance in the Yin and Yang energy of the Five Bodies.**
- **Causes a strong flow of energy along the neural spine.**
- **Purifies thoughts and protects from negative attack.**
- **Aids in the development of compassion and the emergence of unconditional love.**
- **Develops physical stamina and a general attitude of acceptance towards change.**
- **Aligns the Etheric and Physical Bodies, releasing negative programming on a cellular level.**
- **Strengthens character and intentions.**
- **Releases stress and tension from the muscles and bones**
- **Creates a strong energy to rejuvenate the entire body.**

DIAGRAMS
FOR THE
TREATMENT OF SPECIFIC
DISEASES

Treatment For Parkinson's Disease

Having inherited the gene, I manifested this disease in my 35th year, and immediately began my long journey of research to find ways to eliminate this disease. Crystal Acupuncture[sm] was the result. Within weeks, I had stopped the shakes and in the following months, changed my outlook on life. As the years passed, I continued to give myself weekly treatments and to reappraise my attitude and outlook on life. If you suffer with this disease, do the Acu points in the order shown. Recognize that your DNA & early childhood negative conditioning is the cause. Seek counsel and medical advice often as necessary.

(1) Amazonite (2) Carnelian (3) Amethyst (4) Aventurine

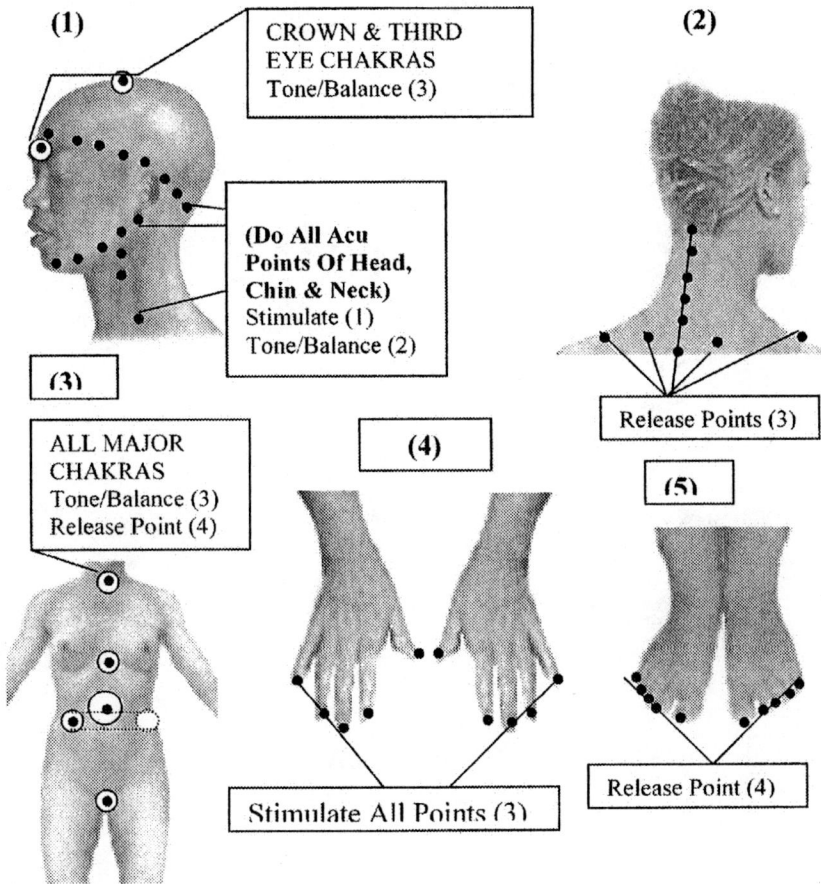

(1)

CROWN & THIRD
EYE CHAKRAS
Tone/Balance (3)

(2)

(Do All Acu
Points Of Head,
Chin & Neck)
Stimulate (1)
Tone/Balance (2)

(3)

Release Points (3)

ALL MAJOR
CHAKRAS
Tone/Balance (3)
Release Point (4)

(4)

(5)

Stimulate All Points (3)

Release Point (4)

121

Treatment for Alzheimer's Disease

As a result of my research, I have come to a conclusion that this disease manifests as a result of emotional and mental restrictions that have either been self-imposed through fear of loss or where these aspects of self have been controlled by close emotional associations through family members. Usually a sufferer of this disease has lived their entire life under the duress of criticism and denial, which ultimately causes them to withdraw. The brain then forms a physical malfunction. Crystal Acupuncture^{sm} will stimulate memories to arise. However, it is imperative that good counseling and emotional support be given frequently. Do points Diagram 1 – 4 in order.

(1) Sodalite (2) Carnelian (3) Amazonite (4) Rose Quartz

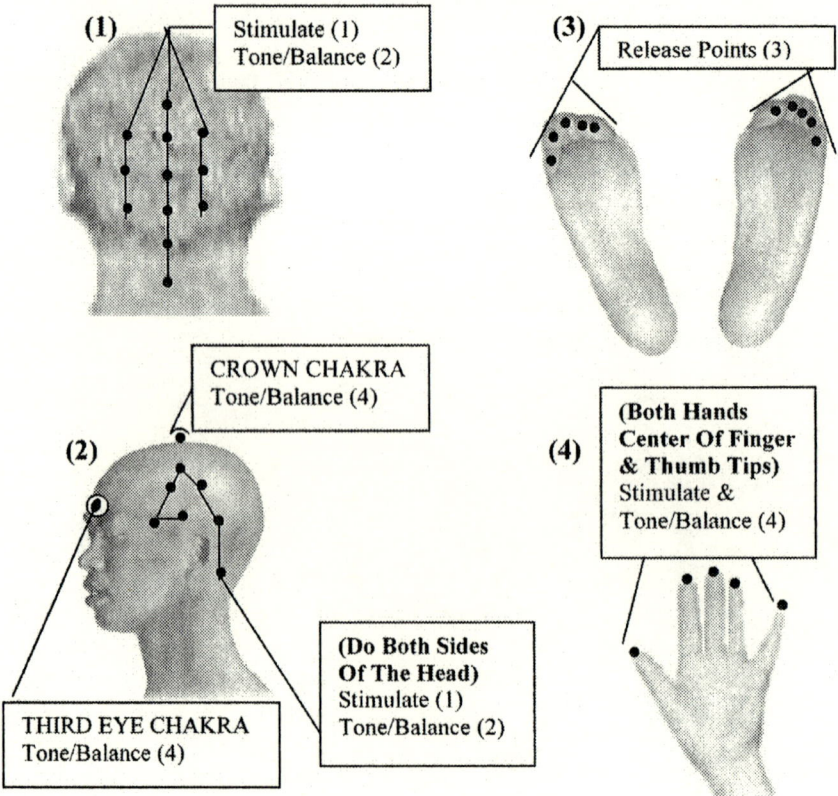

(1) Stimulate (1) Tone/Balance (2)

(3) Release Points (3)

CROWN CHAKRA Tone/Balance (4)

(2)

(4) (Both Hands Center Of Finger & Thumb Tips) Stimulate & Tone/Balance (4)

THIRD EYE CHAKRA Tone/Balance (4)

(Do Both Sides Of The Head) Stimulate (1) Tone/Balance (2)

Treatment For Muscular Dystrophy

This disease while showing deterioration of the brain with pea like forms, in my humble opinion, causes a malfunction of muscles by the manifestation of total fear in the form of inner panic. Usually, the sufferer has a very strong fear of becoming independent and often needs a great deal of emotional support. It is usual to find that the sufferer's mother is also insecure and drastically afraid of her independence and subsequent changes she could make. During her pregnancy, this fear is passed to the child on a cellular level which after birth will affect the Etheric Body. The child will in their own way develop resistance to change, despite their panic. This disease usually begins with a sudden shock caused by an unexpected event. Treatments should be carried out on a daily basis, with intense psychotherapy counseling and massage.

. **(1) Titanium Quartz (2) Amazonite (3) Blue Lace Agate (4) Aqua Aura Quartz (5) Carnelian**

> (All Points on both sides of the head form a series of rings around the circumference of the brain) Stimulate (1) – for mind and/or (2) for emotions on each point and then Tone/Balance (3) on each point before moving onto the next Acu Point.

Treatment of the head should be split up into many treatments over a period of several weeks. Hypnosis and counseling should be included.

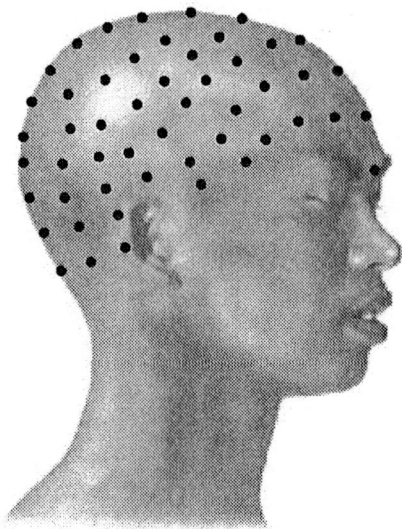

Treatment For Muscular Dystrophy (Cont.)

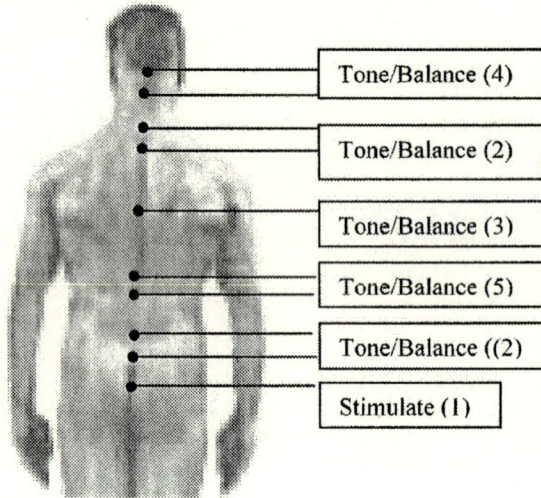

Tone/Balance (4)

Tone/Balance (2)

Tone/Balance (3)

Tone/Balance (5)

Tone/Balance ((2)

Stimulate (1)

Work up the spine to the nape of the neck every day.

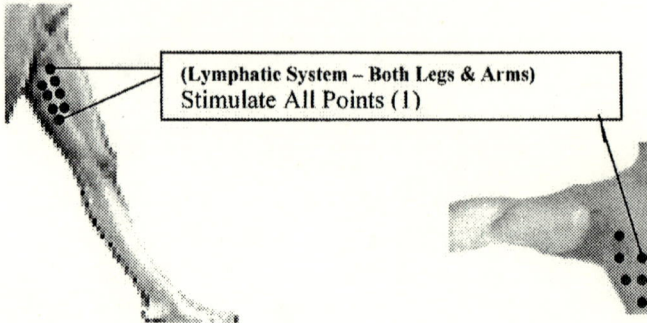

(Lymphatic System – Both Legs & Arms)
Stimulate All Points (1)

Note: Facial & Neck Points can also be worked from time to time.

Treatment for All Cancerous Conditions

All forms of Cancer are a result of an inability to surrender mental and physical control. Although in many cases there may be outside factors such as bacterial or viral infections, the body's inability to rejuvenate is usually a direct result from an emotional fear of being out of control. Judgment with seemingly profound justifications for repeating habitual daily routines along with family conditioning will also prevent healing. These habits include diet, exercise, work, and play activities along with cultural and religious beliefs. Young children, who seem to have no apparent reason for developing Cancer, are in fact running patterns that have been adopted in the womb. Each individual has their own way of storing energy in patterns that are theirs alone. Just as no two snowflakes are the same, so no two humans are the same. Cancer sufferers constantly try to identify themselves with others, resulting in a misguided lifestyle. A radical change of attitude, beliefs and activities is called for in order to heal. Below is a list of the body parts and the aspects of living that need to be looked at.

Bladder: Stubborn retention of information with fear of emotional release
Blood: General negative attitudes concerning new input and adaptability
Bones: Strength of character versus incapability
Brain: Conflict between conscious and unconscious awareness relative to creativity.
Duodenum: Fear of change
Eyes, Ears & Nose: Afraid of seeing and hearing the truth.
General Digestive System: Absorption of other's beliefs causing emotional disruption
General Urinary System: Fixation, dominance and aggression without awareness
Glandular System: Lack of understanding in self and potential development
Heart: General fear of not being loved for being true to one's self.
Kidneys: Inability to discern true reality versus fantasy
Large Intestine: Lack of ability to sort out mistakes and adapt
Liver: Fear of one's own inner power and responsibilities.
Lungs: Paranoia on all levels of existence
Lymphatic System: Lack of belief in life and possible achievements
Muscles & Skin: General negative outlook on skills and abilities
Nervous System: Fear of general experiences in life and their results

Ovaries: Lack of trust and belief in self
Pancreas: Lack of trust and belief in self.
Prostate: Lack of belief in success as a man
Rectum: Unsociable or fixed attitudes and actions
Reproductive Systems: Lack of love and faith in one's spirit and the ability to become an achiever.
Small Intestine: Loss of understanding and emotional/mental wisdom
Spleen: Loss of control in the face of adversities.
Stomach: Storing too many excuses
Throat: Lack of true communication throughout one's life.
Urethra and Ureter: Lack of awareness of retaining misleading information
Vascular System: Lack of connection with The Oneness and the World.
Water retention in the whole body: Fear of drowning in the lifestyles of others.

It should be noted that sufferers of any kind of cancer will need a great deal of counseling with hypnosis to assist them to change their points of view about their entire life. Regular medical treatments may well be essential and should not be avoided. However, in some cases alternative Integrated Medicine can be given to assist in a dual healing. There is no guarantee that any one method will work. The end result will always remain in the hands of the one suffering.

To treat this condition, the first treatment should be to balance all the Chakras and the Five Bodies. See Treatment for Balancing the Chakras with Crystal Acupuncture or Teragram Therapy. This will automatically regenerate the Glandular System and effectively aid in recovery and the building of new cells. Follow-up Counseling is a vital aspect of recovery. The Mindsets of an individual are the cause of illness and so a change of mind and heart is necessary either before or immediately following treatments.

Regular treatments should focus on the affected areas, but there must always be a constant awareness of not treating the symptoms, but rather looking for and treating the cause or causes. Many cancer patients have secondary illnesses. These must be isolated. These secondary complaints are supplementary to receiving help, kindness and support, which can keep the main cancerous disease alive and fixed. This will prevent any kind of healing. So, find out if the patient has secondary gains by being ill.

To treat most of the above areas of the body, please turn to the relevant diagram and follow the instructions. In the following pages are some general suggestions to treat some of the most common cancerous conditions using specific Acu Points. Please always remember to use Teragram Therapy^{sm} as well whenever possible after treatments. Hypnosis can help a patient change their mindsets easily.

It is also essential to find a good wholesome diet, which should follow a period of cleansing. There are many western herbal teas, essences, balms and homeopathic remedies that will help in the development of a more radical recovery.

It must be noted that your medical doctor should be informed about the natural healing treatments and these treatments should be in addition to your regular medical remedies, which may include drugs and chemo etc.

Treatment for All Cancerous Conditions

In every case of Cancer it is important to focus on the energies of the Five Bodies. Points on the hands and feet should always be done first, to open up the Physical Body, which in turn will allow energy to flow in the remaining four Bodies: Etheric, Spirit, Higher Mind and Soul. Use Clear Quartz to stimulate, followed by Rose Quartz to release and lastly use Amethyst to tone and balance. Once this is done, you can continue to treat the affected areas as shown in relative diagrams. Below are some extra areas to work on using different stones.

BLADDER

Citrine: Tone/Balance

Point is center ½ above pubic bone

BLOOD (1)

Red Jasper: Tone/Balance /Release **Spleen**

Point is left rear below rib above hip bone

BONES

Zebra Jasper: Stimulate & Release

Points at base of spine and Atlas at skull edge

BLOOD (2)

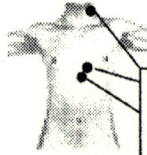

Carnelian: Tone/Balance **Heart, Aorta, Jugular Arteries**

Points between ribs and into muscle line in neck

BRAIN

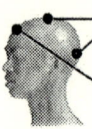

Lapis: Stimulate /Tone & Release

Points are central between the skull plates

DUODENUM & STOMACH

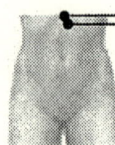

Malachite: Stimulate & Release

Points along edge or rib cage just below Sternum

LIVER

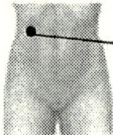

Agate: Tone/ Balance

Point a rib Apex beneath bone

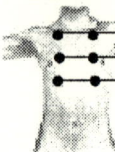

LUNGS

Blue Lace Agate: Tone/Balance /Release

Points below collar bone and ribs

128

Treatments for All Cancerous Conditions (Cont.)

LYMPHATICS   **BREAST**

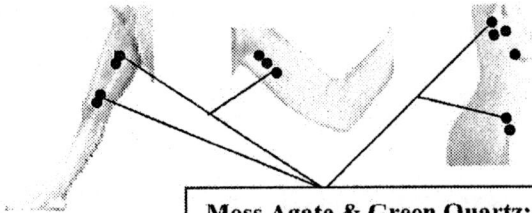

Moss Agate & Green Quartz:
Stimulate/Tone/Balance/ Release

OVARIES   **PROSTATE & TESTES**

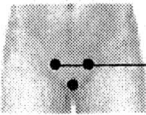

Blue Russian Quartz:
Stimulate/Tone/Release
Green Russian Quartz:
Balance with rotations

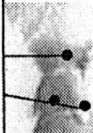

Points on edge of public bone
and top of labia crease

Points central on both testes & below
head of penis

PANCREAS   **ADRENAL GLANDS**

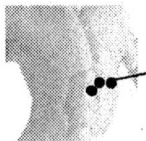

Rainbow Fluorite:
Tone/Balance/Release

Points run below the rib cage in an arc

Points are on the wait line at
edge of rear back

APPENDIX, CEACUM & RECTUM & SMALL INTESTINE

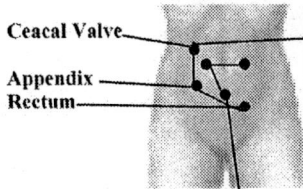

Ceacal Valve

Appendix

Rectum

Hematite:
Stimulate
Malachite:
Tone/Balance

Points for Small Intestine

THROAT & LARYNX

Lapis:
Tone/Balance/Release

Treatment for ADD, ADDH, & mental distraction

Children are easily identified with these types of mental disorders, however it has been my experience to encounter many adults who have struggled and suffered with one or more of these disorders. Where a general attention span is short, and the ability to absorb information is lacking, I have frequently noted that these conditions have been compensated with a powerful ability to store pictorial images in detail. Whenever these images emerged, I noticed that my clients wandered into their associations with their remembered past, making it difficult to keep the present in focus. When the brain is passing images back and forth through the conscious and subconscious at a rate faster than the speed of light, it seems practically impossible for him/her to settle down. The following diagrams will help slow the brain down, so that individual memories can be sorted and understood.

(1) Ruby Quartz   (2) Ametrine   (3) Jade   (4) Amazonite

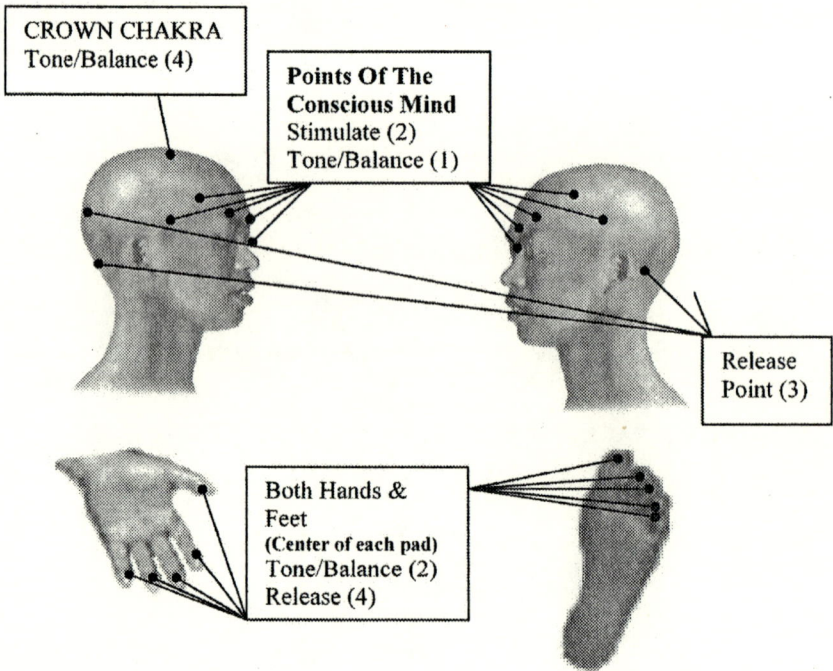

CROWN CHAKRA
Tone/Balance (4)

Points Of The
Conscious Mind
Stimulate (2)
Tone/Balance (1)

Release
Point (3)

Both Hands &
Feet
(Center of each pad)
Tone/Balance (2)
Release (4)

130

Treatment for Lupus Disease

This disease is one of the most devastating as it seems to include many maladies such as sensitivity to any kind of light, swollen limbs, asthmas, chronic pain, muscle fatigue an so on. My research has brought to light the fact that sufferers are afraid of life. Their emotional and mental instability is based on childhood fears and unhappy moments. To treat this disease, which is very real to the sufferer, it is imperative that counseling with hypnosis and plenty of nurturing be given, along with an understanding that the way to true health is through surrender. Fears must be faced and eliminated. Solid education with a strong support system must replace these fears. Below are diagrams to erase fear, and eliminate cellular memory from the Etheric Body. Hypnosis sessions should be integrated into this healing.

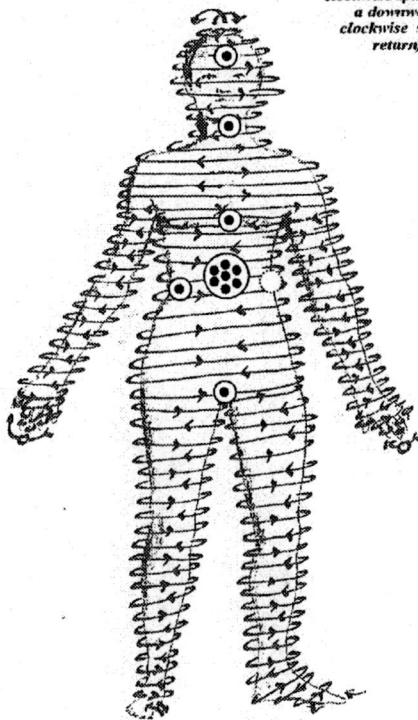

Fig. II
The Etheric Body
Energy Flow
(Ascending anti-clockwise spiral with a downward clockwise spiral return)

Each point should be Toned/Balanced & Released with Titanium Quartz – Both Front & Rear

Treatment for Lupus Disease (Cont.)

Note: All the Chakra Points should be rotated in a clockwise direction to ensure the spiral flow in the Etheric Body.

Releasing the Responsibility Syndrome:

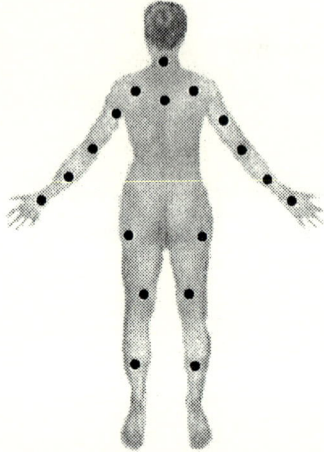

These Acu Points should be stimulated with **Clear Quartz** and then rotated with **Titanium Quartz** and then Released with **Ruby Quartz.** Ideo-Motor responses will cause the body to jerk with many emotional responses that will release in the days to come. Counseling and dream interpretations will be important.

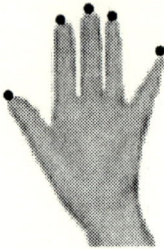

Each Finger tip and toe tip of each side of the body should be rotated in a clockwise direction with **Ruby Quartz** to balance The Meridians.

This Treatment should be repeated weekly in the beginning extending bi-monthly to monthly where necessary. Time must be given for recovery between sessions.

Treatment For Fibromyalgia & Chronic Pain Syndrome

Over the years, I have come to learn and understand that sufferers with these complaints are ill because of mental conditioning received in the womb and later enforced in early childhood. These 'fixed' mindset beliefs have been claimed as the babies' own and as a result, are encoded into the cells of the bone, muscles, ligaments and adjoining tissues. Every physical experience these sufferers have is mentally traumatic which results in constant physiological and psychological imbalances in the way energy flows throughout the Etheric Body. If it often extremely hard for these individuals to let go of all hurtful mindsets and to then embrace a newly found way to express their mental and emotional self. In treating this condition, it is very important to receive counseling and hypnosis treatments along with regular Crystal Acupuncture^{sm} and Teragram^{sm} Therapy sessions.

(1) Calcite   (2) Titanium Quartz (3) Malachite or Russian Green Quartz   (4) Moldavite or Magnetite (5) Rose Quartz

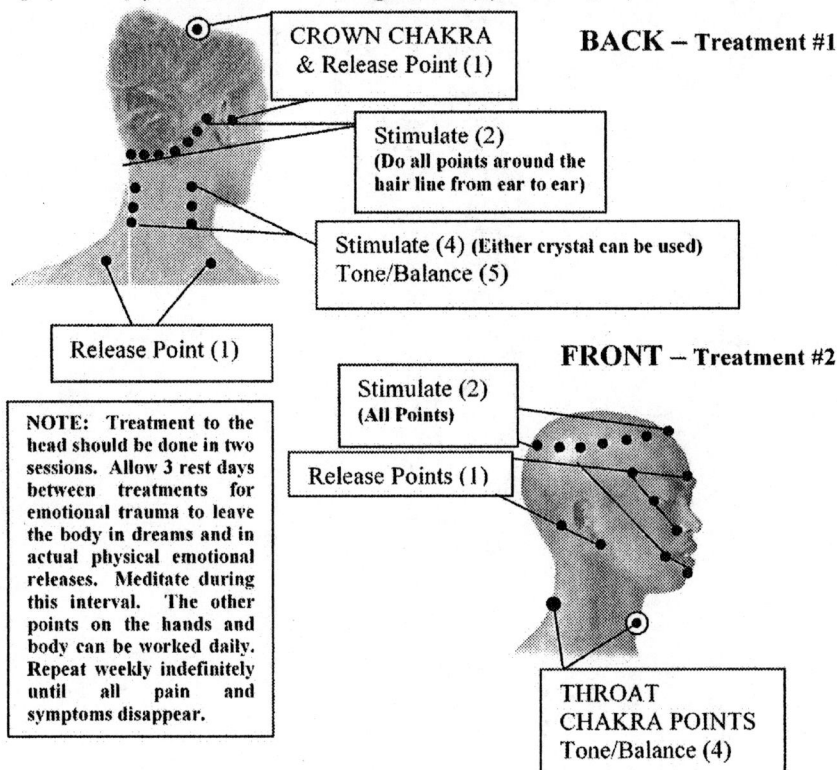

CROWN CHAKRA & Release Point (1)

BACK – Treatment #1

Stimulate (2)
(Do all points around the hair line from ear to ear)

Stimulate (4) **(Either crystal can be used)**
Tone/Balance (5)

Release Point (1)

FRONT – Treatment #2

Stimulate (2)
(All Points)

Release Points (1)

NOTE: Treatment to the head should be done in two sessions. Allow 3 rest days between treatments for emotional trauma to leave the body in dreams and in actual physical emotional releases. Meditate during this interval. The other points on the hands and body can be worked daily. Repeat weekly indefinitely until all pain and symptoms disappear.

THROAT CHAKRA POINTS
Tone/Balance (4)

Treatment For Fibromyalgia & Chronic Pain Syndrome (Cont.)

NOTE: The hands or feet should often be self-treated throughout the day, especially when it is noted that pain and/or emotional and mental anxiety is showing. Each time treatment is given, you should remind yourself that you are releasing history and that the only memory about history worth remembering is what you have learned from it.

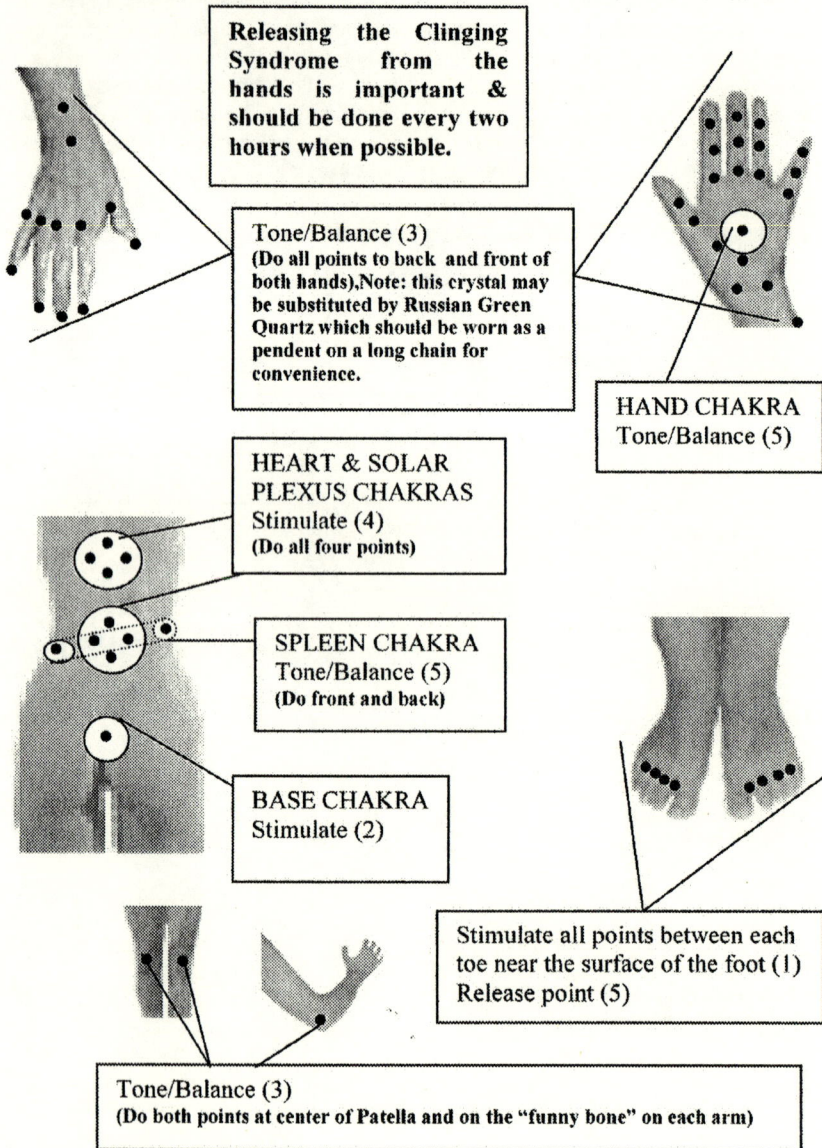

Releasing the Clinging Syndrome from the hands is important & should be done every two hours when possible.

Tone/Balance (3)
(Do all points to back and front of both hands),Note: this crystal may be substituted by Russian Green Quartz which should be worn as a pendent on a long chain for convenience.

HAND CHAKRA
Tone/Balance (5)

HEART & SOLAR PLEXUS CHAKRAS
Stimulate (4)
(Do all four points)

SPLEEN CHAKRA
Tone/Balance (5)
(Do front and back)

BASE CHAKRA
Stimulate (2)

Stimulate all points between each toe near the surface of the foot (1) Release point (5)

Tone/Balance (3)
(Do both points at center of Patella and on the "funny bone" on each arm)

Treatment For Crohn's Disease

In my experience this condition is caused by two factors. (1) Antibiotic given in the first year of life, which killed all acquired natural immunity defenses from the child's mother. (2) Inherited fear of living life on Earth while in the womb. Both aspects of these positive and negative traits are developed into a battle. Good versus bad. The problems that evolve after the first few years of life create an inner battle that affects energy flows in all Five Bodies. This results in an extremely strong allergic reaction to foods with an emotional response to learned taste. Eating is a very important part of learning which should be fun. If the mother is unhappy, then the child absorbs her emotional state. During the first five years of life a child listens and observes everything the mother does. If she is weak and afraid, the child identifies with her and develops these traits in their own personality. Consequently, as the child matures, fearful aspects of awareness develop which compounds the situation. Over several years the metabolic rates of chemical changes in the body affect the rate of digestion which results in mal-absorption and a deterioration of the digestive tract. I have often suggested to those I heal with this condition to put Slippery Elm into a milk drink. Slippery Elm is a very natural balm which will cover the sores and protect the lining of the Digestive System while it heals. But, it is important to treat these Acu Points and Chakras daily as shown in order to eliminate the mother's mental and emotional conditioning from the cellular-neuro-muscular memory.

Note: The Acu Points on the Digestive System pages should be used on and off over the week to help stimulate and balance the normal workings of the Digestive System.

(1) Fluorite (2) Carnelian (3) Sodalite (4) Titanium Quartz (5) Amazonite

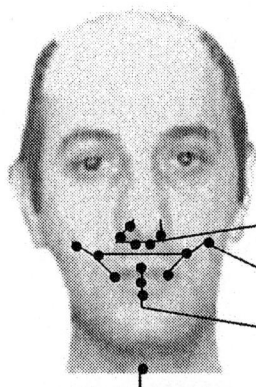

These points are used to release memory for eating by sucking from the breast, bottle and first taste of meals

Rotate each Acu Point and Release (1) & (2)

Stimulate (4)

Stimulate (3)

THROAT CHAKRA --Release Point (5)

Treatment For Crohn's Disease (Cont.)

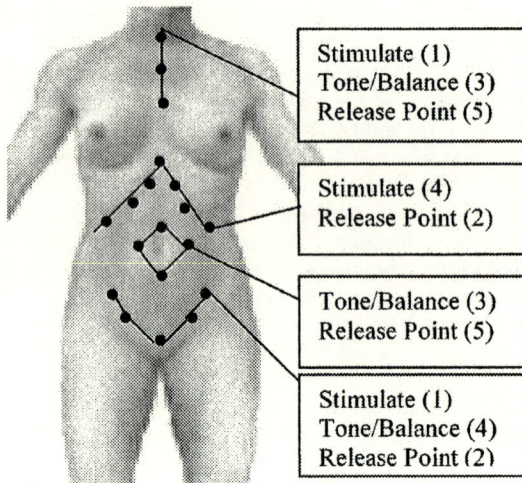

Stimulate (1)
Tone/Balance (3)
Release Point (5)

Stimulate (4)
Release Point (2)

Tone/Balance (3)
Release Point (5)

Stimulate (1)
Tone/Balance (4)
Release Point (2)

These points are all effective in releasing negative past memories that have been stored in the Chakras. Each Chakra has several vortices of energy that will be caused to rotate at a faster speed stimulating growth of the inner child. Sufferers of this disease are still inwardly childlike and in need of nurturing. The body has to mature and improve its own immune system

Stimulate (2)
Tone & Balance (5)
Release (1)

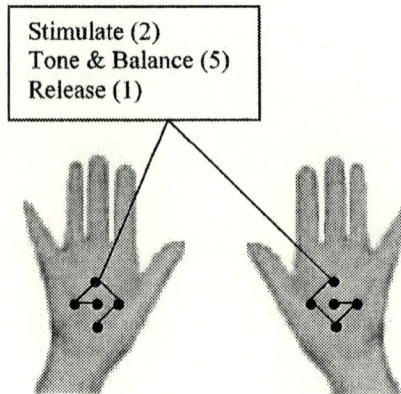

When an infant is feeding he/she holds onto the bottle or clenches his/her fists. During this time a child is sensory only to the act of eating and any unusual sounds can cause shock and fear. The hands grip tighter and those memories are stored in the cellular-neuro-muscular memory as an association that eating is dangerous. The adult equation is that life is dangerous -- even poisonous resulting in allergic reactions to food.

Treatment For Hodgkin's Disease

This disease affects the lymphatic system which is a one way system taking white corpuscles (cells), waste products and various other elements to the main blood supply and on to the Heart. If this system becomes blocked, then deformed lymph nodes develop which results in this type of cancer. I have chosen to show these treatment Acu Points because this disease is not fully understood. Medical science assumes it is originally caused by a virus. I myself feel it is caused through the introduction of certain antibiotics during an early age in life, causing a new strain of cells to develop slowly over what may be many years. While I have no proof of this, it has been shown to me that working the points below can abate this disease. My own personal research with sufferers of this disease has shown them to be very angry, judgmental and often selfish, with a great need for attention. These stones used below will help erase these characteristics. It is also *important to treat the entire lymphatic system. To treat those points, go to Treatment Of The Lymphatic system.* This page is to directly focus on the glands and nodes.

(1) Howlite (2) Fluorite (3) Ruby Quartz

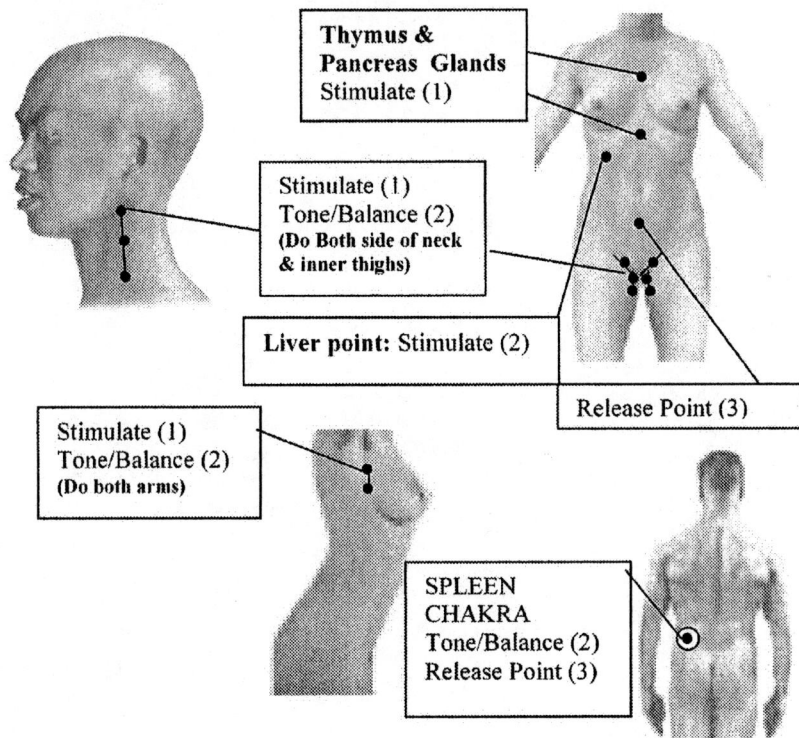

Thymus &
Pancreas Glands
Stimulate (1)

Stimulate (1)
Tone/Balance (2)
(Do Both side of neck
& inner thighs)

Liver point: Stimulate (2)

Release Point (3)

Stimulate (1)
Tone/Balance (2)
(Do both arms)

SPLEEN
CHAKRA
Tone/Balance (2)
Release Point (3)

Treatment For Obsessive Compulsive Disorder

This disorder is very often observed in everyone. However, there are those who are overly concerned with factual evidence that suits the eye. When things are placed correctly, then it is assumed that all is in order. Of course, this is often not the case, especially when one's point of view of order is disturbed and nothing can be located. The real problem with this disorder is the underlying insecurity that is stimulated by emotional fear of rejection. Any OC behavior that causes a disturbance to others is abnormal and will be treated as such. It is necessary to give a great deal of nurturing and counseling is necessary to ensure the sufferer of his/her self-acceptance in the eyes of others. This disorder is primarily activated by the sub-conscious. Therefore, it would be ideal to include hypnosis therapy, with emphasis on releasing parental control. Stimulate points first and then, do release points, followed by tone/balance points. Do daily treatments.

(1) Amazonite   (2) Blue Lace Jasper (3) Red Jasper (4) Sodalite

(Conscious Mind) Release Point (3)

(Mandible Joints) Tone/Balance (2)

Stimulate (1)

(Lt. & Rt. Brain) Tone/Balance (4)

Release Point (3)

(Breath – Both Ears) Tone/Balance (2)

(Brain – Medulla Oblongata – Both Ears) Stimulate (4)

(Both Hands) Tone/Balance (2) Release Point (4)

Crystal Acupuncture℠ Treatment Through The Skull to balance Yin & Yang energy in the 5 Bodies.

It should be noted that the left aspect of the brain has a Higher and Lower Self, being double feminine at the rear and male/feminine at the front. The opposite is true on the right side. (See diagram below). You can use any or all crystals on the brain to create a change in the way energy flows from and back to the brain. Simply rotate an Acu Point in a clockwise direction and then move about half a centimeter further other and do the same rotation. It takes a long time to do the whole head and many changes will occur, therefore it is my advice that only a small area of the skull should be worked on a one time. This type of treatment is always effective.

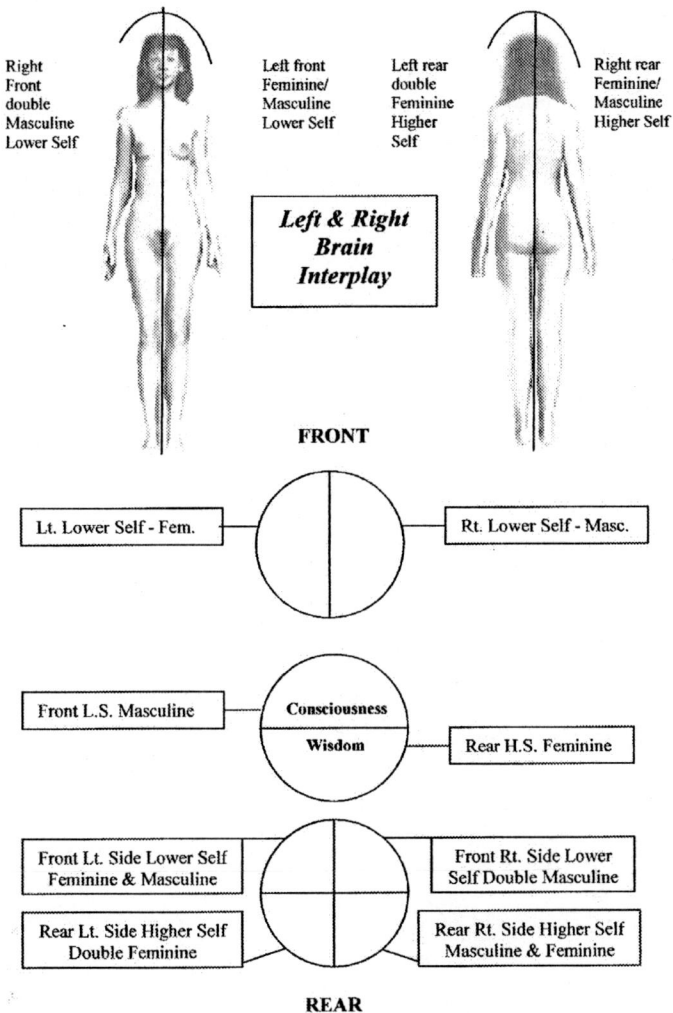

Right Front double Masculine Lower Self

Left front Feminine/ Masculine Lower Self

Left rear double Feminine Higher Self

Right rear Feminine/ Masculine Higher Self

Left & Right Brain Interplay

FRONT

Lt. Lower Self - Fem. — Rt. Lower Self - Masc.

Front L.S. Masculine — **Consciousness Wisdom** — Rear H.S. Feminine

Front Lt. Side Lower Self Feminine & Masculine

Front Rt. Side Lower Self Double Masculine

Rear Lt. Side Higher Self Double Feminine

Rear Rt. Side Higher Self Masculine & Feminine

REAR

139

THE BODY SYNDROMES

The Body Syndromes

The Body Syndromes are present in everyone. Some people show more of one type than another depending on their upbringing and circumstances in life. Each Body Syndrome is established on a cellular-neuro-muscular level by emotional excitement or trauma. When events occur, a child will use all his/her senses to try and understand what is occurring around them. If there is no explanation shown or given, then a child will establish their own opinions and correlate them with any apparent emotions at that time.

There are five Body Syndromes. Each one has its own characteristic traits. These traits can create symptoms of distress, stress and depression, as well as physical abnormalities. Each Syndrome is associated with the Laws of Karma (Rules of God) that have been established throughout all time. They are as follows:

1. Responsibility Syndrome: Affects the Head, Neck, Shoulders and Upper back. The Aura will generate the color red, expressing anger and frustration along with many control issues. This Syndrome is controlled by the 1st.Law – *No fragment may impose its will on another at anytime on any level.*

2. **Crying Syndrome:** Affects the Face, Throat, Chest, Heart and Solar Plexus. The Aura will generate the color yellow, expressing mindsets that are often searching for clues, while hiding many fears. This Syndrome is controlled by the 2nd Law – *Each Fragment shall be responsible for all it creates in positive and negative actions.*

3. **Sexual (Guilt) Syndrome:** Affects the Abdomen (all organs), Groin, Lower Back and Hips. The Aura will generate the color green, expressing jealousy, envy and judgmental attitudes. This Syndrome is controlled by the 3rd Law – *Each fragment shall share itself with all other fragments in unconditional love.*

4. **Clinging (Fight) Syndrome:** Affects the Fingers, Hands, Lower Arms, Armpits, Solar Plexus, Feet and Toes. The Aura will generate blue, expressing an intellectual need to be accepted through a misunderstanding of self-worth and power. This Syndrome is controlled by the 4th Law – *Each fragment shall attract like in the mirror image, either in opposition or support for growth without judgment.*

5. **Flight Syndrome:** Affects the Hips, Legs, Knees, Feet, Hands, Elbows and Back. The Aura will generate the color purple, expressing a need to sacrifice and deny self in all aspects of life. This Syndrome is controlled by the 5th Law – *Each fragment shall, in unconditional love, surrender to The Creator*

If you have the misfortune to suffer from more than one of these Syndromes, then it is important for you to look within on a spiritual level to question your existence and your life's journey. The older a person's Spirit is, the more likely you are to suffer from several of the Syndromes. This is your way of testing yourself on experiencing assimilation to find an understanding of The Oneness while in embodiment. No one is greater or smaller, better or worse than another, but we do have many differences and they are all to be understood if we are to return to God and become one with The Creator.

Each Syndrome by its very nature causes a person to focus on issues:

Responsibility Syndrome: Resistance, Resentment and Rejection
Crying Syndrome: Revelation, Revolution and Resolution
Sexual (Guilt) Syndrome: Perception, Persistence and Power
Clinging (Fight) Syndrome: Agreement, Acceptance and Absolution
Flight Syndrome: Existence, Experience and Evolution

Over the coming ten pages I have shown the Acu Points that you can work on to help yourself eliminate fear, pain, anger, guilt, loneliness and control issues. These diagrams are not in the order of importance, but rather in the order of general experiences. Most people cling to their ideas and hopes and often ignore their irrational attitude. So, I have begun with the Clinging Syndrome.

TREATMENT DIAGRAMS FOR ERASING THE BODY SYNDROMES

Treatment To Erase "The (Fight) Clinging Syndrome"

Throughout our lives we are taught to hold onto what we have, whether it is family, a friend, lover, animal or simply an object. Our belief is that this person or item cannot be replaced as he/she/it is unique. Of course, this may well be the case, but more often than not, those people/things we believe to be unique are in fact eyesores. Yet we still cling to them, hoping against all odds that they/it will save us from a fate worse than death. Just imagine clinging to a ledge, while standing on your tip toes and holding on with your finger tips for hours. This syndrome strains all the muscles of the body just as though you were really on that ledge. Clinging to items/people you have outgrown causes a great deal of stress, depression, low self-esteem and a lack of abilities. The creative self is annihilated along with independence. It is far better to fall, let go of everything while trusting yourself that you will land on your feet again with a better standard of life and relationships. It you are ready to change your life then do this treatment now.

(1) Fluorite (2) Howlite (3) Carnelian (4) Hematite (5) Amazonite

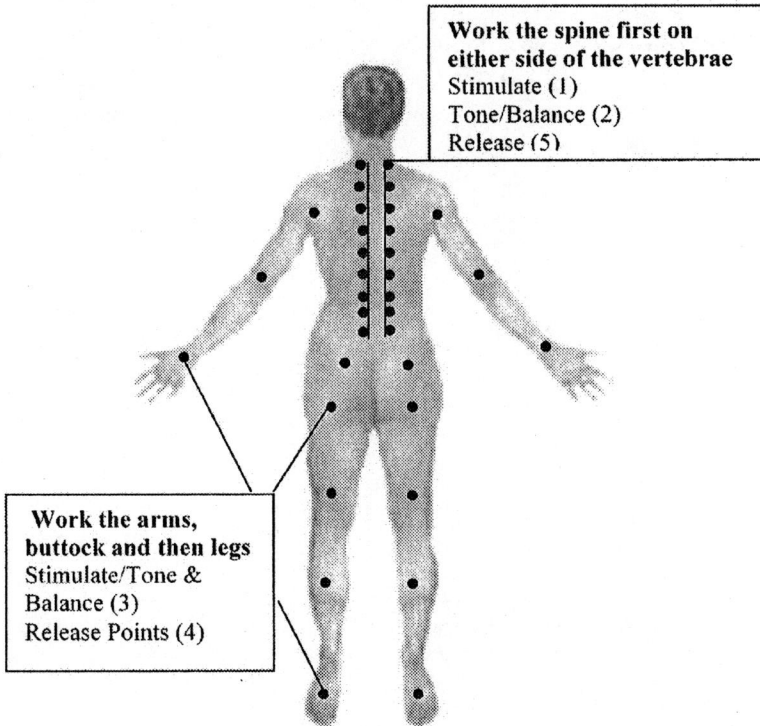

Work the spine first on
either side of the vertebrae
Stimulate (1)
Tone/Balance (2)
Release (5)

Work the arms,
buttock and then legs
Stimulate/Tone &
Balance (3)
Release Points (4)

Treatment To Erase "The (Fight) Clinging Syndrome" (Cont.)

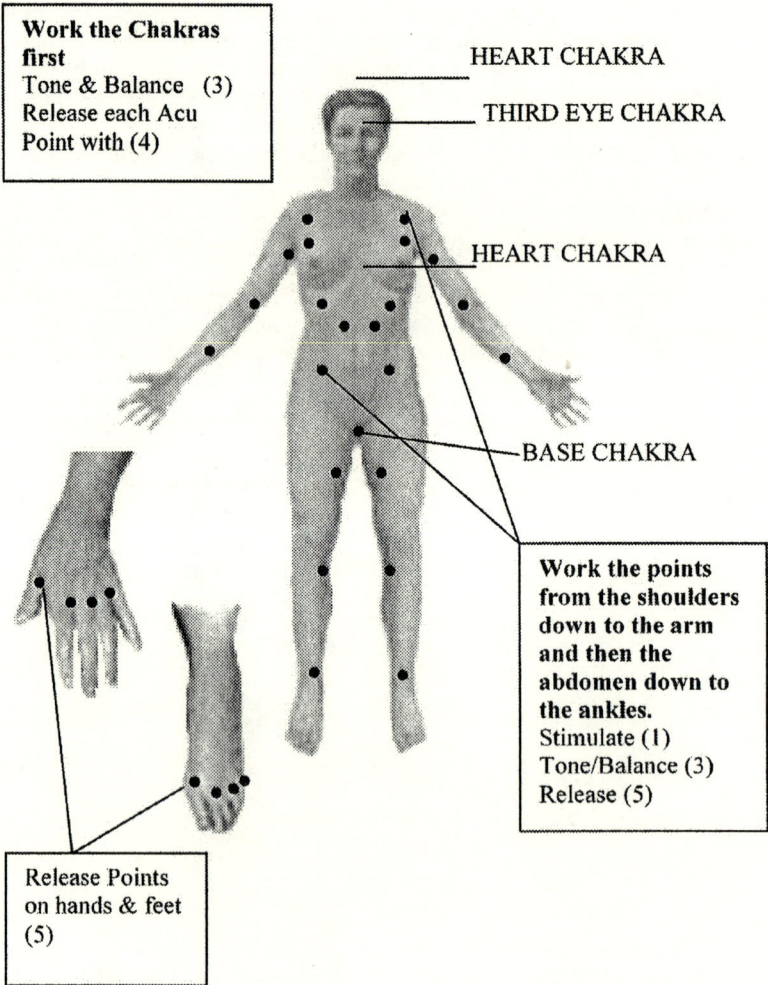

Work the Chakras first
Tone & Balance (3)
Release each Acu
Point with (4)

HEART CHAKRA

THIRD EYE CHAKRA

HEART CHAKRA

BASE CHAKRA

Work the points from the shoulders down to the arm and then the abdomen down to the ankles.
Stimulate (1)
Tone/Balance (3)
Release (5)

Release Points on hands & feet (5)

Meditate using the Teragrams after this treatment and allow the Five Bodies to realign and reprogram mentally to be in *agreement*, *acceptance* and to give self *absolution* from your history.

Treatment To Erase "The Flight Syndrome"

Most often we find ourselves in a situation against odds that suggest that we cannot win. Our natural instinct is to escape and survive yet another day. In extreme places of danger this sense is valid, but in our normal everyday life activities, there is rarely a great deal to be afraid of. Yet despite this fact, there are many individuals who live in fear. Those fears may be based on fact or illusion. It is possible that a robber could snatch a purse, but not very likely that a shark will eat you in the middle of the high street. When we are children, we learn a lot by watching movies, TV and listening to stories. Each piece of information is stored in the brain as an emotional picture that stimulates unwarranted fear.

On occasions, a real fear may manifest as a result of a real happening, such as a fear of being attacked after hearing someone entering your house. These real fears are normal, but unrealistic fears are not. Often, these fake fears cause nightmares that take form in the conscious mind creating panic and terror attacks. Insomnia and many other illnesses can occur. A common result can be a release of excess adrenaline. If you have a history of panic attacks, then this syndrome needs to be eliminated. Make sure you receive counseling and practice developing confident habits.

(1) Fluorite (2) Carnelian (3) Amethyst (4) Aventurine (5) Sodalite

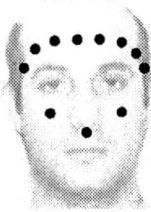

Deprogramming the conscious mind
Front: Stimulate (1)
Tone/Balance (3)
Release (4)
    Back: Stimulate (2)
        Tone/Balance (5)
        Release (4)
(Do all points)

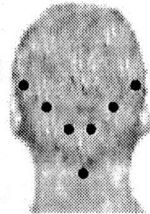

Release fear - all points
Tone/Balance (5)
Release (2)

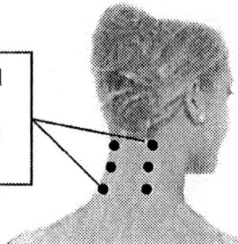

Remember to reprogram in meditation with Teragram Therapy

149

Treatment To Erase "The Flight Syndrome" (Cont.)

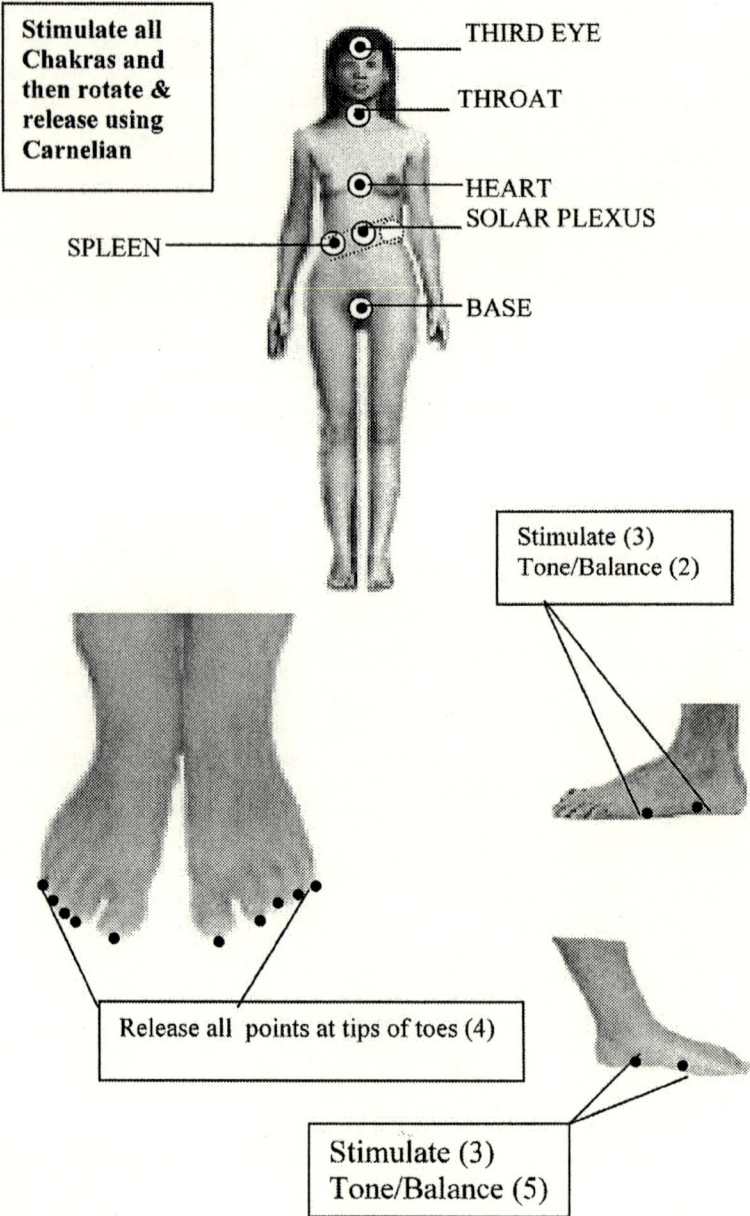

Stimulate all
Chakras and
then rotate &
release using
Carnelian

THIRD EYE

THROAT

HEART

SOLAR PLEXUS

SPLEEN

BASE

Stimulate (3)
Tone/Balance (2)

Release all points at tips of toes (4)

Stimulate (3)
Tone/Balance (5)

Treatment To Erase "The Guilt (Sexual) Syndrome"

When we are very young, we learn to believe everything we see and hear. We all have had many experiences that are now accepted as ultimate absolute truths. Great emphasis is laid upon the rules and regulations which we were taught to accept without question. Our primary programming was and is still tribal. We are trained to fit into the general tribal consciousness as good citizens who will do our utmost to serve and please those who request our aid. We are instructed to obey our elders even when they are wrong. Our peers use these rules to manipulate us to be what they want us to be. Our innermost desire is to respond to all this in the best way that we can. Unfortunately, we often fall short of success and more often than not feel isolated, unaccepted or cast out. In a world of competition, there are many who feel they are unable to keep up the pace. They procrastinate and often mentally and emotionally attack others verbally, casting innuendos that create guilt in others that will hopefully bring them acceptance. Others try to establish power as leaders, only to find that their followers are lacking in support. Yet, still they persist in giving away their power by manipulating themselves to believe in a perception that hides guilt under the surface. If you are ready to face your guilt and establish your gender, then this treatment will help you to eliminate many of your childhood beliefs.

(1) Howlite (2) Fluorite (3) Rose Quartz (4) Amethyst

FRONT VIEW

Use these points for self-help

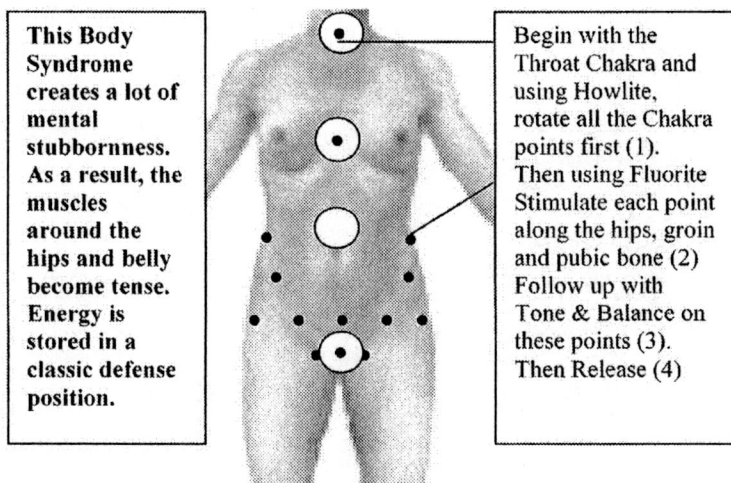

This Body Syndrome creates a lot of mental stubbornness. As a result, the muscles around the hips and belly become tense. Energy is stored in a classic defense position.

Begin with the Throat Chakra and using Howlite, rotate all the Chakra points first (1). Then using Fluorite Stimulate each point along the hips, groin and pubic bone (2) Follow up with Tone & Balance on these points (3). Then Release (4)

Treatment To Erase "The Guilt (Sexual) Syndrome" (Cont.)

REAR VIEW

Use these points if giving a treatment.

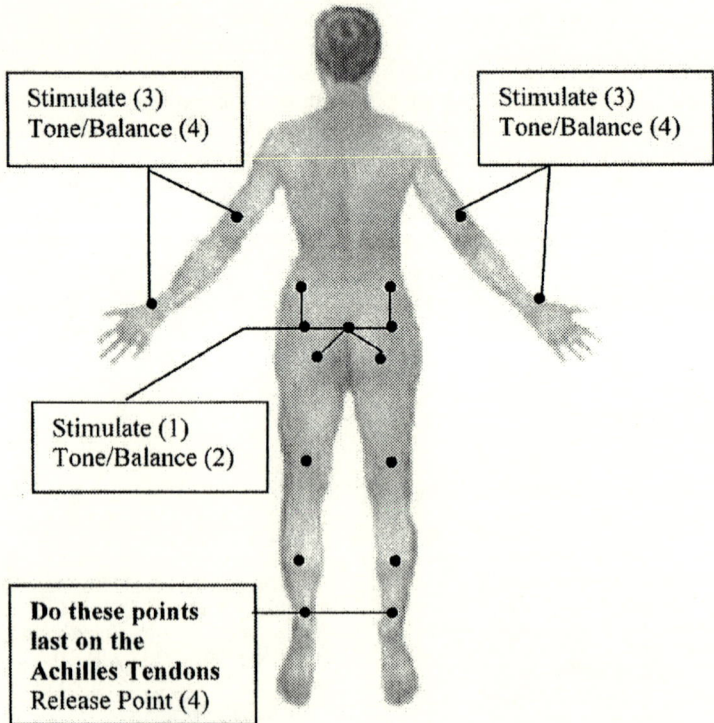

Stimulate (3)
Tone/Balance (4)

Stimulate (3)
Tone/Balance (4)

Stimulate (1)
Tone/Balance (2)

Do these points last on the Achilles Tendons Release Point (4)

Use Teragrams and meditate after this treatment has been completed to re-align the Five Bodies

Treatment To Erase "The Crying Syndrome"

This condition is very exhausting for the sufferer. Everything they do seems to take a tremendous amount of effort with little energy to complete their tasks. Everything is in a state of flux as projects are never completed and successes are rare. These individuals embrace fear of failure every day of their life. They expect to fail and yet live in fear of experiencing failure. They often resort to emotional outburst and mood swings. To those who know them well, they seem to be out of balance. They whine, complain and judge their family and friends. They constantly demand attention and feel bitter about many events in their lives. These people *"hate"* everything and everyone at some time or other. The world seems too big a place and they feel lost in it. These sufferers are the children who never grew up. Such diseases controlled by this syndrome are Bi-Polar Disorder, Obsessive Compulsive Behavior, ADD and ADDH. In many of these types of disorder the mind is unable to deal with realties. The emotions are therefore swinging back and forth in unexplained mood swings.

The Body holds everyday energy in patterns that are locked into cellular neuro-muscular memory. These patterns need to be broken with regular treatment and hypnosis. Below are some of the treatments that will help. Anxiety and phobias can also be treated with this condition. Seek a counselor and learn to erase those negative aspects of your character that cause your mind to respond in *revolution*, *revelations* and in making unfit *resolutions*.

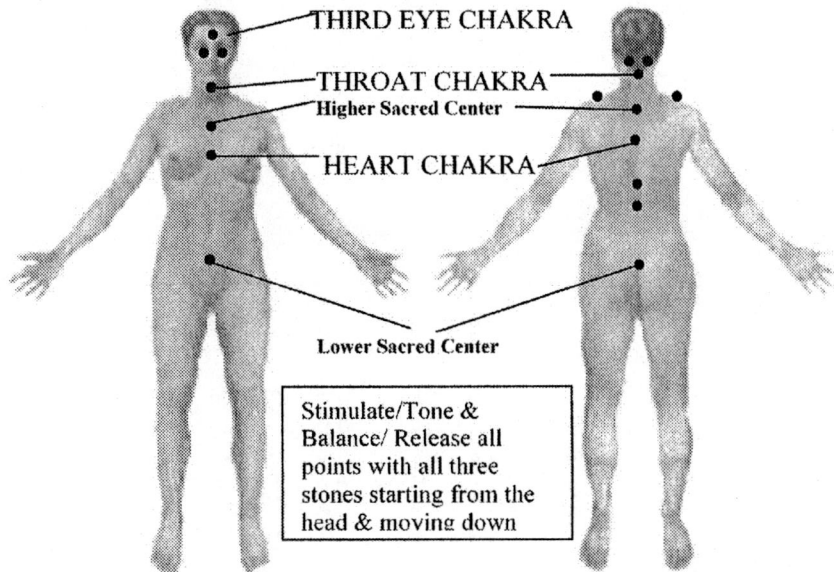

THIRD EYE CHAKRA

THROAT CHAKRA

Higher Sacred Center

HEART CHAKRA

Lower Sacred Center

Stimulate/Tone & Balance/ Release all points with all three stones starting from the head & moving down

(1)   AQUA GOLD QUARTZ (2) RUBY QUARTZ (3) RAIBOW QUARTZ

Treatment To Erase "The Crying Syndrome" (Cont.)

Note: Each point should be worked on individually. This treatment may be done on two separate days. Do the front first, and then the back the next day.

AQUA GOLD – Stimulate Tone & Balance all points of both hands and feet.

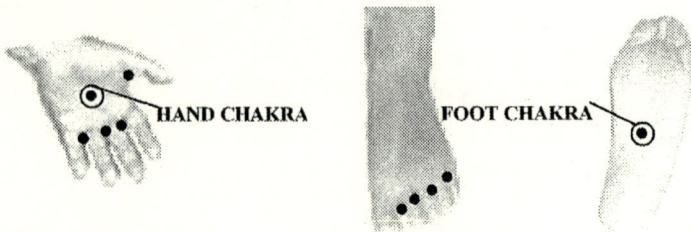

HAND CHAKRA   **FOOT CHAKRA**

Note: Release Point is right in the center between fingers and toes

Treatment For Bi-Polar Mood Swings

(1)Hematite (2) Magnetite –

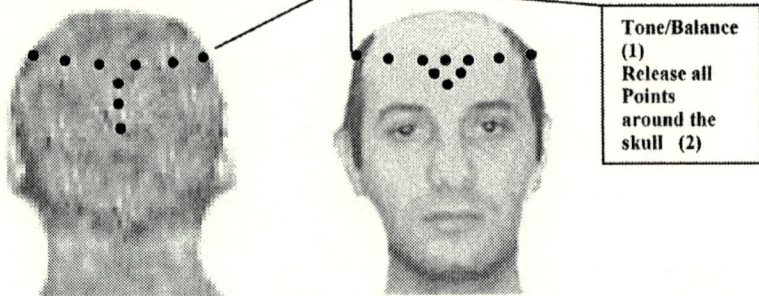

Tone/Balance (1)
Release all Points around the skull (2)

Note: Frontal Lobe Acu Points will relax the conscious mind. The rear three descending Acu Points will release visual tension and emotional stress and tension.

Treatment for Obsessive Compulsive Disorder

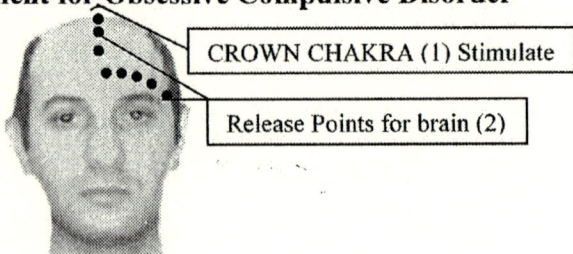

CROWN CHAKRA (1) Stimulate

Release Points for brain (2)

Treatment To Erase "The Responsibility Syndrome"

The Responsibility Syndrome is a learned patterning that has caused an individual to store energy in a particular place. That stored energy is likened to becoming Atlas holding up the world. The fingers, wrists, arms, back of upper back and neck ache continually, with lower back trauma which often results in the vertebrae going out of alignment. A person suffering with this physical type of disorder will often have vocal/throat/migraine and back pain illnesses with a great sense of tiredness/weakness. If it is time to put your load down, then do this treatment. In the days to come you will release, fear, pain, anger and guilt along with your attitude of control. At that time you must seek counsel and learn how to live your life without taking on the responsibilities of others. Learn to erase thoughts of *resistance*, *resentment* and *rejection*. You are no longer required to be the "fixer" child. You and you alone are responsible to make yourself happy.

(1) Fluorite (2) Carnelian (3) Amazonite

REAR VIEW

With this diagram, it is impossible to treat yourself completely. Simply treat the Acu Points that you can reach comfortably. If you have someone to help you, all the better. If you are helping someone else, be sure to treat all the Acu Points in a downward direction beginning at the nape of the neck. This will force negative energy into the ground and ensure a release of energy without discomfort.

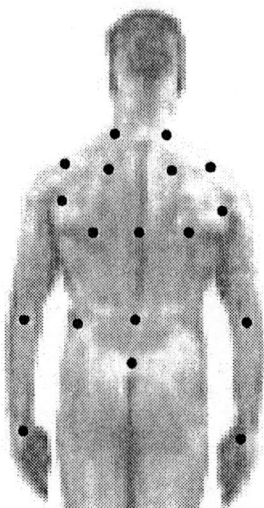

Take each stone in turn and treat each Acu Point as shown. First Stimulate with Fluorite, then Tone & Balance with Carnelian and then Release with Amazonite. Note: If you are treating yourself, focus on sending energy out through your Foot Chakras. Energy will still move giving you further relief.

Note: Use Teragrams to rebuild and Balance the Throat, Heart, Solar Plexus & Spleen Chakras.

155

Treatment To Erase "The Responsibility Syndrome" (Cont.)

FRONT VIEW

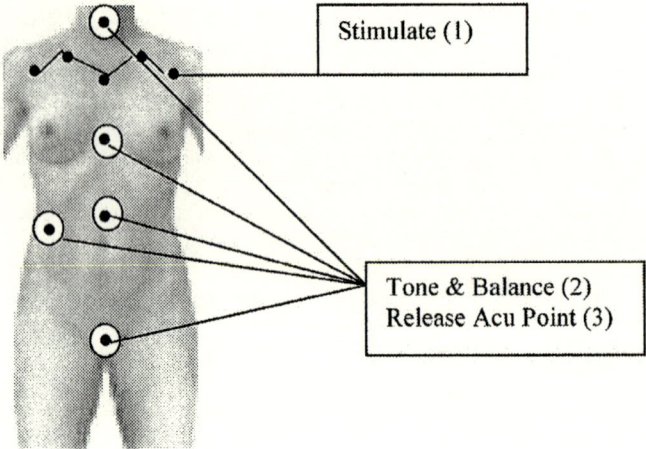

Stimulate (1)

Tone & Balance (2)
Release Acu Point (3)

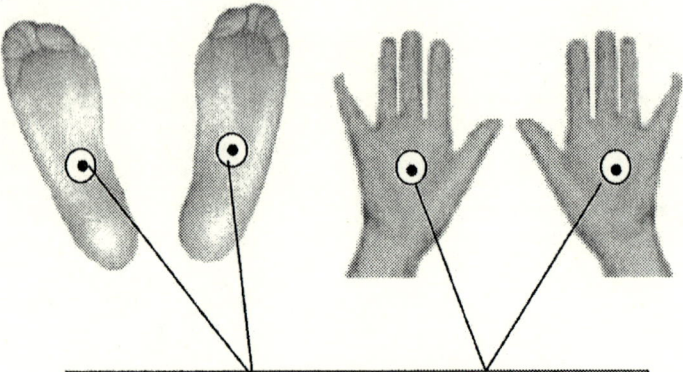

The Foot & Hand Chakras should be the last thing to treat. Use Fluorite to Release. Rotate in a clockwise direction until the body physically shifts. You may feel strange and familiar sensations during this part of the treatment.

TERAGRAM^{SM} THERAPY

They didn't want to know

As a child, whenever I spoke about energy and the way it followed people around, I was called stupid or imaginative – a silly child with a lot of pretend ideas! You can imagine my frustration! I often asked myself the question, "Why couldn't those people see what I see?" To me, they were "pathetic" adults with fixed ideas and no room to grow! They just didn't they want to know what I had to tell them and I always wondered why?

Well, a lot has changed since 1950. Today, people actually do *understand* that the body is a working machine that generates energy. Some doctors in various fields of medicine do take this into consideration when helping individuals back to full health. Unfortunately, many more do not understand the way energy flows and where it is created and why it flows the way it does.

I spent my life looking. Yes, literally watching and recording my findings. But even so, the medical profession is still unwilling to trust metaphysicians such as I.

The Medical profession says Sorry!

"We know there is an energy flow. Acupuncture has proved that, but because we can't see it, it is impossible to tap into it and understand it. We haven't got the time or the funds to investigate. **Sorry!**"

I guess from their point of view, it's no different from electricity. We know we have it, we know it works when the light bulb goes on, but we can't see it. Often their education has narrowed their point of view and anything outside the box is a dangerous area for them to explore. In the meantime millions of people grow sicker, even die! They take pills to ease the side effects of other pills. Suddenly they are caught in a loop - a mindset that is fixed. It says, "I need a medical doctor to cure me. So I need to keep going back to get his advice". The problem is the Doctor does not necessarily have the cure. Just because he got us out of measles or chickenpox when we were small, doesn't mean he has the cure withal for everything else. Can we do anything about that? I say we can.

But you can make a difference yourself

My work with individuals, both with Medical supervision and on my own, has over the years, proved that **changes can be made in a person that**

will help them return to full health, no matter what the complaint. Yes, we are all our own healers at heart. **We each can free ourselves from pain and disease!**

How, you may ask?

What I saw through the eyes of my childhood was a world of negativity in which people focused on what was wrong with their lives. They complained constantly about their lifestyles, their loved ones' lack of support or understanding, their country's economy leaving them practically penniless, and all the ailments that resulted from such a bad life.

Watching these "miserable" wretches, I saw that the more they complained, the more their energy flared in anger. Dark red explosions ruptured from the surface of their faces and hands, seeming to flare towards me as if they intended to gobble me up. Sickly greens skimmed off their skin to slip and slither around them as they complained about their pain. Yellow ochre spilled forth from their brains like oozing slime. No wonder I was afraid of these people! But something inside me said, "search deeper, find the cause."

Today, I'm happy to say, I understand!

In my book "Breakthrough Therapies – Crystal Acupuncture^{sm} & Teragram^{sm} Therapy" I explain how mental and emotional conditioning has caused everyone to develop many restrictions, limitations and repressions of the true self. Expression of truth is paramount if we are to remain healthy.

Now that you know that you are composed of five bodies, it is important to understand that these five bodies need to be kept in harmony with one another.

Etheric body is the key!

In the early days of my research, my question was, "What kept the Spirit Body in the Physical Body?" My studies lead me to understand the existence of the "Etheric Body". This body often goes unnoticed both by the layman and the doctor. How can there be such a body if you cannot see it? Well, you can. Every time you feel an emotion or think an intense thought, you are actually feeling this body. It is the summation of all of your existence in this life. All your feelings and thoughts are impregnated into this body.

The more negative you are, the heavier it is. Imagine a balloon filling with water. It will expand and enlarge until a weakness appears. At this point, the balloon will burst. The Etheric Body is much the same. When it is overloaded with negativity, it spills over into the physical body, causing a disruption in the flow of this body, which could result in any illness from a mild headache to a stroke.

In fact an illness will manifest in the weakest part of the body – anything can happen! In extreme cases, the Etheric Body will spill over into the Spirit and then acute depression and suicidal tendencies can arise.

Don't forget there are two more bodies!

The other remaining bodies, The Higher Mind and Soul/God self (Unconditional Love) are strong and extremely capable of rebalancing the lower three bodies. *Yes, a miracle can happen from these two bodies.* All it takes is a catalyst, which allows you to let go of negativity. When negativity is released, the dam is unlocked and energy flows from these two bodies to realign and harmonize the Spirit with the Physical Body. It does this by cleaning the Etheric Body of negativity and filling it with positive polarity, which affords a new beginning and, in turn opens you up to changing your emotional outlook, your physical point of view and your lifestyle.

My new discovery!

Teragram Therapy is a simple technique. By placing a colored Teragram on certain parts of the body, where the major chakras (Energy vortices where the five bodies meet) effective colors can be amplified and absorbed into the body. Each Teragram is made from natural agate. Agate is a healing stone that has long been recognized for its ability to calm and relax. What I was able to see and prove was that this natural mineral is a conductor and transformer. It is able to hold and transform energy from negative to positive. Each Teragram is capable of creating an exceptionally powerful rotation of each Chakra that in turn causes a shift in all the Five Bodies.

Etheric energy can be transformed!

Each of the Chakras consists of multiple vortices that rotate and interact with one another. When a Teragram is placed on any one or all of the Chakras, energy in the vortices are changed. This changed energy causes a faster spin in the Chakra as a whole, which in turn causes the flow of energy around the Physical body and the Etheric body to release tension and stress, while at the same time releasing old memories and emotional conditioning.

Actual case studies

I also discovered that visual, olfactory and auditory input during a session with Teragram   Therapy acted as a stimulus to release even deeper issues. For example, a woman who was afraid of sharks was watching a program about sharks while sitting with two Teragrams , one on her abdomen and the other over her heart. She noticed several days later, that sharks no longer horrified Her. Her fear had turned into a normal healthy respect of them.

Another client told me that she could not forget her past relationship, even though it had been over for years. I left her in a meditative state with all six Teragrams   on her body. When I returned, she was totally relaxed. During her meditation, she found herself saying goodbye to her former lover and planning her future. That lady went on to build a successful business and find a new relationship that ended in a happy marriage.

Teragram   Therapy helps individuals to re-focus and redirect their energies. They can be used while relaxing with a favorite pastime, like reading, writing or watching a movie. They can be carried in a pouch or pocket during physical exercise or while working. Every thing your five senses take in is a stimulant within your brain to evolve spiritually. As you experience each event, energy is moving throughout your Aura. As this happens, the Teragrams continue to balance your energies over and over again. Whatever your choice of experience, moving energies will in due time change your mind and heart allowing your body to heal rapidly.

Why Use Agate?

Agate is a member of the Quartz family and is known as the *"Gem of the Earth"*. Since early times men have been attracted to agate in its variety of colors and have used them to decorate themselves and their temples. In spiritual ceremonies, early civilizations used highly polished slabs of agate as ritual tables in which to present their offerings to the Gods. In these rituals, it was understood that when agate was held, it would transmute any earthly negative energy, even from the densest of forms. When presented to the gods, it would become a catalyst to rid the transgressor of his sins. It was believed that whoever surrendered in this way would receive something else – positive energy and a new way of life. Many talismans were made of Agate, which made the wearer feel protected and at peace.

Agate is still considered a beautiful stone. Technology has made it possible to enhance its beauty by dying it as well as by grinding it to a highly polished surface. Geodes are sliced thinly and chemically dyed. Various colors are produced that are in keeping with modern tastes. While today there is a vast market for clocks, ashtrays etc., few people give credit to the valuable healing qualities of agate or the trace minerals that lie within this powerful healing stone.

Dispel the madness!

Teragrams are agate slices and taking time to relax with them can help dispel the madness. You are in a hurry. Nothing seems to go right for you. No matter how hard you try, there always seems to be something negative happening. In trying to cope with difficulties, many of us make our situation more desperate by trying to solve our problems through illusions and fantasies. By lying in a comfortable position with Teragrams on your body, it is possible to bring in stillness of mind and to draw upon inner peace. This wonderful state of relaxation will allow you to find your inner truth and make adjustments in your attitude.

There is an AURA about you

I stated earlier, each of us is a source of energy that is manifested into human form. Human form, composed of Five Bodies: Physical, Etheric, Spirit, Higher Mind and Soul, is a unique pattern of energy that creates a combined energy discharge called the Aura. These Five Bodies normally fit nicely inside one another, with a slight overlap that creates a whirlpool of energy that results in an egg shaped emanation. The Aura should be full of vibrant brilliant colors that radiate outward from the Physical body three feet or more. Many people only radiate about half that distance and only emanate dull, dismal colors. These people feel lonely and misunderstood. Their Etheric Bodies are loaded with negativity.

The Etheric Body is where all of an individual's misunderstood learning is stored stimulated by the rotations of the Base Chakra (Root). If the majority of lessons have been negative, then this person will be depressed, angry and unhappy. The Base Chakra will be loaded and the Etheric

Body will be blocked. Taking time to relax with Teragrams can help dispel this. If the Physical Body is denied a good link with the Spirit Body because of a negative Etheric Body, the Physical Body's energy fails and illness occurs. The Etheric Body's negative energy controls the conscious mind, creating false beliefs. These beliefs prevent the Spirit Body from true self-expression. When this occurs, the Chakras lose their balance. By meditating with the Teragrams, the Etheric Body can be cleaned and recharged to open channels for the Spirit Body to harmonize with the Physical Body. Then a new consciousness can develop providing a positive attitude and a new way of looking at life.

What's a Chakra?

The Chakras are vortices of energy that tie the five bodies together. There are seven Major Chakras. (See Diagram).

CROWN – (Top of Head) Lets energy flow from God-source into the five bodies.

THIRD EYE – (Middle of Forehead) Allows a person to perceive truth

THROAT – (Over Larynx) Allows a person to communicate truth.

HEART – (Over Heart) Allows a person to feel truth and creativity.

SOLAR PLEXUS – (Over Abdomen) Lets a person exchange energy with others

SPLEEN – (Runs diagonally through body from back left to front right) Creates an alignment of the 5 bodies.

ROOT – (Over Reproductive Organs) Old lessons are reworked to create spiritual revelation and new ways to be.

The energy in each Chakra rotates in a clockwise direction and should flow forcefully from front to back and then return from back to front maintaining the clockwise rotation. This creates a shield of energy that prevents negativity from entering. Most of us may experience a slowing down of the rotation of one or more of the Chakras. This is often caused by self-doubt and/or fear allowing negativity to enter. When this occurs, the natural energy flow is interrupted and blocks occur that create imbalances, which prevent enjoyment of self.

By placing Teragrams on the Chakras, the flow of energy in each Chakra is stimulated to rotate faster, creating a strong vortex of energy, which then circulates through the body and expels negativity.

My Teragram^{sm} Therapy Kit

I have managed to obtain 6 different colored Teragrams. (1 each natural, blue, violet, red, green and pink), These colors are primary colors that together synchronize white. The primary color of yellow is within the red and green colors and is therefore present. Since Earthly colors are different in vibration in the Spirit World, the colors of the Teragrams affect the Spirit Body and Higher Mind Body differently. With a psychic eye observation, silver, gold, bronze, copper and radiating sunset colors can be seen in the Aura when an individual is in a state of grace.

Meditations on Audio

Many of my clients have repeatedly informed me that they find it hard to meditate and even harder to focus on their Five Bodies. So, I created a special meditation CD to help those who feel stuck. I have also written a book called *50 Spiritually Powerful Meditations,* which is written in a way for a student of meditation to read aloud onto a tape. By listening to your own voice leading you into a deep meditation a true sense of self-empowerment is established. If you require this CD, it is obtainable from me at the back of this book.

TERAGRAM CD CONTENT

Track 1: A guide to placing the Teragrams on the body and a directed focus on the absorption of the colors to obtain deep healing.

Track 2: An in-depth guide to rebuild the chakras and harmonize the five bodies with emphasis on rejuvenation and revitalization.

Using your Teragrams

Choose a quiet time with no one around to disturb you. Lie on a bed or on the floor and place a Teragram on each of the five Chakras from the Third Eye to the Root. Begin with violet on the Third Eye, Blue on the Throat, Green on the Heart, Pink on the Solar Plexus and Red on the Root. The Spleen and Crown Chakras will be done separately afterwards.

Take several deep breaths and relax. Concentrate on your body. Feel its tension and stress. Acknowledge these feelings and then attune to the Teragrams. Feel the Teragrams on your body and be sensitive to the energy that is flowing through them. Know that your own energy is being recycled and rejuvenated.

Feel your tension and stress leaving you. Listen to and follow along with your CD or just do your own favorite meditation. You may simply wish to just lie there until you have achieved a wonderful sense of well being.

At this point, ask yourself if you want to change the Teragrams around. (Some Chakras may need more than one color). If so, change them and meditate again as before. When you are satisfied with your self-healing, you are finished and may remove the Teragrams.

Next, take the natural Teragram in your left hand and hold it at the rear left side of your body, (Over the spleen). At the same time, take the red Teragram in your right hand and hold it over the right front side of your body (Just below the ribs). Relax and feel the energy flowing through your hands and body. Stay in that position and imagine yourself balancing your energies by visualizing a meter with a scale of 0 – 100. Push your energy to 50 (which is the middle balancing point). When this is achieved, set the Teragrams aside.

Finally, take the natural Teragram and hold it over the Crown Chakra. With both hands covering this Teragram, allow your energies to flow downward towards your feet. Sense your excess energy flowing into the ground and when you feel ready, remove the Teragram and sit up slowly.

Closing and locking down the chakras

Focus your mind on your Third Eye Chakra and frown. Say close. Relax.
Focus on your Throat Chakra. Swallow three times. Say close. Relax.
Focus on your Heart Chakra, breathe deeply three times and say close. Relax.
Focus on your Solar Plexus Chakra. Pull the muscles in slowly and say close. Relax.
Focus on your Root Chakra, squeeze the genital muscles and say close. Relax.
Focus on your Spleen Chakra. Pull your lateral muscles in. Say close. Relax.
Finally, attune to your Crown Chakra. Visualize a daisy closing up for the night, leaving a small part open. Say, "I am connected to God". Relax.

Affirm how good you feel. In the days to come, look for the positive aspects of your life and avoid negative thinking and confrontations. People will be nicer to you and more helpful when they feel how mentally calm and physically relaxed you are. Be receptive to the many opportunities that can now enter your life that would not have happened before you treated yourself to Teragram Therapy.

PROTECT YOURSELF.
CLOSE YOURSELF DOWN FREQUENTLY

Healing Yourself The Lazy Way

You can use your Teragrams while watching TV, listening to the radio, reading a book or any other pastime or hobby. Teragrams work even when you are not meditating. Everything you hear, see, smell, taste, touch and sense is an automatic catalyst that allows you to release old mindsets and emotions and to re-program new thought with positive feelings. Simply place the colored Teragram of your choosing over the chakras of your choice. Sit back and relax and let it work for you. If you are more active and wish to walk or involve yourself in sports, then place them in your pockets or strap them with tape to your body. As you use your muscles, you will reconnect with old memories that will be deprogrammed. As you consciously connect to your movement, you can and will create new thoughts with positive affirmations. You will change subtly for the better.

Additional Help

You may have a family member or pet that seems to be low in energy. Hold the red Teragram on the Heart Chakra and allow your energy to flow through the Teragram into the person you wish to help. If you wish to help further, other Teragrams may be placed on their body and your energy can be directed through those Teragrams too. This can also be done while a person is asleep because an individual's energy is constantly moving and will automatically pass through the Teragram, simulating them on an unconscious level to release negativity through their dreams. Try sleeping with them taped to your own body or simply lie on them and watch how your own dreams help you release unwanted conditioning from early childhood that has prevented you from becoming successful, strong and healthy.

Teragram Color Connections

Violet – Spiritual, Psychic attunement
Blue – Mind clarity, Focus
Pink – Emotional harmony, Peace of mind

Green – Healing of Mind, Body and Spirit
Red – Vitality, Life force, Energy, Motivation
Natural – Grounding, Stabilizing, Calming

TERAGRAM^{SM} THERAPY TREATMENT DIAGRAMS

TERAGRAM THERAPY BLACK & WHITE COLOR KEY

Teragrams are colored agate slices. As this book is not in color, below are photos of each colored Teragram. Notice how the circles and shapes vary. Each Teragram in a kit is varied in size and shape. Nature does not make everything exactly the same size and form. This makes Teragrams uniquely powerful. Each Teragram is carefully chosen for its quality and the rings within its make-up. In the pages to follow are diagrams showing how you can apply them to yourself. Enjoy discovering the power of each one individually, or as a group of two or more.

Blue

Green

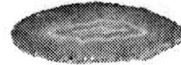

Natural

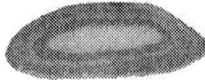

Pink

Purple

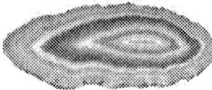

Red

Treatment To Balance And Align The Seven Major Chakras

Having frequently used Crystal Acupuncture^{sm} to remove blocked energy, it is always extremely important to rebalance the Major Chakras over and over again. Even when it seems that a person is healthy, it is still important to rebalance the Chakras from time to time to eliminate any negativity that has been unconsciously collected. Every encounter with another individual leaves an imbalance in the energy flows of the five bodies. Even an extremely wonderful event can disturb the equilibrium of the Etheric Body.

Once all Teragrams are in position, listen to your favorite meditation music or a guided meditation CD. I have one available for those interested in reaching deeply into their psyche. On this CD the first meditation is a color meditation to help you to become familiar with the use of the Teragrams and the major colors that dominate each Chakra. (As seen below). The second hypnosis meditation is to rebuild each Chakra, realign the five bodies, balance the left and right brain, then to lift your vibration and connect with your Spirit Guides to receive inspiration and help in healing yourself. With this meditation, you choose the Teragrams and place them on the Major Chakras according to you intuition of that day. It maybe entirely different the next time you use them.

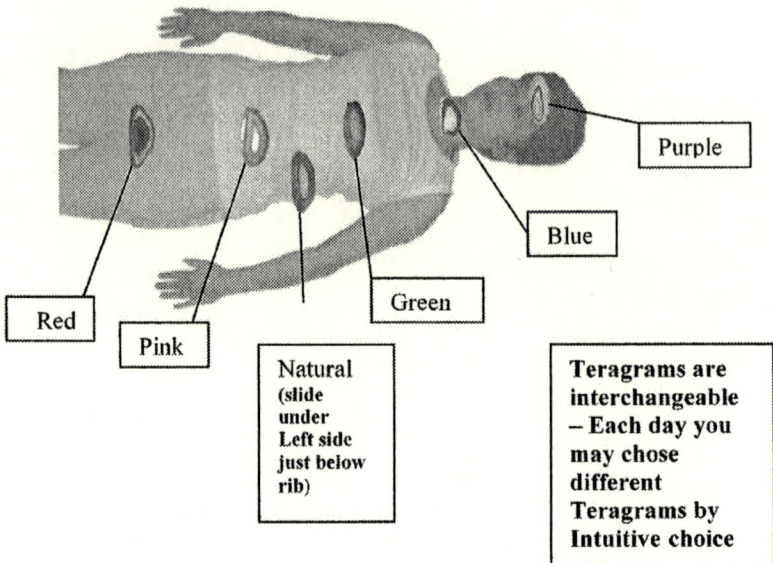

Purple

Blue

Green

Red

Pink

Natural (slide under Left side just below rib)

Teragrams are interchangeable – Each day you may chose different Teragrams by Intuitive choice

Teragram Treatment For The Rear of Major & Minor Chakras

The Minor Chakras are found in the center of the palms and sole of the foot. The Hand Chakras are used to transfer energy from self to another or to receive energy from another person who cares. The Foot Chakras are for grounding. Negative energy is passed into Mother Earth where it is revitalized and reprogrammed to be positive. Then this energy is drawn back up through the Foot Chakra and on into the other Major Chakras.

During middle age, the Minor Elbow and Knee Chakras at the joints become activated. In negative circumstances the knees become painful, and bending is difficult, while the arms swell and muscles ache preventing the raising of the arm. In both these cases the sufferer is being forced to surrender control and allow someone else to take the lead. In extreme cases, the emotional and mental mindsets are causing a disbelief in the desire to surrender. The conscious mind continues to hold onto unwanted mindsets that govern control issues.

Teragrams should be placed on the rear of the body. This will first induce a balance between the Higher and Lower Selves and then when this shift has occurred, the Teragrams should be placed on the hands and feet.

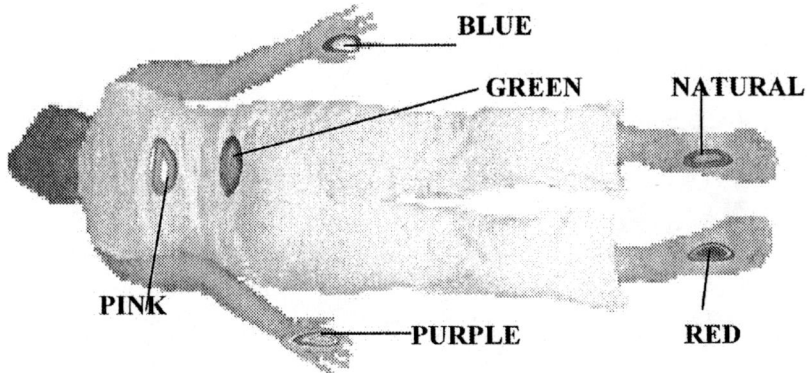

BLUE GREEN NATURAL PINK PURPLE RED

Note: The Teragrams can be placed on different Chakras as needs arise

Teragram Connection For The Crown & Base Chakras

Often individuals find their minds overloaded with information that is constantly being considered with a judgmental attitude. During this unfortunate state of confusion, the mind stimulates the Base Chakra to release conscious and unconscious fears, pains, angers and guilty memories from past history. These general releases of negative emotions cause an imbalance in the state of the Five Bodies. By using the Teragrams to create a vortex of energy between the Crown and Base Chakras, energy surges up through the spine and out to the other Major and Minor Chakras of the Body, resulting in a renewed awareness and a change of mind and heart.

This treatment can be carried out in the prone or sitting position. If the sitting position is chosen, simply place the red Teragram at the base of the spine and sit on it, while placing the natural Teragram in the palm of the right hand and rotate the hand in a clockwise direction on top of the center of the head. A general warming throughout the body will lead to strong heat sensations in the Solar Plexus and Heart Chakras. If you are a healer, then the client should face down and both Teragrams can be rotated clockwise at the same time.

Or, you can treat yourself in a prone position by rotating each one alternatively in clockwise directions. This will cause a powerful shift in the Five Bodies immediately.

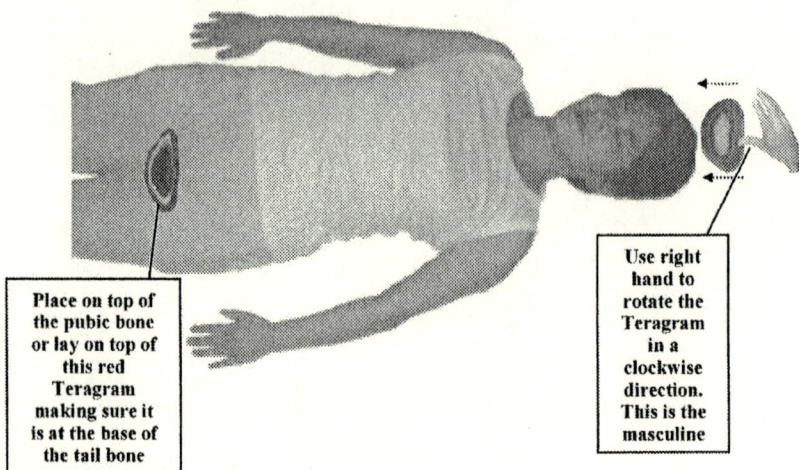

Place on top of the pubic bone or lay on top of this red Teragram making sure it is at the base of the tail bone

Use right hand to rotate the Teragram in a clockwise direction. This is the masculine

Teragram[sm] Therapy To Balance The Spleen Chakra

Earlier in this book, there are diagrams to show the positions of the Major Chakras and how they interact. The Spleen Chakra is the most over-looked, and therefore abused, Chakra of them all. So often it has been confused with the Lower Sacred Center which lies midway between the belly button and the pubic bone. This Spleen Chakra is constantly balancing all the energy waves made by the other Major Chakras. As each person interacts with another, or with their own memories, energy moves and the Spleen Chakra needs to rebalance all the energy flows of all Five Bodies. It is important to regularly correct and rejuvenate this Chakra with a once-a-week treatment. This simple technique explained below can save your life and prevent serious illness. For further information please read my book *Breakthrough Therapies*.

Left Rear View **Right Front View**

Spleen Chakra runs diagonally through the liver, pancreas and spleen as well as the kidneys, adrenals and transverse large intestine. To treat another, hold one Teragram in the palm of each hand and place over the chakras at rear and front

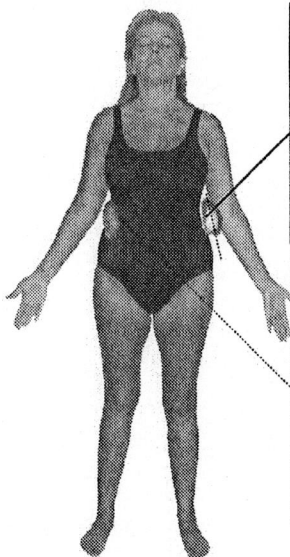

Blue Teragram to be held at rear of body and rotated in a clockwise direction while looking from the rear

Green Teragram to be held at front of body and rotated in a clockwise direction while looking from the front.

The Spleen chakra has two double helices that run diagonally through he abdomen. One Teragram should be placed in each palm and held at the spleen Chakra sight. Then the hands should rotate together back and forth in clockwise and anticlockwise directions to balance the two helices. The client should feel a glowing warmth in the Solar Plexus Chakra. Then the Spleen Chakra is balanced,. Simply instruct your client to visualize driving a car at 50 m.p.h. and lock in this perfect speed. Then close this chakra mentally.

Balance mind and emotions after treatments – calming nerves and mind

Teragram^{sm} Therapy To Balance The Spleen Chakra (Cont.)

If you are alone and treating yourself, then hold a Teragram in each hand up against the body and rotate in parallel rotations back and forth from clockwise to anti-clockwise, ending with clockwise rotations. A general sense of power and well-being will return, along with a glowing warmth that will spread from the abdomen to the far extremities of the head and toes.

Note: The Teragrams can be changed according to your state of mind, emotions and physical senses. When you use the Teragrams in pairs of your own choice, spiritual changes in your attitude will occur.

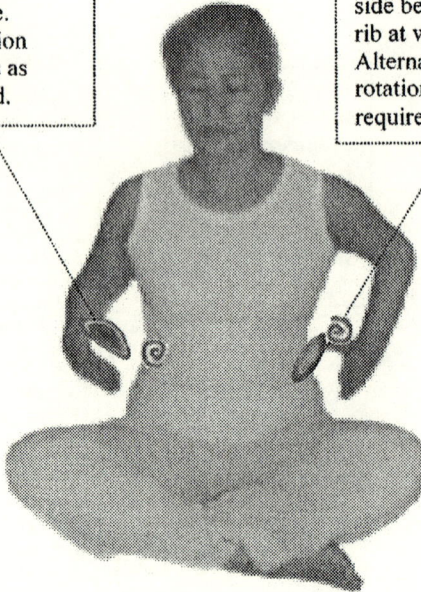

Use red for energizing lower-self. Apply clock-wise rotation at front right below rib at waistline. Alternation rotations as Required.

Green for rejuvenation of Spirit following trauma. Apply clockwise rotations to rear side below left rib at waistline. Alternate rotations as required.

Teragram^{sm} Therapy Treatment to Balance the Crown Chakra

The Crown Chakra is the most important Chakra of all. It has 144 neural pathways entwined with the cerebrum and cerebellum. These 144 neural pathways are cone shaped. Seven are elongated and extend to the Lower Sacred Center. The remaining neural pathways are small vortices of energy that allow our brain to exchange information and awaken our realizations along with our involuntary automatic neural system that defines our natural health. With the Crown Chakra is the Pituitary Gland. This Master Gland controls all the other glands of the body. It is also sensory to the Pineal Gland that lies close by and is connected to the Third Eye Chakra. The combination of these two Chakras awakens inner awareness and lifts negativity and depression.

Below is a diagram showing the use of a natural Teragram held in the palm of one hand, while the other hand rest across the lower hand. The Teragram is then held on the central part of the head. In a state of meditation, you should focus on energy coming from both hands, passing through the Teragram and on down to the Sacred Center. An inner knowing will emerge when the healing is complete.

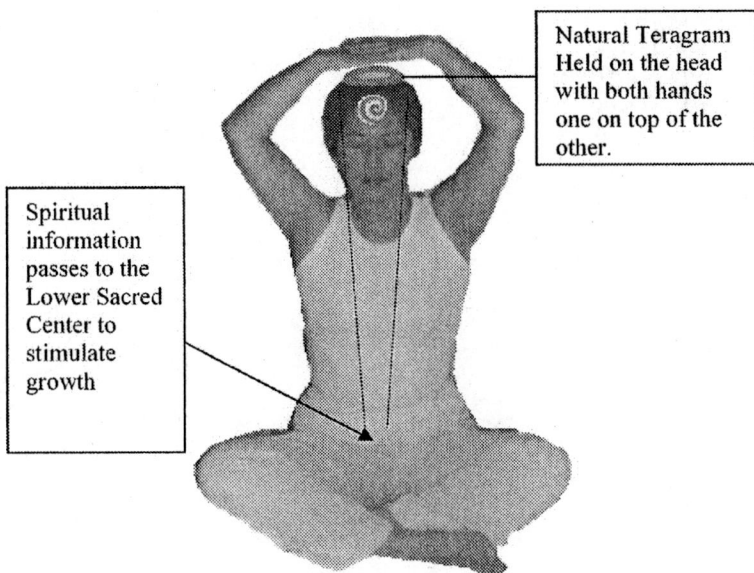

Natural Teragram
Held on the head
with both hands
one on top of the
other.

Spiritual
information
passes to the
Lower Sacred
Center to
stimulate
growth

Teragram℠ Therapy Treatment to Align the Crown Chakra with the Base Chakra and Lower Sacred Center.

Place a Teragram at the base of the spine and hold a Teragram on the Crown Chakra and then allow your energy to flow in an upwards direction until the Crown Chakra feels energized and then concentrate on sending that same energy down to the feet. When the feet become energized, the treatment is complete. At the same time the Lower Sacred Center will become energized. Feelings of warmth with tingling sensations may be felt.

Note: Your choice in Teragrams may change daily because your Aura is constantly shifting as all the Chakras realign themselves as a result of inner and outer influences. Trust your instincts when you choose your Teragrams. Each color has a different influence. For example: Blue at the Base Chakra will cause a shift in how you respond in your actions, while natural at the Crown Chakra, will shift your point of view. The result is a more responsible you.

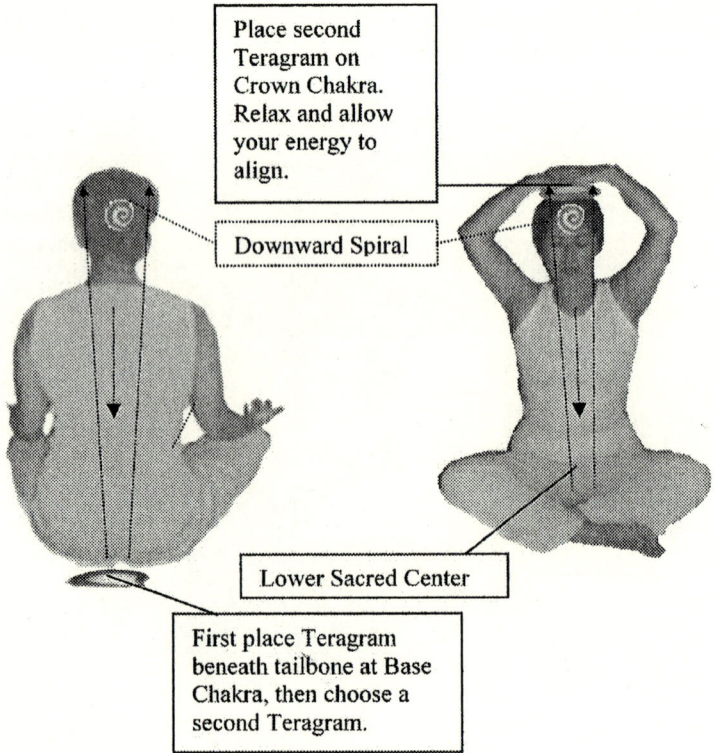

Place second Teragram on Crown Chakra. Relax and allow your energy to align.

Downward Spiral

Lower Sacred Center

First place Teragram beneath tailbone at Base Chakra, then choose a second Teragram.

Teragram^{sm} Therapy Treatment To Align The Crown Chakra With The Base Chakra And Higher Sacred Center.

Place a Teragram at the base of the spine and hold a Teragram on the Crown Chakra and then allow your energy to flow in a downward direction until the Base Chakra feels energized and then concentrate on sending that same energy up to the head. When the head becomes energized, the treatment is complete. At the same time the Higher Sacred Center will become energized. Feelings of heat/with electrical sensations may be felt.

Please note: Your focus on centering the energies from the Base Chakra will automatically stimulate the Higher Sacred Center and the Third Eye. During stimulation and with the natural rotations of the Chakras, the Throat Chakra will be affected and coughing and swallowing is not unusual during which time blocked energy is being cleared. In this case shown, a natural Teragram at the base of the spine will stimulate early memories and emotional blocks to rise. While a purple Teragram on the Crown Chakra will stimulate psychic awareness with inspirational answers. During this time the Higher Sacred Center will be activated allowing closeness to Spirit Guides.

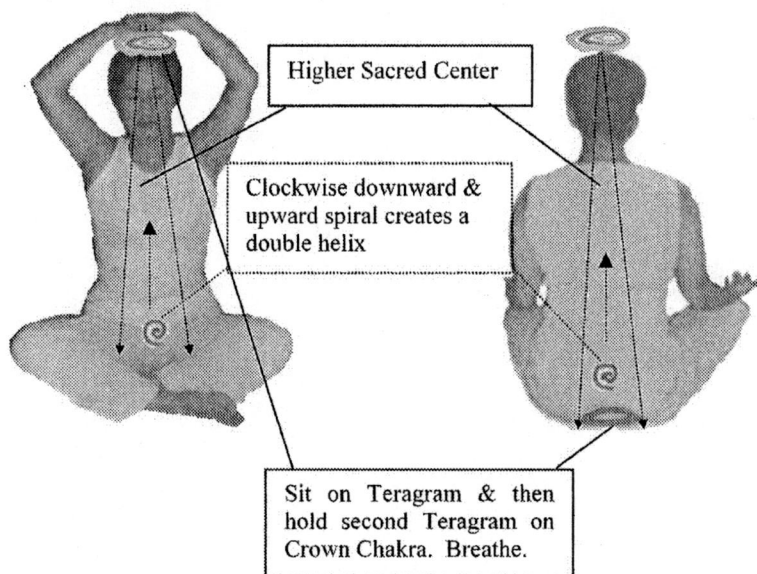

Higher Sacred Center

Clockwise downward & upward spiral creates a double helix

Sit on Teragram & then hold second Teragram on Crown Chakra. Breathe.

SPIRITUAL CRYSTAL ACUPUNCTURE^{SM}

Powerful Spiritual Crystal Acupuncture^{sm}

What you need to know!

In my book *Breakthrough Therapies- Crystal Acupuncture^{sm} & Teragram^{sm} Therapies* there is a great deal of information, but since I have to assume that you have not read that book, the following guidelines will help you to use your Spiritual Crystal Acupuncture^{sm} Kit or other similar stones. In each of my ready-made kits are four specially chosen points and five small equilateral triangles. The idea of this kit is to help those aspiring to become more psychic and actively more aware of their own spiritual journey. (If you have your own stone triangles, please make sure that they are suitable for spiritual work. Some stones are better for material and lower-self problems.)

Remembering that there are seven Major Chakras, which keep your Five Bodies in alignment, each of the triangles in my kit have been specially chosen to help you maintain that balance as well as to transform this balance into a more spiritual one.

To start, only one crystal should be chosen along with one triangle. Each Chakra should be treated (one at a time) with these two chosen crystals during which time you observe changes that occur. You are likely to face many of your fears that will arise while facing the unknown.

Many of my students try to run before they can walk with their triangles by using them all at once. They often have wonderful, but fearful occurrences that remain unexplained afterwards. It is far better to evolve with conscious awareness and guidance. So, take your time and enjoy. First choose a crystal that suits your current choice of growth. Below are the purposes and uses of each point:

THE POINTS
Tiger's Eye: (Black and yellow)
- **Stimulates higher consciousness to awaken the Physical Body's senses.**
- **Synthesizes the energies of Earth and Sun as our bodies absorb their energy.**
- **Clears away mental chaos and opens up the Third Eye Chakra.**

- **Naturally balances the energy flow of the Base (Root) Chakra stimulating physical activity**
- **Lifts the vibration of the Etheric Body by harmonizing Yin and Yang energy.**
- **Balances the left and right brain and stimulates awareness of changing perceptions**
- **Stimulates desire to be fulfilled and connected to The Oneness and Spirit Guides.**

Leopard Jasper: (Spotted brown and black)
- **This "The Supreme Nurturer," crystal provides protection by stimulating inner light from the Spirit Body.**
- **Aids your inner light to attract light beings from the Spirit World to assist you.**
- **Stimulates the Solar Plexus Chakra by aligning it with the other Chakras, causing the Physical, Emotional and Mental attitudes to agree.**
- **Creates a state of inner harmony.**
- **Cleanses and releases negativity from the cellular-neuro-muscular memory and stabilizes the Aura.**
- **Develops rejuvenation of the Physical Body.**

Rhodonite; (Pink with black marks)
- **This crystal brings true blessings by its own energy.**
- **Balances the Yin and Yang energies and makes it possible to connect to the Universal Consciousness.**
- **Awakens spirituality and brings in receptivity to unconditional love from God.**
- **Opens and stimulates the Heart Chakra to manifest one's greatest potential. Helps stimulate confidence and emotional contentment.**
- **Aids the growth of intuitive abilities to receive guidance through connections with Spirit Guides.**

Snowflake Obsidian: (Black and white)
- **This present from God helps us awaken to the unnecessary patterns that negatively hold us back throughout our lives.**
- **Stimulates to naturally desire a change for the better.**
- **Helps in producing a deep state of meditation.**

- Effectively lifts the vibration of the Five Bodies into a state of serenity.
- Stimulates a sense of isolation and observation of self, which then directly leads to a focus on one's sensitivity around earthly love.
- Inspires the user to connect with the acceptance of self-love and self-beauty in which a state of grace can then manifest.

THE TRIANGLES

Picture Jasper: (Brown with black lines)
- Awakens memories in picture form from the past.
- Stimulates the recall of old ideas for review.
- Creates a deep state of change by facing original injury causes.
- Inspires understanding and a release of grief, negative thoughts, phobias and fears.
- Induces creative visualization and the ability to tap into the unknown for insight and direction.
- Enhances appreciation of one's environment and motivates individuals to harmonize with others for a positive physical result.
- Business and family interactions are oriented towards success.

Red Jasper: (Red)
- Reveals mental and emotional obstacles that block the truth about your self.
- Increases perception and stimulates the desire to find a solution and a release of blocks.
- Provides an excellent tool for remembering dreams.
- Stimulates the Third Eye Chakra and the conscious mind to remember important aspects of dreams upon waking.
- Also helpful for returning into the dream state and repeat it for further insight.
- Allows old memories to rise into the conscious mind for reevaluation and, if necessary, elimination.

Hematite: (Silver-gray black)
- Calms the Conscious Mind and assists in awakening the Spirit Mind in meditation.
- Improves the right brain activity giving focus and connection to Spirit Guides.
- Balances the meridians of the Physical Body, and has a calming effect on the nervous system.
- Produces true harmony in the Physical, Etheric and Spirit Bodies creating a harmonic vibration lift that allows unconditional love to flow.
- Inner peace and happiness arise, giving a strong sense of self-trust.
- Balances the magnetic forces of the physical form.
- Provides protection from negative attack.

Unakite: (Pink and Green)
- Influences the Third Eye Chakra to open wide and focus on the ethereal planes of the Spirit World.
- Aids in balancing earthly emotions with spiritual one's which then creates a need to rebirth.
- Stimulates the rebirthing process that removes earthly conditioning and physical blockages.
- Awakens a new growth in awareness that ultimately results in a change of approach to life.
- Assists in the connection with Spirit entities in preparation for birth and rebirthing.
- Aids a new mother to talk to her child-to-be
- Aids a therapist in "Rescue Work" to release a lost soul from a client's Aura and direct it toward the Spirit World.

Calcite: (yellow)
- This natural amplifier aids in helping the mind to remember spiritual experiences such as astral traveling.
- An aid in harmonizing the conscious, sub-conscious and deep-subconscious parts of the mind to connect with Spirit Guides and to have total recall.
- Assists the Spirit Body's physical experiences in the Spirit World to be remembered as a Physical Body experience.
- Establishes a link for healing and a need to perfect one's way of life.

- **Polarizes and activates all the Chakras to cleanse and rebuild without negativity.**
- **Excellent crystal for stimulating the Crown Chakra and connecting to God and Spirit Guides.**
- **Is an effective generator and stimulant that can cause the physical growth of new cells throughout the body.**

Become familiar with your Crystals

Lay all the crystals out in front of you and investigate them thoroughly. Hold each one in turn and notice how it feels in your hand. At the same time, notice how it affects the rest of your body. Let your crystals become your friends.

When you become more familiar with your crystals and the effects they have on you, you will be able to work with several crystals at one time. Ultimately ideally you will be able to work crystal points with both the points and corners of the triangles before meditation. You may even wish to include your Teragrams as well.

Preparing for Meditation

The need for meditation comes from dissatisfaction that arises from an imbalance in the way you assimilate information. If you are fearful, angry, in pain, guilty or lonely etc. then you can confidently see a need for change. Change in itself is often the cause of panic, terror or phobia. Whatever your problem, Spiritual Crystal Acupuncture^{sm} will help you to make those changes that instill confidence. This unique therapy will help you empty your mind of problems, whether trivial or large. It is important to let go of history by selecting one of the Crystal Points and using them on the tip of the fingers and thumbs of each hand. (Imagine you have drawn a small circle of the top of each finder and find the center point.)

To select the right crystal, look at all four Crystal points and allow your instinct (Psychic Sense) to select the one that seems to pull you towards it. Do not question your choice. Trust you have chosen the right one. Now Place the crystal point approximately 1-3 millimeters away from the back of the nail in the center of your imaginary circle at the top of the thumb and/or fingers, depending on how deep you want to go.

Get the energy flowing

Energy flows around your Five Bodies. If you are emotionally, mentally or physically in a bind, then your energies are not flowing well. You may be blocked. When energy cannot flow through a meridian, it will flood over into another meridian causing a riptide reaction. Each meridian in the Physical Body feeds into invisible meridians in the other Four Bodies. Meridians are like conduits that hold energy and keep it on its correct course.

To correct your flow of energy, it is important to allow yourself to be in a reclined position, where arms and legs are uncrossed, and all tight clothing is removed. You can lie with your head supported with a pillow or in a comfortable sofa seat with your legs raised. Make sure you have your chosen crystals beside you.

Once you are comfortable, spend a moment in contemplation of your problem(s). Then in your own way, ask God for insight. Then attune to your Guardian Angels and Spirit Guides and ask them to help you with your meditation and healing. Take several deep breaths and relax. Now you are ready to begin.

With your chosen Crystal Point, treat the Acu Point at the top center of each thumb. Hold it there and allow yourself to sense your energy flowing from the hand that holds the crystal. Feel that energy passing through the crystal, on out and along the meridian. Watch your body for signs that energy is moving. If you feel nothing, impound the Acu Point by gently pushing the crystal into the point three or four times. Wait and watch your body again. You may do this several times until you feel something. Now rotate the Crystal Point on the Acu Point as through drawing a dot with a pencil. Rotate continually until you feel a sensation in your feet, especially your big toe on the same side as the thumb. You will notice yourself becoming more relaxed and in a hypnotic state. Then proceed to do each of your fingers on both hands.

When you reach this state, chose a triangle to place on the Chakra you have chosen to work on. Position it in an upward pointed direction and allow your energy to rise. Focus on the triangle and then let go and enjoy your journey. (Turning the point toward the ground will draw your energy downward – only do this if you are very erratic and over-excited.) .

If you have a very specific focus, make sure you choose the crystal point and triangle that will most likely help you with your focus to find inner answers. Simply place it on your Third Eye Chakra and then settle back to relax and meditate. You will be in meditation for as long as you need it. When you awaken, try to recall your experience. Sit up and write it down as soon as you can. Always remember to close your Chakras after meditation.

Over the following pages are some diagrams that will help you to focus on certain issues. However, there are many ways to explore with these crystals.

Major Chakras & Their Spiritual Connection

In the beginning of treatment when using Spiritual Crystal Acupuncture^{sm}, each Major Chakra needs to be dealt with separately. It is important to locate their positions and to feel the sensations of each one. For convenience each chakra is listed below together with their ascended vibration:

- **Crown:** **Center of top of head – Spiritual connection to God**
- **Third Eye:** **Center of forehead – Spiritual awareness**
- **Throat:** **Over the Larynx – Clear communication**
- **Heart:** **Center of the breast bone – True emotional expression**
- **Solar Plexus:** **Center of upper Abdomen (waistline) - Earthly awareness**
- **Spleen:** **Runs diagonally through Liver to Spleen -Total harmony**
- **Base (Root)** **Over the Genitals – Assimilation of experience**

Also, All Of The Five Bodies Have Energy In Ascension Listed Below;

- **The Physical:** **The human form in re-creative mode**
- **The Etheric:** **Erasing of Lower-self (mental & emotional) conditioning**
- **The Spirit:** **The Eternal true form expressed in embodiment**

- **The Higher Mind: Universal Consciousness manifested as inspiration**
- **The Soul:`   Universal unconditional all knowing and embracing Love**

Meditation

Once you are ready for meditation, I suggest you begin with focusing on your Heart Chakra. Place the triangle of your choice on your Heart Chakra (Point upwards) and close your eyes while taking several deep breaths and then mentally and emotionally surrender to your Spirit Guides and to God. In this state of mind you will allow healing to take place. It is important to stay aware and watch as waves of emotions or mental pictures leave you. This will allow you to release past history from the cellular-neuro-muscular memory.

What to expect while raising your past history

As energy moves along the meridians, the triangle is empowering the Chakra. The Chakra will dilate and rotate slightly faster causing neuro-muscular reactions, such as twitches and jerks.

For more information please read my book "Breakthrough Therapies". This powerful healing causes changes on many levels to the bio-chemical and metabolic rates.

The brain has stored every experience you have ever been through, along with your spiritual history. In Meditation, you can tap into many layers of information, including Past Lives and the Worlds between. So, allow yourself to watch the events that cross the screen of your mind and constantly say to yourself "I am releasing." Let your body do what it wants to do as it lets go.

You will instinctively know when it is time to end the meditation. During the course of the meditation, the other Major Chakras will have opened. They too are busy helping you to let go of history. Now is the time to close down.

Closing Down The Chakras

- **Take several deep breaths, allowing your whole self to become conscious of the room.**
- **Focus on your Third Eye Chakra and frown. Say "Close" and relax the brow.**

- Next, focus on the Throat Chakra. Swallow several times and then say "Close."
- Let yourself then focus on the Heart Chakra. Breathe in and then as you exhale say "Close." Do this several times if you feel a need.
- Next focus on the Solar Plexus Chakra. Pull the stomach muscles in. Feel the tension there and say "Close." Relax the stomach muscles.
- Now you are ready to close the Base (Root) Chakra. Contract all the muscles around the Genitals. Say "Close." Relax.
- Become aware of the Spleen Chakra and then focus on the Crown Chakra. Allow yourself to visualize god's golden healing energy flowing down throughout your body to the toes. Feel every cell in your body being replenished. Accept that you have been changed. Make an affirmation/promise to yourself to improve.
- Next visualize your Crown Chakra closing up, rather like a large open daisy closing up on your head that turns into a tulip. Say "close."
- Lastly, remember your Spleen Chakra. Say "Balance" and visualize yourself driving down the road at an even 50 miles an hour (This is a good speed for your body to function). Now say, "Close" and know that you will have enough energy to function correctly.
- Now make a fist and close the Hand Chakras and then wriggle your feet and close the Foot Chakras as you say, "Close."
- Mentally thank your Guardian Angels and Spirit guides.
- When ready sit up and contemplate your experience.

Working with the other Chakras

The above meditation can be done with each Major Chakra in turn. Do not try to do them all at once. This would cause too much of a radical change. You would find yourself in a state of stress as you release your past too quickly. It is far better to work on yourself a little bit at a time. Remember that it took your whole life to get into the state that you are now in. It will take several months, even years to undo all your wrong thinking and to reprogram yourself into a positive state and manner to develop the way you desire to be.

Allow several days for changes that you have made in the meditation to manifest. Keep a diary and make notes to yourself about your observations. Accept that it is you who have changed, not your family and friends, so do not expect them to understand what you are going through. However, given time they will notice that you are different and may well become different themselves as they adapt to you.

Useful Hints

If you wish to work on the Crown Chakra with a triangle, then it will be necessary to sit upright, or find a way to stick it to your hair so that it will stay in position when you lay down. I have used a piece of sticky tape, which has not affected the potency of the crystal. Another way might be to place a thin scarf or band around the head tied under the chin. If you do decide to sit up, then make sure your back is well supported. Once you move into a deep state of meditation, you will no longer be aware of your body. However, if the body is uncomfortable in the beginning, it will prevent you reaching this great state of meditation.

These Spiritual Crystal Acupuncture℠ Triangles can be used to help many people who are suffering. For more information concerning the stones and their powerful effects, please read my book ***Breakthrough Therapies***. Over the following pages you will find diagrams that will help you understand how to use these crystals.

It is possible to use Spiritual Crystal Acupuncture℠ to awaken someone from a coma, even if it has been many years. With the combination of regular Crystal Acupuncture℠ and Teragram℠ Therapy followed by a placement of all the triangles on all five Major Chakras (Root/Base - Third Eye) it is likely that a person will awaken three or four days later, once the Spirit has bonded with the Physical Body again. Two cases of this occurring, which have been reported to me by my students.

In the following pages, there are several diagrams showing you placement of the triangles. I have chosen not to show the Crystal Points, assuming you are now familiar with them. The triangles have been shown proportionately larger on the body. Each triangle is in reality 2mm in size. It is the stone and not the size that makes them powerful. These triangles are obtainable in a complete kit from me.

SPIRITUAL CRYSTAL ACUPUNCTURE^SM TREATMENT DIAGRAMS

Spiritual Triangles

Red Jasper is brick red with
some black spots

Hematite is metallic gray

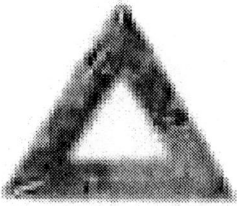

Unakite is mottled green & pink

Calcite is sand yellow

Picture Jasper is brownish pink
with black lines

Treatment With Triangles To Erase Depression & Ascend Vibration

Acute depression is usually caused by low self-esteem – not liking self, low self-worth – not appreciating what you can do and low self-value – not appreciating your time and effort. It is important to like and love who you are for all these factors. Many people spend a great deal of time trying to find their direction and purpose in life, but find themselves falling into an emotional dark pit instead. This is caused by erroneous beliefs that have been made and accepted during an emotional negative event. That person probably felt sorry for h/herself and worried over the results of such an event, which ultimately became a self-hypnotic suggestion that things can only get worse. To change your mind, and lift this depression, first select the Rhodonite Crystal Point and treat each finger and thumb tip as shown in the Crystal Acupuncture^{sm} Section of this book. Once this is done, you will feel relaxed. Then lie down and place the small equilateral triangles on your body as shown below. Relax for about 10 – 15 minutes. You will notice your depression lift and your mind become clear. Because these crystal triangles are specially chosen for their power, you will feel a connection to God and to your Spirit Guides/Guardian Angels.

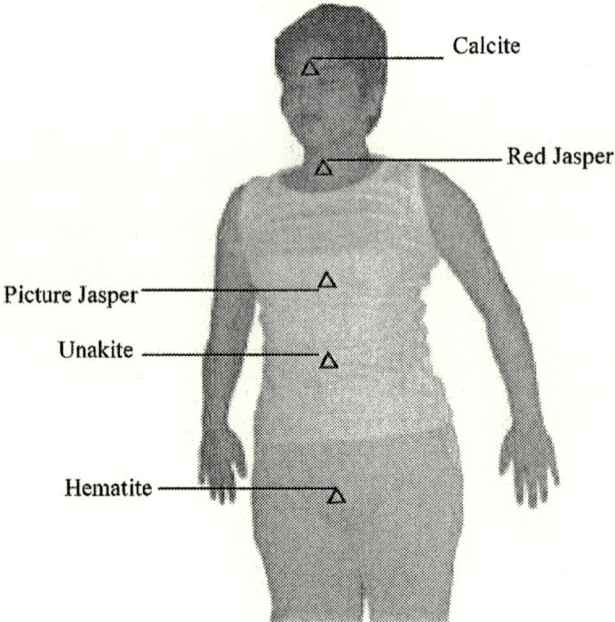

Calcite

Red Jasper

Picture Jasper

Unakite

Hematite

Treatment With Triangles To begin A Healing Meditation

Most individuals find it extremely difficult to switch off the ravings of the conscious mind. Even when one is tired, the mind is busy checking out the body, aligning the emotions and mental states with past history. So dreaming becomes a compound mixture of past, present and future hopes. Confusion often is the only conclusion at the end of a meditation.

Using a single Crystal Triangle on the Crown Chakra will help you switch off that constant noise of your own mind talking back at you. You can drift into a state of clear minded, unconditional acceptance of yourself. The moment you reach this state, your meditation can truly begin. You can focus on healing some part or all of your body, or find a true answer to some question that has been bothering you.

In meditation, you can contact your Spirit Guides/Guardian Angels and receive inspiration that will lead you to understand that they can inspire you to follow direction and manifest your heart's desire. Each crystal triangle, though small, is powerful. You can choose any one of them to place on the center of your head. I suggest you use a piece of sticky tape to make sure it stays on your head. Or, you can wrap it in a scarf and tie the scarf around your head and then lie down and begin your meditation. But remember to choose and use one of your Crystal Acupuncture Points to open up the meridians first. I suggest Picture Jasper to start. You can try the others later.

You can also place one Spiritual Crystal Acupuncture^{sm} triangle on any other of the Chakras when you meditate at different times. As you work on each Chakra, relax and allow yourself to flow into a deeper meditation. **Never try to meditate with all five triangles on the Chakras at once. You could go too deep and face too many fears too quickly. This is for the Shaman to do! So practice with a gradual increase in using one, two, three etc. making sure you feel comfortable.**

Select a Triangle of your choice and place it on top of the center of your head while sitting supported (To lie down, use tape to secure it.)	Δ 	TO WORK ON EACH CHAKRA Select a Triangle of your choice, lie down and place it on the relevant Chakra of your focus.

It may take many years to master the use of all these Spiritual Triangles!

Dr. Margaret Rogers Van Coops

Treatment With Triangles To Harmonize Lower & Higher Selves

Equilateral triangles are very powerful shapes. The inside and outside of each crystal used in this healing are actually forming two triangles. In Sacred Geometry the triangle is the most important shape. It is the basis upon which our form is made. The energy in all our Five Bodies is stimulated and balanced by the power of these triangular crystals.

Your Lower Self is the everyday you that focuses on the issues of everyday living. Your Higher Self is your Spiritual self that focuses on your journey of Ascension into The Oneness and your relationship with God. This part of your consciousness is only concerned with truth. By harmonizing these two aspects of yourself, you can become confident and active in ways you never dreamed of.

> **By stimulating, toning & balancing your meridians with a Tigers Eye point first, you will move into a very calm state in preparation for harmonizing these two aspects of self**

I have shown these triangles on the body in the Buddha position as a symbol of spiritual Ascension.

When you do this meditation, be sure to lie down before placing the Triangles. This will take about 15 minutes to complete. When you are finished you will have a feeling of completion.

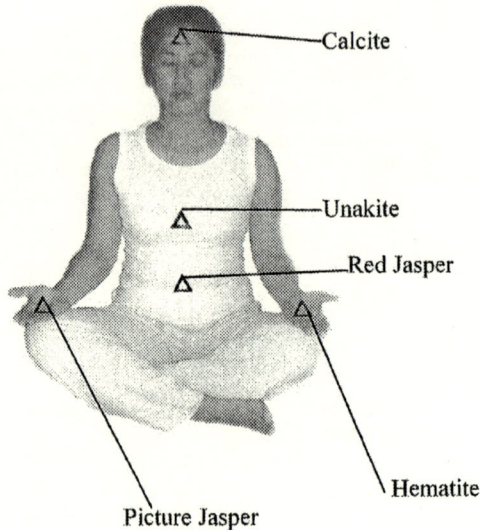

Calcite

Unakite

Red Jasper

Hematite

Picture Jasper

198

Treatment With Triangles To Develop Creativity

So often I hear people tell me that they have no creativity within them. They will swear up and down that they are useless when it comes to expressing themselves in form. Of course, I tell them the truth. Everyone has creative skills, you just need someone to inspire and teach you how. While this kind of spiritual growth will inspire your own Spirit to express yourself, you will still need to attend a few classes to help you take those baby steps. Once you understand how easy it is to be inspired, your passion and desire will well up in such a way as to excite and stimulate you into action.

Your choice can be writing, music, art, etc. Only you know deep inside you what you like best. Like all things it takes time to search. Try a little bit of this and that and then when you really like something, try it again and again until you become a master that satisfies you. Use your Spiritual Crystal Acupuncture^{sm} stones and triangles to connect you to your Spirit Guides/Guardian Angels who will become your teachers and help you improve your skills.

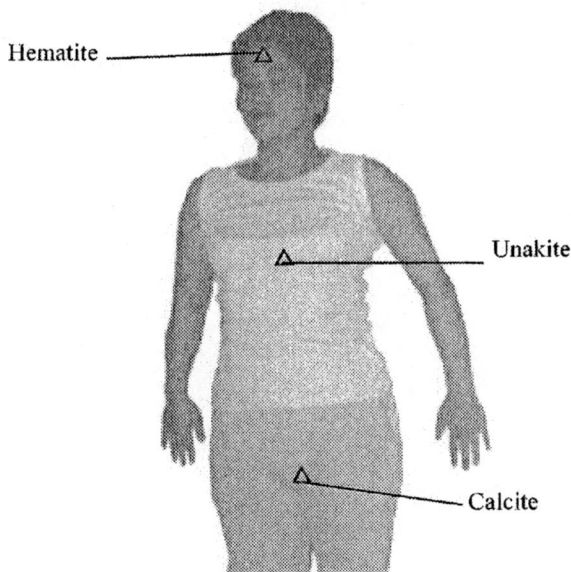

Hematite

Unakite

Calcite

Use Snowflake Obsidian to tone/Balance the
Meridians on all the tips of the fingers first

Treatment With Triangles To Balance The Spleen Chakra

The Spleen Chakra is the most important Chakra of all. Its job is to constantly monitor, and rebalance the energy movements of the other Major and Minor Chakras as well as to harmonize the Five Bodies. Any imbalance in the energy in any Body or Chakra will affect the health of an individual. Lying within this Spleen Chakra are the kidneys, spleen, pancreas and liver, parts of the colon, as well as the adrenal glands. If this Chakra is out of balance then an individual is steeped in fear and will have many adrenaline rushes resulting in panic attacks and hyperglycemia. The Solar Plexus Chakra will also be weak which results in an inability to protect self from negativity coming at him/her.

Everyone should balance this Chakra at the end of a day. By using the Spiritual Crystal Acupuncture^{sm} triangles, energy in this Chakra is not only balanced but also recharged. You can do this treatment without having to open and rebalance your meridians first. However, should you be very negative, then it would be best to use Leopard Jasper on the fingertips to rebalance the meridians.

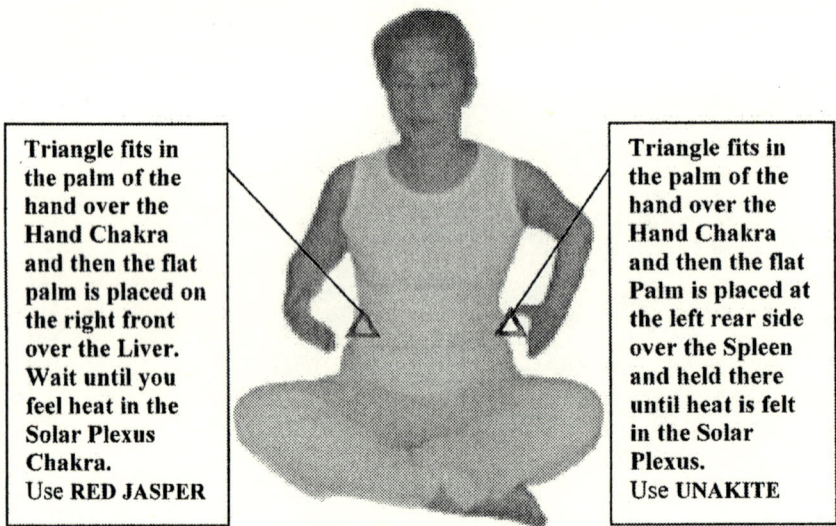

Triangle fits in the palm of the hand over the Hand Chakra and then the flat palm is placed on the right front over the Liver. Wait until you feel heat in the Solar Plexus Chakra. Use RED JASPER

Triangle fits in the palm of the hand over the Hand Chakra and then the flat Palm is placed at the left rear side over the Spleen and held there until heat is felt in the Solar Plexus. Use UNAKITE

Mentally think of energy flowing back and forth between the two Triangles. Continue until the Solar plexus is energized.

200

Treatment To Erase Hysteria Or Catatonic States

There are times when Hysteria seems to be overpowering both for the client and the practitioner. In the 'olden days' the answer was to give a highly potent tranquilizer. The beauty of the power of the equilateral triangle is that it has the power to create such a change in a person's energy that it will effectively calm a person down within seconds. Another aspect of a stone triangle's power is that it stimulates such a change generally throughout the Five Bodies, that it causes any blocks that could prevent healing from occurring to be broken open wide, which is rather like breaking a dam and letting the water free. Energy flows everywhere in an unrestricted way that allows the spirit of an individual to return to the body and aid self in recovery. When all the equilateral triangles are placed point down, this causes a flush of energy to earth. A person in a coma will take about three days to awaken fully into the Alpha state and then later into the Beta state. Though I have never had this opportunity to work with someone unconscious, a few of my students have and with great success.

These triangles are extremely powerful in this order when laid upon the Chakras. It does not take long for them to create an astounding effect. Do not leave them on the body for longer then ten minutes. When this is done replace them with Teragrams that will balance the Chakras

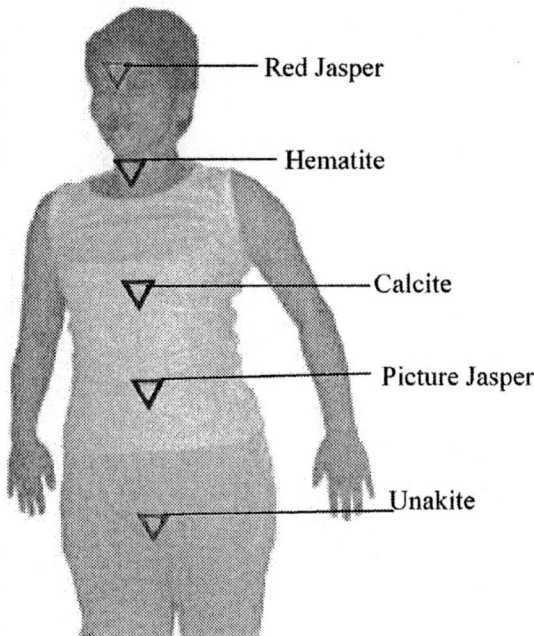

Red Jasper

Hematite

Calcite

Picture Jasper

Unakite

201

Treatment With Triangles To Activate Third Eye Images

If you are interested in developing your clairvoyant sense, then this quick meditation with the triangles will help you to overcome your Lower Self fears and accept your Higher Self consciousness that will allow you to perceive images. All the images you will see will be taken from your entire life's experience. If you have not seen it, then you will not see anything you do not understand. Your own Spirit and your Spirit Guides can only work with what you have experienced in this life. It is up to you to understand the meaning of the images you see. For example, if you see a child's diaper, then you know it has something to do with your childhood. It may be that there are memories within your consciousness that have caused you to carry unfounded fears, pains, angers and guilty beliefs. By spending time with your triangles, you may well uncover your initial beliefs and then redirect them towards a positive attitude. The types of stones and the order you use the triangles can be changed according to your intuitive sense at the time of meditation and relaxation. So give yourself several times to meditate with the different triangles in different places on the Chakras.

It is important to only work with the Heart, Throat and Third Eye Chakras during this meditation. Begin first by stimulating the fingertips and thumbs with Rhodonite and then Release energy from the day by rotating the Acu Point. Then lie down, place the triangles and relax. Say your prayer of protection and surrender to your Spirit Guides/Guardian Angels.

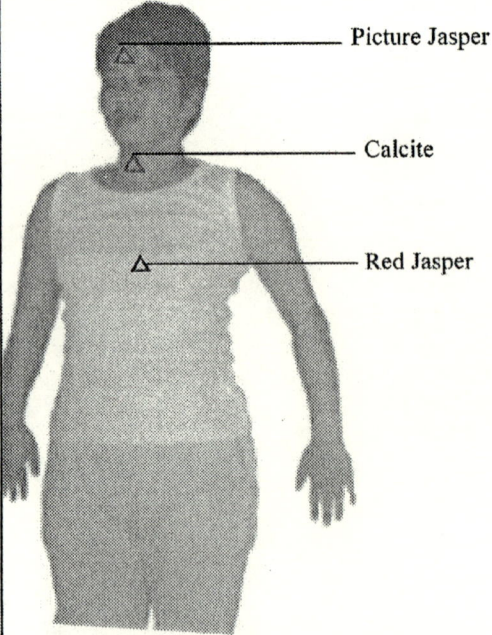

Picture Jasper

Calcite

Red Jasper

Lie in this position for as long as you need and when you have finished, close all your Chakras down and awaken to feel refreshed. Write your experience down.

Treatment With Triangles To Open Up Your Heart & Release Negative Emotions

Negative emotions are accumulated throughout our lives. We often allow these bad emotions to lie hidden, keeping them suppressed in order to protect ourselves. We tell ourselves that they don't matter and if we try harder they will simply be forgotten. Of course, this is not true. Those negative emotions fester and affect everything we do. Our beliefs are borne out of those old stale memories of pain, fear, anger and guilt. Every time we try to fool ourselves that all is well, up comes an emotion to remind us that we still harbor bad feelings. Using the Spiritual Crystal Acupuncture points and equilateral triangles as shown below will help you to let go of unwanted memories that color your choices and hold you back from changes that normally, should be made with ease. First use Tigers Eye on your Acu Points on the tip of each finger and thumb. Balance the meridians and then release negativity from your current day. Then lie down and place the triangles (point up) on your Chakras and let yourself surrender and release.

You may have a great deal of negative emotions to release. It is quite in order to cry and tremble, while your body twitches and releases. When you have finished this release, reprogram yourself with positive emotions. Remember that you are loved by God, family and friends.

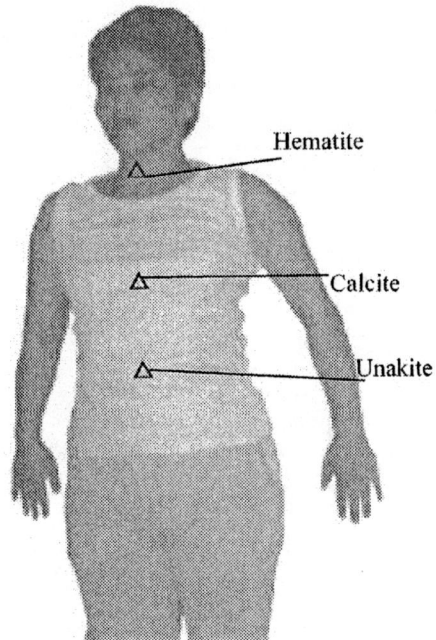

Hematite

Calcite

Unakite

Some emotional releases may be very traumatic. Please make sure you see a counselor to help you make mental and emotional positive changes and to establish some new boundaries for yourself and to set new standards to live

Treatment With Triangles to Awaken Sexuality

Often we grow up with many false ideas about our bodies, our skills and our abilities to express our emotions in general. So, when it comes to sexual expression, this part of ourselves is often skipped over, ignored and washed into areas of sin. Those who do have an active and apparently positive attitude about themselves and sex are often covering up many aspects of low self-esteem. Sex becomes a way to hide from self or to try and earn attention or gain love. Though this is not the place to write much about the many problems in our attitude about sex, it is appropriate to show this diagram to help those who believe they are ready to face some of these early childhood fears, beliefs, hopes etc. around their ideas of sex and love. Before entering into your releases, make sure you are ready to relax and let go with an empty mind. Thinking about issues is not necessary with this type of healing. Simply Rotate each Acu Point on the top of each finger and thumb with Leopard Jasper. Then lie down and place the triangles as shown in the diagram. The triangles are placed in alternating positions to create a disturbance in the force – the way you allow your energy to flow. You will feel great shifts of energy or fall asleep. Either is appropriate. Let your body twitch, itch etc., and if necessary cry until you feel better. Once you feel that the shift has occurred, remove the triangles and replace them with the Teragrams in any color order on all The Chakras and breath and relax. When you sense that you feel really good, sit up and affirm to yourself how much better you are. Close your Chakras and get on with your life.

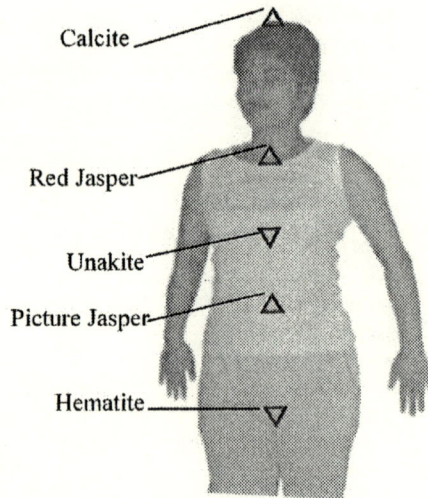

Triangles in this position will cause the Chakras to swirl their vortices within them to flow energy from front to back and back to front while stimulating the Five Bodies to adjust their speed and then balance and harmonize.

Calcite

Red Jasper

Unakite

Picture Jasper

Hematite

Sexual activity after this kind of release and relaxation will be more acutely sensory and less embarrassing as enjoyment takes over

Treatment With Triangles To Protect From Psychic Attack

Because the area of Psychic Development is often shunned by many, few realize that they are under attack. Strong religious beliefs prevent them from searching their own energy and mindsets to find out why they think negatively. They assume it is because of the people and circumstances around them; that all the things they say and do appear to be wrong. Often this is not the case. There are many Spiritual Entities that are 'lost in the twilight zone' drifting between this world and the next. Whenever they find a sensitive person, they attach themselves to that person and through various negative states of mind, begin to harmonize and then to control that person's emotions. Soon that individual is lost in negativity. Fear, pain, anger and guilt emerge. They blame everyone for their state of mind, emotions and health. During this time they generate energy that is food for the Spirit Entity to gain more strength and a stronger hold. That Entity is simply trying to survive by using up its host's energy. Of course, this poor Spirit needs to be sent into the light and on into the Spirit Realm where they will receive help. By doing this treatment below, you will be able to free yourself of any unwanted presence that has been 'bugging' you. As you use the triangles, your energy and vibration will shift and transform you, leaving the Entity out on a limb. You can then meditate and ask your Spirit Guides/Guardian Angels to help the lost Entity to go into the Spirit Realm that is equal to their vibration.

First select one of the four Acu Point crystals: read what they do and decide which one feels right to use on this day. (There may be more than one Entity and each may need a different stone). Rotate the crystal/s on the finger and thumb tips and then lie down and place the triangles as shown below. Take deep breaths and relax and watch as your energies transform. It is important to feel safe and protected. So say your own form of prayers and acknowledge God within yourself. Meditate for 10 mins.

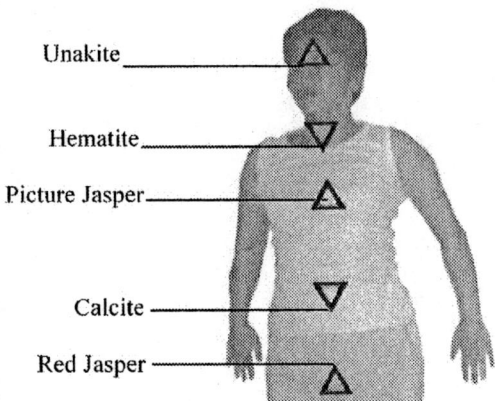

If you feel out of sorts, have strange sensations in your body, think unusual negative ideas, develop sudden passions -- drugs/alcohol, can't sleep because of bad dreams or nervous attacks, feel miserable for no reason or seem to hate everything, then you are being haunted by a negative Entity.

Unakite

Hematite

Picture Jasper

Calcite

Red Jasper

Remember to close Chakras after you release.

Using Triangles To Raise The Kundalini
(Not to be attempted without supervision)

So often my students ask for advice on how to raise the Kundalini and my immediate response is to tell them not to do it. The reason I have included this in this book is to make sure that those students who do insist on doing this meditation will at least do it in the right way with the help of their teacher. Raising the Kundalini is not easy. In fact it is highly unlikely that it will occur. However, it is important to know that when it does occur it must be done in a state of grace and calm. Do not attempt this if you are in any state of fear on any level. Fear generates heat and heat when raised can cause internal combustion and in extreme cases can cause your body to burn from the inside out. Raising the Kundalini must be done with generated cool/cold energy. As the Kundalini begins to arise, all Five Bodies move through their own orgasmic shift which cause a wonderful feeling of elation and surrender. The ultimate energetic orgasm is a beautiful sensation of freedom and connectedness to The Oneness and God while watching a variety of geometrical shapes pouring out of the Crown Chakra. Only a Master Teacher can obtain this state of ecstasy.

When the ultimate and final orgasm is complete, it is vitally important to bring your raised energy back down to the Base Chakra. Meditate on returning energy to the ground and then harmonizing the Five Bodies into your Lower Self. If you do not do this, you will find it difficult to function and to sleep. Again I stress the importance of practicing with a teacher.

Orgasms:
PHYSICAL BODY –
Sexual sensations
ETHERIC BODY –
Pins and needles
feelings
SPIRIT BODY –
Warm shivers fading
to cold
HIGHER MIND
BODY –
Waves of energy
flowing and a
drifting upward
sensation
SOUL BODY –
Energy explosion
with mixed feelings
of euphoria and
delight

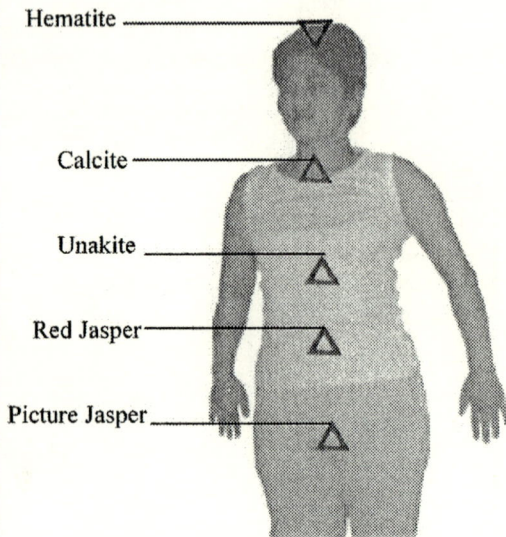

Hematite

Calcite

Unakite

Red Jasper

Picture Jasper

Treatment With Triangles to Develop Vocal Expression

Whether you speak in a low or high voice, your memories from childhood have copied those adults who influenced you the most. The resonations that your voice gives can be powerful and influence others. If you are feeling insecure and unsure of yourself, then your voice can often appear ineffective whether it has been heard or not. Vocal expression also includes singing. Since we usually speak with expression our speech patterns cause our voice tones to rise and fall. Singing is simply taking the next step to talking with expression and resonance. Many people will say without hesitation that they are unable to carry a tune. This is an erroneous belief. Everyone can sing. Like everything else in life, it has to be learned. If you feel that you wish to put more power into your voice or to improve your singing skills, then this meditation with the triangles will help you evolve your voice into a more confident and powerful resonance. Begin by using Snowflake Obsidian to open up all the meridians on the tips of thumbs and fingers. Then impulse – Place point of crystal on the center of the first crease in the fingers and thumbs to stimulate the Throat Chakra. Then lie down and place the triangles as shown below. Focus on your throat and your voice. Talk and sing and then relax and allow your mind to adapt in thought. Then allow energy to flow through the Chakras. In the days to come you will find an improvement in the sounds you make.

In a relaxed state you can speak aloud and listen to the sounds you make. You can say the same thing in different tones. Look for the resonation that feels easy and natural. Then sing your childhood songs and listen to how you sound. Allow your adult voice to emerge as you sing. You will be amazed how different you can sound.

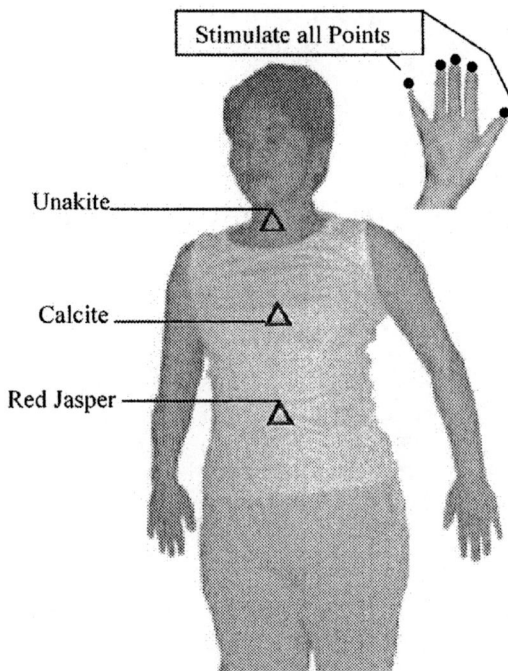

Stimulate all Points

Unakite

Calcite

Red Jasper

Use Triangles To Align The Five Bodies

All the triangles in the Spiritual Crystal Acupuncture kit are very powerful. It is amazing just how much they cause a transformation in the way energy flows throughout the Five Bodies. If you are unable to spend time in meditation, then you can choose two of the triangles and set them on the floor about a foot apart from one another. Have the apex of the triangle furthest away from your feet. Then step onto the triangles, placing the center of the arch of your feet right over the triangles. Then stand with your hands at your side, close your eyes and feel your energies moving and shifting as the Five Bodies harmonize. You can also do this with two triangles placed in the palm of the hands (wrists and lower arms extended in front of you comfortably) with the apex pointing away from the body. If you choose to use four triangles at once, you will cause a major shift and in the days to come you will feel and understand many things about yourself that went unnoticed before. You can also expect to have emotional releases. So, warn your family because they are sure to do some button pushing by just being their usual selves.

On different days you may feel drawn to different triangles. There is no need to do any Crystal Acupuncture^{sm} when using the triangles this way.

When you have completed balancing the Five Bodies remember to close all your Chakras down. Make muscular movements with each part of your body to remind you that you are closing them. Note: It is advisable to always close down when with negative people.

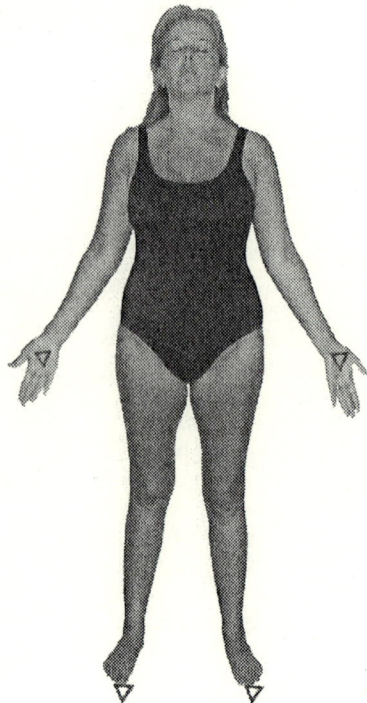

HEALING ANIMALS

HEALING ANIMALS FROM THE HEART

There will always be times when your pet needs a healing hand. Since they cannot speak to us and tell us how badly they feel, where the pain is, or what they need, it is often up to us humans to pay special attention to their habits and general behavior. We have to listen to our hearts and sense what they need.

Some animals find change stressful and hide, while others become over-excited. Yes, there is such a thing as an ADD dog, or an Obsessive Compulsive cat. Just like humans they have their habits and their ways that can be most loving and most annoying.

When you attune to your miserable pet, you will feel an energy change in them. They will make you feel uneasy and full of discomfort. If you are empathetic, you may well feel their moods, pains and mental anguish. For example, a new food dish for dinner may be a disruptive thing for your fussy cat. Smells and familiar old things mean comfort and less stress.

If the animal has something seriously wrong, it is always a good idea to take it to the vet, but you can also help it make a rapid recovery by giving the animal a Crystal Acupuncture[sm] and Teragram[sm] Therapy treatment.

Every animal has a different nature, just like humans. Their healing care will vary. If the creature is very small, then a very tiny impulse will be sufficient, with a simple rotation or two to balance the energy flow. Or, perhaps just a release will be all that is needed. The more muscle there is in an animal, the more healing will be needed. Large animals, such as horses, dogs and farm animals can need a great deal of impulses and rotations to move blocked energy. Whatever the animals illness, it should be remembered that they store imbalances in the Five Bodies too.

Pay attention to the Spleen Chakra after every treatment. Be sure to balance the animal's Five Bodies by rotating the Chakras in a clockwise direction with a Teragram or two. Your instincts will tell you which colors are pertinent at the time of healing. In extreme cases where the animal is really sick, anticlockwise rotations are in order when beginning, then follow-up with clockwise rotations. This will allow the core of each Chakra to rebalance all the vortices within it.

Even reptiles respond well to Crystal Acupuncture[sm] and Teragram[sm] Therapy. Though they are cold blooded, their energy flows are very similar. Simply give them your time and attention. Within moments you will begin to feel them respond.

Every animal will use its own psychic senses to protect itself from harm. When you heal your animal, they may fret and fuss as they feel unusual energy flows within their body. If this is the case, wait until they are sleeping and then do the healing. Usually, they will incorporate the changes without waking up. Of course, if the animal is really sick, then there will be no resistance to your healing them with a crystal.

Where an animal has a paw, it is good to do Crystal Acupuncture℠ to the pads and between the pads. Just like humans, this is where the main Acu Points are for the meridians. By exploring your own hand and applying pressure with the crystal, you can use the same amount of pressure to the paw when doing this type of healing. This is always a good way to help your animal. If you are dealing with a very large animal, it is of course advisory to have supervision. – have someone who can hold the animal still.

Animals that have hoofs have sensitive points within the center of the hoof. This is an excellent point to gain a strong energy pulse into the animal. Otherwise, points around the top of the hoof are also excellent Acu Points that connect with the Main Meridians that supply energy to all parts of the body.

Even Birds, bats and other clawed animals, whether webbed footed or not, are also receptive to Crystal Acupuncture℠. Simply place the point of the crystal underneath the claw/nail and impulse gently once or twice and then rotate and hold, allowing a release to follow. Often birds have wing problems. Using a crystal point and stimulating, toning and balancing the energy in the wing, you can expect a fast recovery.

Animals have no judgment. They do not consider what is being done to them, and so just like babies, they are open and very receptive to any type of healing. You can expect a quick response immediately, since any block in energy will be dispersed without any strings attached. Humans rationalize, explain, excuse and justify their illness. Animals have no idea why they are ill; they simply know they want to get better. There is no secondary gain to be had either. They are not manipulative like humans can be.

In the pages that follow are some diagrams that will help you to heal your animal. Always remember to use the Teragrams whenever possible to keep the healing going in between Crystal Acupuncture^{sm} treatments. You can even tape a Teragram to your animal or bind it inside a dressing. It will continue to stimulate, tone and balance the Acu points beneath it. If you have a desire to use different crystals, it is quite in order to do so. Many animals respond to many different kinds of earth stones. I have used the same ones that you have now become familiar with over the next few pages. However, if you have some other crystal stones, feel free to use them. Your pet will be receptive no matter what the stone.

HEALING ANIMALS
TREATMENT DIAGRAMS

Crystal Acupuncture[sm] & Teragram[sm] Therapy For Cats

(1) Carnelian (2) Hematite (3) Sodalite (4) Aventurine

BALANCE MAIN MERIDIANS

Do Acu Points on all four feet just below each claw.
Stimulate (1)
Tone/Balance (3)
Release Point (4)

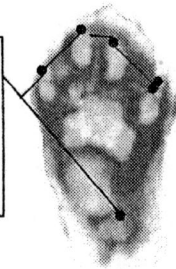

DIGESTIVE & NERVOUS SYSTEM

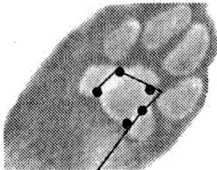

Neural Spine
Release
Points (2)

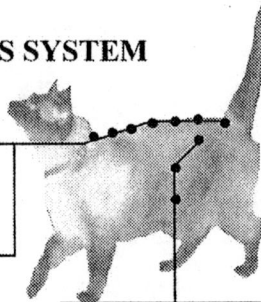

General Digestive treatment
Stimulate (1)
Tone/Balance (3)
Release Point (4)

Kidney, Spleen, Intestine
Tone/Balance (2)

Balance all Chakras Rotate until hands get hot
Release Point (4)

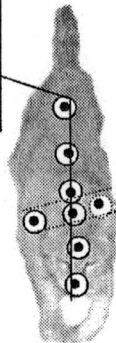

BONES

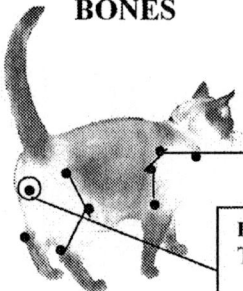

Do both sides
Stimulate (1)
Tone/Balance (2)
Release Point (3)

BASE CHAKRA
Tone/Balance (4)

Crystal Acupuncture^{sm} & Teragram^{sm} Therapy For Cats (Cont.)

CALMING TEMPER/NATURE

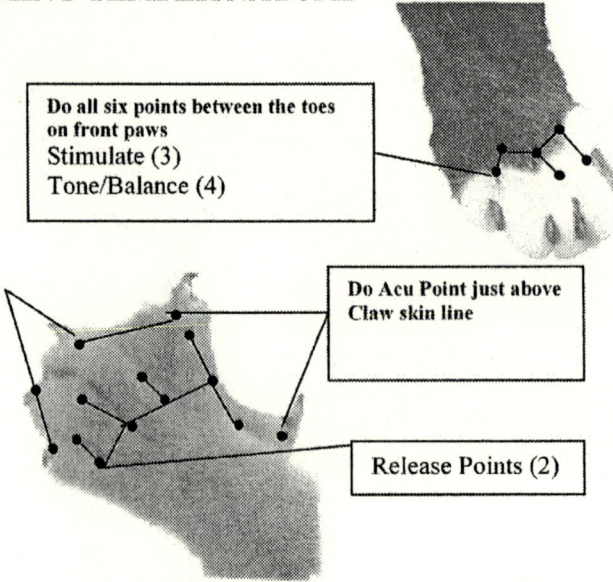

Do all six points between the toes on front paws
Stimulate (3)
Tone/Balance (4)

Do Acu Point just above Claw skin line

Release Points (2)

Teragram^{sm} Therapy to harmonize the Five Bodies

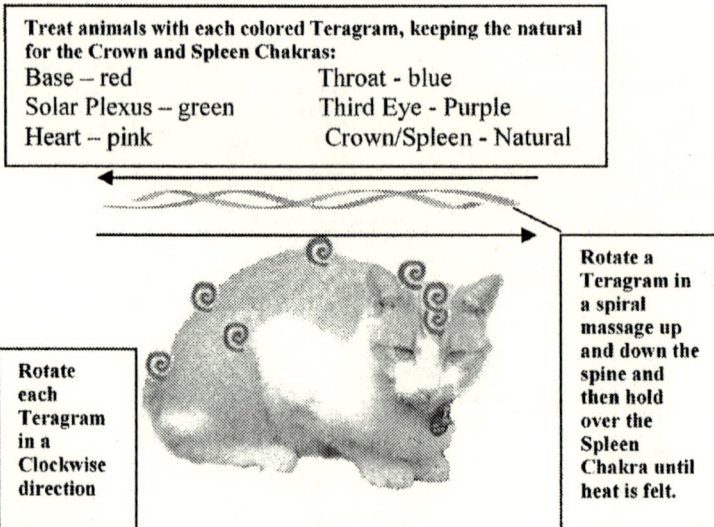

Treat animals with each colored Teragram, keeping the natural for the Crown and Spleen Chakras:

Base – red　　　　　　Throat - blue
Solar Plexus – green　　Third Eye - Purple
Heart – pink　　　　　Crown/Spleen - Natural

Rotate a Teragram in a spiral massage up and down the spine and then hold over the Spleen Chakra until heat is felt.

Rotate each Teragram in a Clockwise direction

218

Crystal Acupuncture^{sm} & Teragram^{sm} Therapy
Treatment For Dogs

(1) Quartz (2) Amethyst (3) Sodalite (4) Amazonite

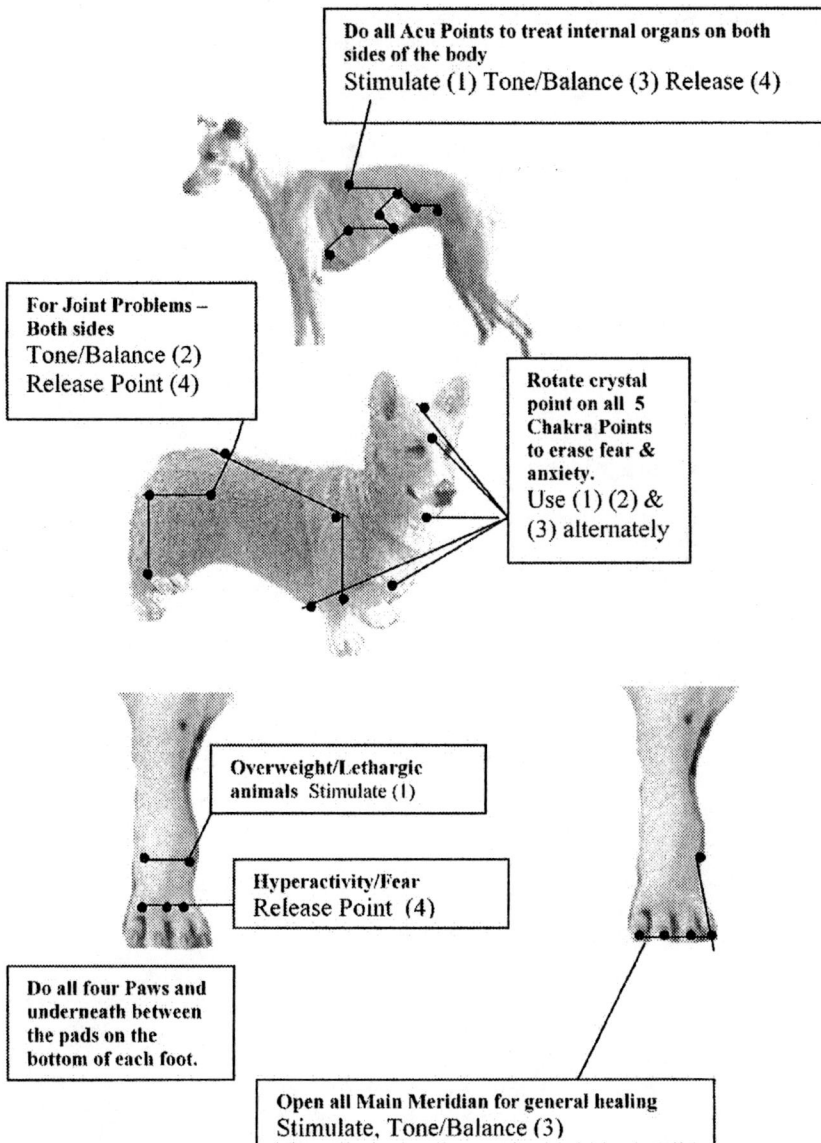

Do all Acu Points to treat internal organs on both sides of the body
Stimulate (1) Tone/Balance (3) Release (4)

For Joint Problems –
Both sides
Tone/Balance (2)
Release Point (4)

Rotate crystal point on all 5 Chakra Points to erase fear & anxiety.
Use (1) (2) &
(3) alternately

Overweight/Lethargic animals Stimulate (1)

Hyperactivity/Fear
Release Point (4)

Do all four Paws and underneath between the pads on the bottom of each foot.

Open all Main Meridian for general healing
Stimulate, Tone/Balance (3)

Crystal Acupuncture^{sm} & Teragram^{sm} Therapy Treatment For Dogs (Cont.)

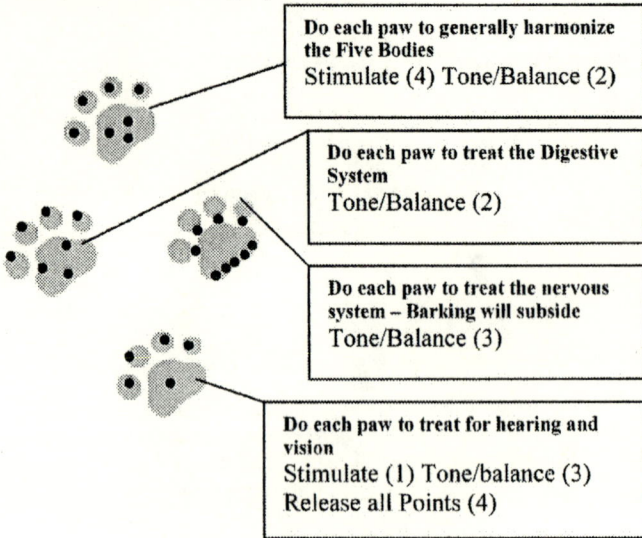

Do each paw to generally harmonize the Five Bodies
Stimulate (4) Tone/Balance (2)

Do each paw to treat the Digestive System
Tone/Balance (2)

Do each paw to treat the nervous system – Barking will subside
Tone/Balance (3)

Do each paw to treat for hearing and vision
Stimulate (1) Tone/balance (3)
Release all Points (4)

These points have the same affect with any animal that has a paw. Be intuitive and use the crystals that seem to tell you to use them if you do not have any of these crystals

Teragram Therapy Chakra Balance

Rotate in an anti-clockwise direction from head to tail and then in a clockwise direction from tail to head to remove fear and rebuild Chakras

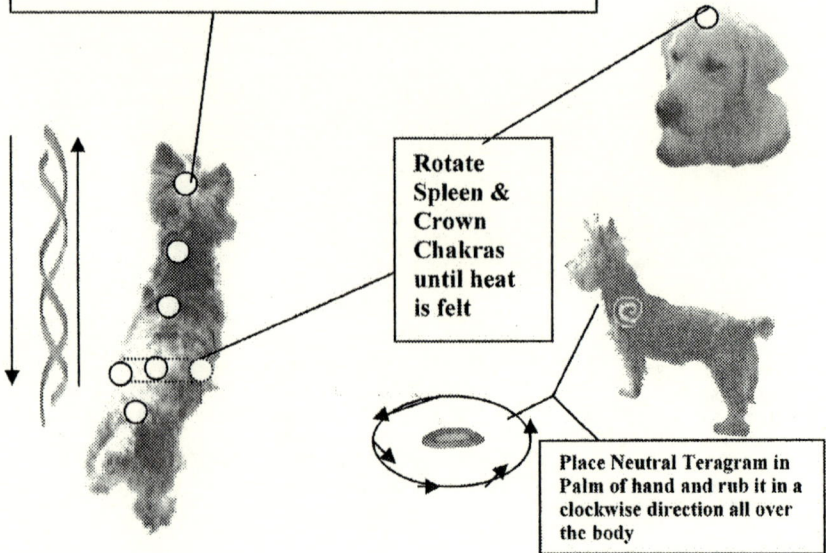

Rotate Spleen & Crown Chakras until heat is felt

Place Neutral Teragram in Palm of hand and rub it in a clockwise direction all over the body

Crystal Acupuncture[sm] and Teragram Therapy Treatment For Horses

(1) Amazonite (2) Amethyst (3) Aventurine

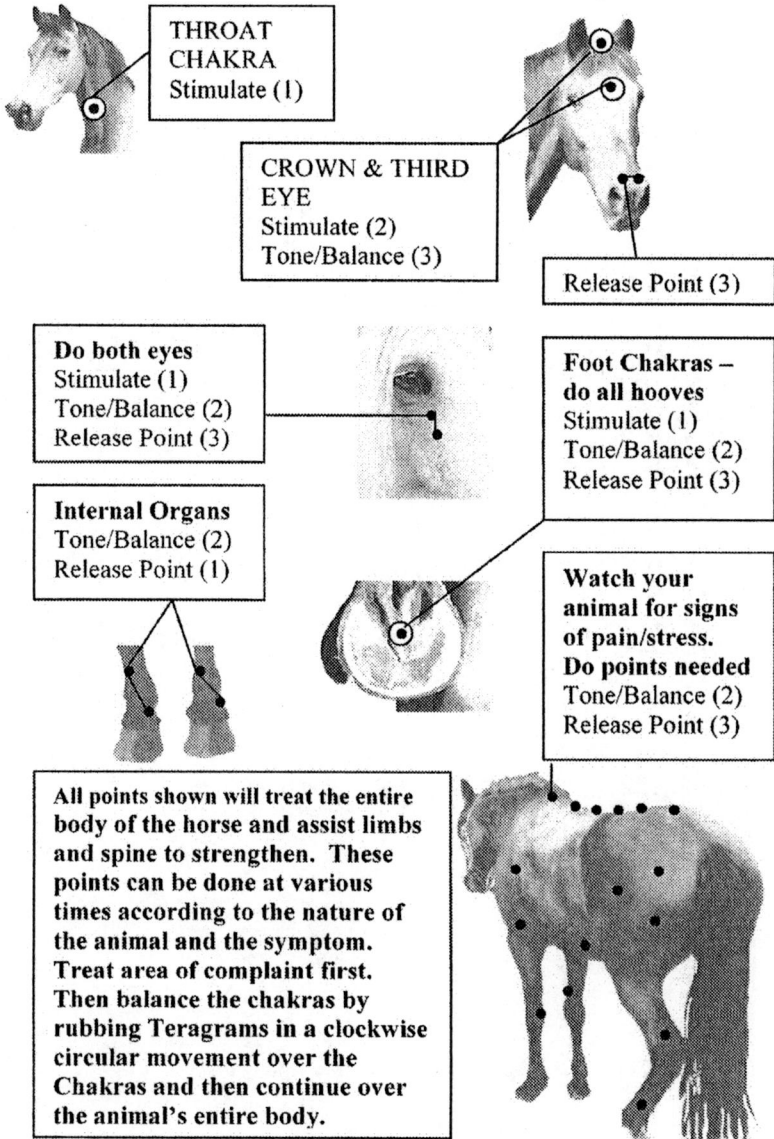

THROAT
CHAKRA
Stimulate (1)

CROWN & THIRD
EYE
Stimulate (2)
Tone/Balance (3)

Release Point (3)

Do both eyes
Stimulate (1)
Tone/Balance (2)
Release Point (3)

Foot Chakras –
do all hooves
Stimulate (1)
Tone/Balance (2)
Release Point (3)

Internal Organs
Tone/Balance (2)
Release Point (1)

Watch your
animal for signs
of pain/stress.
Do points needed
Tone/Balance (2)
Release Point (3)

All points shown will treat the entire
body of the horse and assist limbs
and spine to strengthen. These
points can be done at various
times according to the nature of
the animal and the symptom.
Treat area of complaint first.
Then balance the chakras by
rubbing Teragrams in a clockwise
circular movement over the
Chakras and then continue over
the animal's entire body.

Crystal Acupuncture^{sm} & Teragram^{sm} Therapy
For Small Mammals (Cont.)

RABBITS

(1) Rose Quartz (2) Amazonite (3) Natural Agate

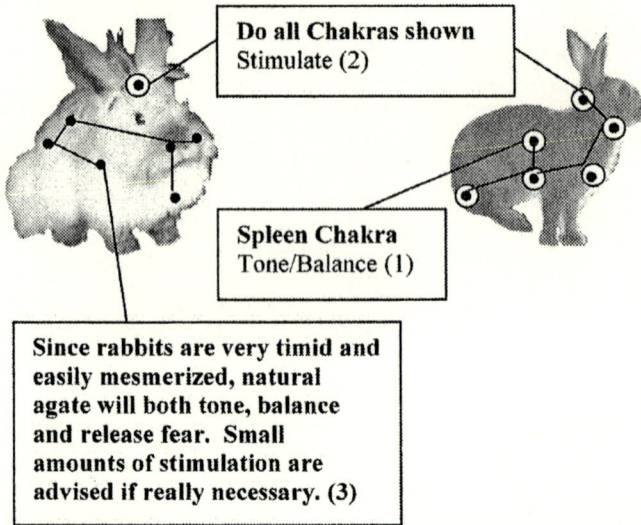

Do all Chakras shown
Stimulate (2)

Spleen Chakra
Tone/Balance (1)

Since rabbits are very timid and
easily mesmerized, natural
agate will both tone, balance
and release fear. Small
amounts of stimulation are
advised if really necessary. (3)

TERAGRAM^{SM} THERAPY FOR ALL ANIMALS

The Spleen
Chakra should
be balanced
last to
harmonize
The Five
Bodies. Hold
until hot
tingles are felt.

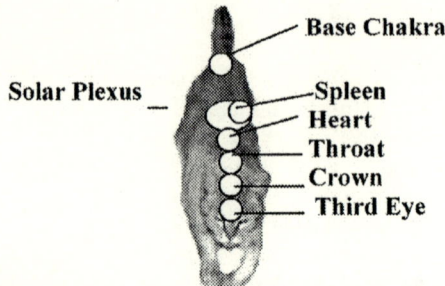

Base Chakra
Solar Plexus
Spleen
Heart
Throat
Crown
Third Eye

Intuitively choose any colored Teragram and in a
clockwise spiral rotation, move the Teragram up and
down the spine several times. The animal will want
to get away when all is balanced.

222

Crystal Acupuncture^sm & Teragram^sm Therapy For Birds

(1) Amethyst (2) Ruby Quartz (3) Sodalite (3) Hematite

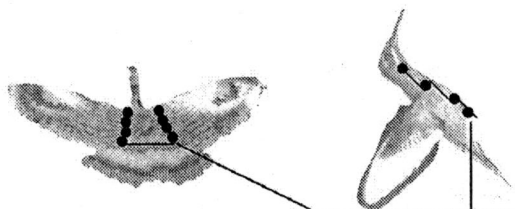

(Most birds suffer broken wigs with an imbalance from shock and fear. Treat all the Acu Points shown)

Stimulate (1)
Tone/Balance (3)
Release Point (4)

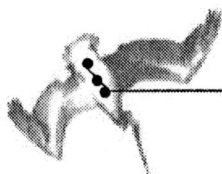

(Waterfowl often eat something poisonous. Treat these points taking care to allow the bird to relax)
Release All Points (3)

(Sometimes birds get damaged lungs. Treat the bird with care, trying not to hinder their breathing)
Tone/Balance (2)
Release Point (1)

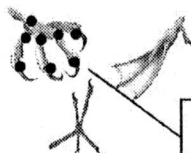

Whatever type of bird you have, do the foot points shown here. (3)

Teragram Therapy

Take any one colored Teragram and place it over the head or on the chest of the bird. Allow heat to build and when the animal fidgets, that is enough.

Crystal Acupuncture^{sm} and Teragram^{sm} Therapy for Reptiles

(1) Titanium Quartz (2) Sodalite (3) Carnelian (4) Agate

Note: These animals rely on the sun for warmth and so the crystals used will generate healing heat. Be intuitive and use the crystal points anywhere where the animal seems to hurt.

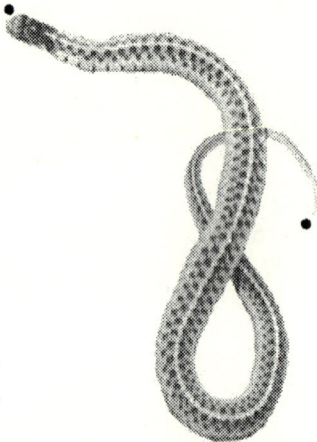

Crystal Acupuncture -snake
Crown Chakra Point at center of flat of head
Stimulate (1) **(3 impulses)**
Tone/Balance (2) **(Hold until warmth is felt in fingertips)**
Release Point (3) **(rotate until release is seen in the animal as it wriggles or twitches)**
Do the same to the end of the tip of tail

Teragram Therapy
Take two Teragrams and hold on either side of the body of the snake around the affected area until you feel heat

Crystal Acupuncture-turtle or Tortoise
Do all toes points beneath the nail on all feet or flippers
Stimulate (3)
Tone/Balance (2)
Release Points (4)

Do around neck and tail points to align the meridians
Stimulate (1)
Tone/Balance (3)
Release Points (4)

Teragram Therapy
Take any two Teragrams and hold one on top of upper shell center and one below on lower center shell -- allow hands to become really hot and finish treatment

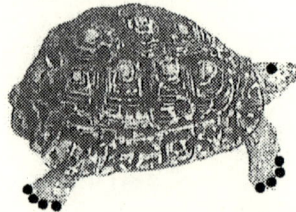

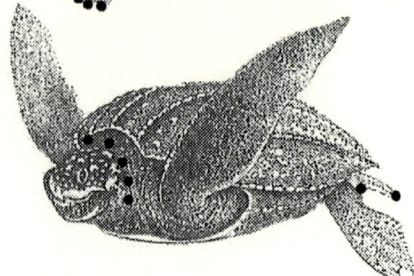

224

PRODUCTS & SERVICES

PRODUCTS AND SERVICES
FROM SUMARIS ENTERPRISES

THERAPY KITS

Crystal Acupuncture^{sm} Therapy Kit

This amazing set contains 8 crystals and 3 pendulums attractively packaged in a satin purse which can be easily carried in a handbag or pocket. Included in the kit is The Book of Crystal Acupuncture Diagrams. *This clear and detailed work gives directions on the use of the points and pendulums and also presents valuable information on the Chakras, the Five Bodies and the acupuncture meridians. $50.00*

Teragram^{sm} Therapy Kit

Dispel the Madness with our kit containing one each of Natural, Blue, Violet, Red, Green and Pink Agate plates attractively contained in a satin drawstring pouch. A simple instruction booklet provides directions and tips. As a special bonus, we include a CD by Dr. Margaret Rogers Van Coops with a color meditation and a meditation for Chakra and Five Bodies balancing. **$30.00**

Dr. Margaret's "Core" Teragram^{sm} Therapy Kit

Releases Negative History stored in your body's cells. Banishes effects of old issues. Strengthens you to deal with emotional and mental issues. Stimulates more efficient energy flow. Generates inner sense of well-being. Margaret Rogers' *"Core" Teragram^{sm} Therapy Kit* contains 3 specially selected Agate slices with a Basic Relaxation Meditation CD featuring the nurturing voice of Steve Van Coops. You will quickly enter into a deep alpha state ideal for releasing old emotional habits and irrelevant mind conditioning. **$15.00**

Spiritual Crystal Acupuncture^{sm} Kit

Five small triangular stones combined with four specially selected pointed stones to refine dense energy and to redirect it according to your desire or need. Kit includes detailed booklet with instructions and diagrams. Spiritual Geometry leads to focus on Spiritual reality beyond your previous physical awareness. **$30.00**

Trinity Stone Healing Kit

This unique kit allows auditory memory to stimulate and shift negativity from the body. The five specially selected large open equilateral triangles are used on the Chakras, one at a time, and then all together to erase fear and illusions stored in associations with sounds. Each triangle, when added, will enhance your perception, vision and positive sensations. Included is a booklet with instructions and diagrams and two Serpentine isosolese triangles that are useful in raising the Kundalini and stimulating and harmonizing the Higher and Lower Sacred Centers. When all seven triangles are used together, an awakening may be realized that will result in an explosion of self-confidence. **$50.00**

BOOKS

Breakthrough Therapies: Crystal Acupuncture^{sm} & Teragram^{sm} Therapy

While most people today vaguely realize that the body is a working machine that generates energy, most of us don't understand the way that energy flows, where it goes, and what it does. ***Breakthrough Therapies*** is the product of Dr. Margaret's research with her clients and under medical supervision. Her research has validated the integration of the energies of The Five Bodies. The book reveals how the principles of Oriental Acupuncture, combined with the use of specially cut crystals and semi-precious stones, will unblock energy flow in our Five Bodies and will tone, stimulate and balance the Chi energies. Using natural resonating energy stones and crystals such as, but not limited to Hematite, Jasper, Citrine, Amethyst, Carnelian and Quartz, has opened the door to drug-free, inexpensive solutions to emotional and psychological issues ranging from addictions to depression to stress. Dr. Margaret's powerful, non-invasive healing methods also provide remarkable relief from minor physical ailments like headaches to major illnesses and syndromes such as AIDS, Cancer and Multiple Sclerosis. AuthorHouse Publishing Co. **$13.95**

The Way to Oneness

This inspiring work delves into the cosmology of multi-dimensional spiritual existence. Beginning with the "Word" as vibrational consciousness, this book takes you on a journey through the principles of creation, separation, the descending and ascending currents, faith, intuition, belief and evolution. The various sub-divisional cosmologies of the seven archetypes and planes of existence are viewed. Also, incarnation, reincarnation and the Akashic Records are explained as an inter-relationship with the deep subconscious and the Chakras. Of particularly unique interest is the principle of soul fragmentation that the book discusses throughout the text. ***The Way to Oneness*** concludes with practical steps and techniques for emotional balancing and relaxation, disciplinary exercises and various other psychic tools such as astrology, numerology, graphology and palmistry. Recommended for all practitioners seeking insight into higher knowledge

-- *James Ravenscroft* <u>*Whole Life Times*</u> *March 15. 1990* **$25.00**

The Rejection Syndrome

In our daily lives, all of us experience moments of rejection that create an internal impasse, either by ourselves or by others. My intent is to assist those wishing to be free of those encumbrances brought about by ***The Rejection Syndrome***. This is about a pattern of existence that compounds habit, routine and conditioning, leading to limitation, restriction, judgment and competition. Learn about the soul structure and how you can use it to be aware of yourself and to perform to the best of your ability without negativity or rejection. **$20.00**

50 Spiritually Power ul Meditations

In the stillness of the mind lies the answer to your purpose. Dr. Margaret has tested all of these meditations herself. By doing each of these meditations, you can find true direction for your life and release fears, pains, restrictions and anger acquired through conditioning. These meditations work! Develop your psychic ability, fine tune your healing skills, mend relationships, empower yourself and much more. This should be a book on everyone's shelf. Jaico Publishing **$12.95**

Pro-Life, Pro-Choice, Pro-Spirit

Spirit's truth is clearly shown through Margaret's own personal experiences. Is everything pre-ordained? The word "abortion" evokes emotions in almost all normally rational minds. Right or wrong? Moral or immoral? Should it be legal or illegal? One of the most burning issues of our time: Advocates of both sides have thrown themselves at each other's faces even to the point of violence. This book is a must read for women who have been, are now or are likely to become pregnant. Without being judgmental, Dr. Margaret provides the wisdom of Master Teachers to assist women to acknowledge, accept and deal with their circumstances. She has crossed the worldly boundaries to discover just what really happens from the point of view of the child-to-be's Spirit and Spirit Master Teachers. **$15.00**

FOCUSING TOOL

The OmniCard™

The OmniCard™ is the simplest way of doing a psychic reading for yourself, your friends or your clients. This revolutionary tool lets you easily tap into images that apply to the question being asked. This can be a wonderful new adventure in learning and psychic awareness. Simply attune to a question and then let your eyes scan the images until one looms up at you. Visualize the significance of the image and all of the meanings it draws forth. It's like having an entire Tarot deck of cards in one stylistic full-color painting, which evokes vivid, literal and symbolic images. These images are the focal points for you to create a psychic reading that will entertain and amaze your friends and clients. Try closing your eyes and letting your hand move over the OmniCard. Your fingers may point to some image of interest or significance. There are many ways to interpret the answers to questions. Try experimenting with them and discover how effective you can be. Special bonus! We are including *Expanding Images,* a special book and glossary of symbols with your OmniCard™ that will make it even easier for you to match the pictures with their meanings. **$20.00**

EDUCATIONAL TOOLS

AUDIO TAPES & CD'S
Dr. Margaret Rogers Van Coops has given many informative and interesting lectures, which are available on audiocassettes. She also provides hypnosis and meditation CD's for focus on specific problems, issues and conditions. Please contact Sumaris Enterprises for titles and prices.

PERSONAL SERVICES
Dr. Margaret is available for private consultations and is also available to do audiotaped readings by mail or over the phone. Call: (928) 453-7974

All listed prices are US Dollars (USD). Please allow for $7.50 S&H for each item order in the United States. $15.00 S&H for Overseas orders. Arizona residents must add 8.00% for sales tax. Visa, Master, Amex and Discovery Cards accepted. All orders to be in US Dollars or equivalent amount.
Send orders with correct amount to:
Sumaris Enterprises
321 Farallon Dr., Lake Havasu City, AZ 86403, USA.
Website: www.sumariscenter.com or www.twocommas.com
e-mail: sumaris@sumariscenter.com

ı

ABOUT THE AUTHOR

Dr. Margaret Rogers Van Coops has been an ordained minister and missionary of the Universal Christ Church (School of Spiritualism) since 1983. She is currently the Director of Education for UCC. Margaret has a Ph.D. specializing in Medical and Clinical Hypnotherapy and Behavioral Sciences. She is also a DCH(IM), a Doctor of Clinical Hypnotherapy and Integrated Medicine. She has practiced successfully in Spain, France, Switzerland, India, Egypt, Japan, England, Mexico and the United States. Her professional affiliations include the Spiritualist Association of Great Britain, the British Astrological and Psychic Society, The American Board of Hypnotherapy, the International Hypnosis Federation, the Professional Board of Hypnotherapy and The American Counseling Association. Margaret was among the co-founders of the International Psychic Forum and the American Metaphysical Society. Her dynamic lectures and workshops in Japan and the U.S. have led to regular invitations to speak and participate in international events, including Whole Life Expos and Lifeways/BMSE Expos in various American Cities and The Festivals for Mind, Body and Spirit in London and Los Angeles.

She is the author of six metaphysically oriented texts, including *The Way to Oneness, The Rejection Syndrome, 50 Spiritually Powerful Meditations, Pro-Life, Pro-Choice, Pro Spirit, Breakthrough Therapies and Expanding Images*. She has authored two novels: *Regenesis* and *Henry's Secrets*. Her books have been published in Western and Eastern Europe as well as Russia, China, Mexico and India. Dr. Margaret has written screenplays including *The Regenesis Trilogy, Seeing Blind* and *The Survivor,* and she is negotiating production of several reality TV series treatments. Margaret's TV series, Psychic Chit Chat, has been aired weekly on many public access channels in Southern California and Arizona. The show features Dr. Margaret and her husband, Dr. Stephen Van Coops, also a Metaphysician and collaborator on her works.

Printed in the United Kingdom
by Lightning Source UK Ltd.
109401UKS00002B/73-78

9 781420 862935